The SOCIAL PROBLEMS *of*
AN INDUSTRIAL CIVILIZATION

International Library of Sociology

Founded by Karl Mannheim
Editor: John Rex, University of Warwick

A catalogue of the books available in the **International Library of Sociology** and other series of Social Science books published by Routledge & Kegan Paul will be found at the end of this volume.

The SOCIAL PROBLEMS
of AN
INDUSTRIAL CIVILIZATION

*WITH AN APPENDIX
ON THE
POLITICAL PROBLEM*

by
ELTON MAYO

Foreword by Professor J. H. Smith

ROUTLEDGE & KEGAN PAUL
London

First published in 1949
Reprinted in 1952, 1956, 1962 and 1966
Reprinted with a new foreword in 1975
by Routledge & Kegan Paul Ltd
Broadway House, 68-74 Carter Lane,
London EC4V 5EL
Printed in Great Britain by
Lowe & Brydone (Printers) Ltd
Thetford, Norfolk
© Routledge & Kegan Paul Ltd 1949
New foreword © J. H. Smith 1975
No part of this book may be reproduced in
any form without permission from the
publisher, except for the quotation of brief
passages in criticism
ISBN 0 7100 8196 0 (c)
ISBN 0 7100 7723 8 (p)

This book is dedicated to

M. L. PUTNAM
H. A. WRIGHT
W. J. DICKSON
A. C. MOORE
D. D. DAVISSON
H. HIBARGER

the team that worked through the Hawthorne experiment to its interesting conclusion. They will understand if I add the name of

GEORGE A. PENNOCK

CONTENTS

THE SOCIAL PROBLEMS OF AN INDUSTRIAL CIVILIZATION

(*Oct. 1st, 1945*)

PART I

SCIENCE AND SOCIETY

PART II

THE CLINICAL APPROACH

APPENDIX I

THE POLITICAL PROBLEM

(*May 10th and 11th, 1947*)

APPENDIX II

FOREWORD TO THE 1975 EDITION
THE SIGNIFICANCE OF ELTON MAYO

ELTON MAYO's *Social Problems of an Industrial Civilization* was published on the eve of his retirement, after twenty-one years as Professor of Industrial Research at the Harvard Business School. His reputation was then at its peak. An article in *Fortune* ranked Mayo as a modern social thinker with Thorstein Veblen and John Dewey; it further hailed him as an academic whose views directly challenged the basic assumptions of the practical world of industry.[1]

Scientist and practical clinician, Mayo speaks with a rare authority that has commanded attention in factories as well as Universities. His erudition extends through psychology, sociology, physiology, medicine, and economics, and his experience comes from a lifelong, firsthand study of industry. . . . Mayo's view gives promise of exerting through the field of business administration a significant influence on the future relations of U.S. management and labor. Indeed, many believe that Mayo holds the key to industrial peace.

Among academics, however, there was already more than one view of his contribution and the first of a stream of critical articles had already appeared.[2] Mayo's critics soon placed him in more ambiguous company. Clark Kerr, also writing in *Fortune*, saw Mayo's solution to the problems of industrial conflict as too narrow and monolithic in its implications, threatening the freedom of the worker–citizen: society must devise a pluralist framework for the accommodation of conflict, as against "the all-embracing party of the Communists and the Fascists, the all-absorbing corporation of Elton Mayo, the all-absorbing union of Frank Tannenbaum, the all-absorbing church of T. S. Eliot."[3]

[1] "The Fruitful Errors of Elton Mayo", *Fortune*, Vol. 34, November 1946, pp. 181–3 et seq.
[2] Of these, the most significant was to be R. Bendix and L. H. Fisher, "The Perspectives of Elton Mayo", *Review of Economics and Statistics*, Vol. 31, 1949, pp. 313–21.
[3] Clark Kerr, "Whatever Became of the Independent Spirit?", *Fortune*, Vol. 48, July 1953, pp. 110–11 et seq.

A quarter of a century after his death, Mayo's name is still remembered and he himself is still the centre of controversy. The vigour of the criticism directed against him demonstrates the importance of his views for the social scientist concerned with industrial behaviour. By the 1950s, the stream of criticism had swelled to a flood. Writing towards the end of the decade, Landsberger was moved to remark "that among a large number of sociologists and economists, 'taking a shot at Mayo'—and at human relations—seems to be a favoured practice of several years' standing."[1]

Since then there has been some reduction in frequency, but none in intensity. Mayo's name has become synonymous with a narrow (and, to some, ethically questionable) view of social relations in industry; so much so that the terms "Mayoite" and "Mayoism" have passed into the pejorative language of social science. A recent appraisal of research needs in industrial relations in Britain tartly reproduces what is now the received wisdom concerning Mayo's contribution and outlook.[2]

> From the middle of the 1950s, industrial sociologists and psycho-logists began to show that they could contribute to industrial rela-tions. "Human relations" had a considerable following among British practitioners of industrial relations, but academics were initially sceptical. For especially as expounded by such writers as Elton Mayo, human relations concentrated on the primary work group and labour-management cooperation, ignoring or belittling most of the topics in which students of industrial relations were interested.

All of which suggests that Mayo's work could only be of limited interest today; of little value perhaps except as a paradigm offering a rather threadbare interpretation of the social needs of the industrial worker. Viewed in this way, the best that might be said for him is that Mayo's critics have found an analysis of his shortcomings an essential stimulus in clarifying their own views about the proper scope of industrial sociology.

There is of course much more than that to Mayo as the reader of this volume will discover. Indeed, some of the features of Mayo's writings which so upset his posthumous critics—his

[1] Henry A. Landsberger, *Hawthorne Revisited* (Cornell University Press, Ithaca, New York, 1958), pp. 28–9.

[2] G. S. Bain and H. A. Clegg, "A Strategy For Industrial Relations Research in Great Britain", *British Journal of Industrial Relations*, Vol. XII, No. 1, March 1974, p. 99.

suspicion of state power, his distrust of politicians, his scepticism about the faith in formal procedures designed to solve problems of human co-operation—look very different in the 1970s. One is reminded of the fluctuating reputation of Herbert Spencer, whose arguments and concepts continue to enrich present day sociology.[1] The comparison should not be pressed too far—Mayo cannot really be put in the same class as Spencer, except possibly on grounds of intellectual arrogance—but there are some interesting similarities. Like Spencer, Mayo is a representative product of his age. Spencer fashioned the essential vocabulary of sociology and social anthropology: Mayo, without ever himself using the term "industrial sociology" defined its essential point of view in an unmistakeable and (his critics notwithstanding) inescapable form. Amid the pessimisms of the post-welfare society some of Mayo's ideas—like Spencer's—are beginning to be in fashion again: while his views on the methods of social science and their limitations are unconsciously shared by many of those who may have assumed, on ideological grounds, that he is a writer of little interest.

The Social Problems of an Industrial Civilization is not Mayo's most satisfactory book. It is clear that he had misgivings about writing it and that he was not very pleased with its final form. It was written under the stress of war and of worries about his family and about himself. Nevertheless it tells us a great deal about the man and what he did. In particular, it gives us Mayo's own version of the intellectual and social context in which he made his name and in which he came to exert a singular influence. It is also a record of the development of a point of view without which the subsequent histories of sociology and of management thought and education would inevitably have been different.

MAYO'S LIFE AND WORK

Early Life and Education

There is as yet no reliable biography of Mayo, but even an incomplete account of his life shows that his career and interests could at no time be classed either as settled or conventional.[2] He was born George Elton Mayo in Adelaide in December 1880.

---

[1] See the introduction by Donald MacRae (ed.), *Herbert Spencer: The Man Versus The State* (Penguin Books, Harmondsworth, 1969), pp. 8–12.

[2] I am indebted for much of the personal information used in this section to the generous help of Patricia Elton Mayo and Professor George F. F. Lombard.

The Mayos were well-established in Australia, a comfortably-off professional family. Mayo's father, George Gibbes Mayo, was an engineer. There were seven children, of whom Mayo himself was the second-born. His sister Helen trained as a doctor and by the turn of the century Mayo himself was studying medicine in Britain.

The details of Mayo's academic career up to that time have yet to be fully established. From 1896 to 1898 he was at St Peter's College, Adelaide and he was a student at the University there in 1899. Following this, he went to Edinburgh University, but left without completing the course, apparently impatient of the routine requirements of a Scottish medical education. Despite a subsequent interest in the personal difficulties of students, Mayo does not refer to this phase of his life in his writings, although he was fond of using anecdotes involving himself to illustrate an argument (usually of a clinical nature). The next year or two (1903–4) was an unsettled period. He was first in London, where by his own account he did voluntary work at the London Working Men's College.[1] He then tried his luck in West Africa in the Ashanti goldfields but returned to London now apparently hoping to go to Canada. Instead he was restored to the family fold in Australia: it was to be more than seventeen years before he finally landed in North America.

Once more in Adelaide, he went back to the University and became a student of psychology with Sir William Mitchell. The attraction for Mayo, as reported later by one of his students, was that "the professor could answer his questions."[2] In 1910 he gained his B.A. with honours in philosophy, winning the Murray Scholarship as the best student in his class.

University of Queensland

Mayo's career as a university teacher began in 1911, with his appointment at the University of Queensland at lecturer in Logic, Ethics and Psychology. He built up a small but vigorous school of Mental and Moral Philosophy, during the first three years of which he appears to have been responsible for all of its teaching, including that on economic theory.[3]

---

[1] Elton Mayo, *The Psychology of Pierre Janet* (Routledge & Kegan Paul, London, 1951), pp. 9–10 (hereafter referred to as Mayo, *Janet*).
[2] W. M. Kyle, obituary note in the *University of Queensland Gazette*, No. 15, Brisbane, December 1949.
[3] Ibid.

Mayo established a reputation as an outstanding lecturer, both inside and outside the university. He took a particular interest in trade union education and was a keen critic of the reluctance of Australian universities to develop the social sciences.[1]

A principal influence on Mayo's approach to psychology during this period was the work of the French psychologist, Pierre Janet. Janet's work on hysteria and obsession stimulated and guided Mayo's own teaching and research. This interest found practical expression in the psychotherapeutic treatment of shell-shocked soldiers returning from the First World War. This work had a profound and lasting impression on Mayo's approach to the problems of the individual in industrial society; it also marked the beginning of some thirty years as an active practitioner with individual patients. Clinical psychology in Queensland seems to have developed directly as a result of this pioneering work (psychiatry as such barely existed in Australia) since it led directly to a grant from the British Red Cross Society to finance a Research Chair in Medical Psychology at the University.

Mayo meantime had himself been appointed Professor of Philosophy. He was beginning to focus his attention on the problems of monotonous and repetitive tasks in industry. Work published by him at about this time shows that he was already familiar with industrial questions.[2] By the early 1920s Mayo seems to have decided that he could make a distinctive contribution through the investigation of industrial problems, especially the adaptation of the normal individual to industry.

Arrival in the United States

He was also keener than ever to visit the United States. Mayo was dissatisfied with the opportunities for research and for academic development in Australia and took up a Laura Spelman Rockefeller Fellowship, arriving in San Francisco in August 1922. Mayo was encouraged by his reception, but his sense of frustration

[1] Ibid. Elton Mayo, "The Australian Political Consciousness", in Meredith Atkinson (ed.), *Australia: Economic and Political Studies* (Macmillan & Co., Melbourne, 1920), pp. 142–4.

[2] Despite the later criticisms that Mayo was ignorant of or indifferent to existing industrial studies, especially of trade union questions, he showed a close familiarity with the institutions of Australian management-labour relations. See his chapter in Meredith Atkinson (ed.), op. cit., pp. 126–44. In his chief work in this period, *Democracy and Freedom* (Macmillan, Melbourne, 1919), Mayo is closely concerned with the problem of realizing political ideals in the context of an industrial society committed to continuous change and adaption.

with Australia was deepened by the refusal of the University of Queensland to grant six months' extension of his leave. He had left his wife and two young children behind; it was to be over a year before they were with him again in America.[1] By then he had resigned from his Chair at Queensland. Mayo never returned to Australia.

His first academic post was a Rockefeller Fellowship, held at the Wharton School of Finance and Commerce at the University of Pennsylvania; his first empirical investigation in America was concerned with the causes of high labour turnover in the mule spinning department of a textile mill near Philadelphia. Mayo subsequently used the course of this study to illustrate the short-comings of conventional approaches, including his own, to questions of worker behaviour. At the same time it enabled him to demonstrate to his own satisfaction that studies involving experimental changes in working conditions were both feasible and worthwhile.[2]

During this period, Mayo wrote a number of articles for the general reader, including some for *Harper's Magazine*.[3] It was these that first aroused the interest of Dean Wallace B. Donham of the Harvard University Graduate School of Business Administration, as a result of which Mayo was invited to Harvard as an associate professor of industrial research in the Business School.

Harvard and Hawthorne

Mayo took up his post at Harvard in 1926. He was to remain there for twenty-one years, becoming one of the best-known (and one of the most controversial) members of the University. Despite this, his precise role in the development of the Business School and of its research programme is difficult to evaluate.

In particular, the famous Hawthorne Experiments, the set pieces of his two best-known books, and with which his name is always linked, were neither designed nor directed by Mayo.[4]   A

---

[1] Mayo had married Dorothea McConnel in 1913. They had two daughters Patricia (b.1915) and Gael (b.1921).

[2] Mayo's first account of this study was given in an article "Reverie and Industrial Fatigue", *Personnel Journal*, Vol. III, No. 8, December 1924, pp. 273–81. See also Chapter III of this volume.

[3] An example is "Should Marriage be Monotonous?", *Harper's Magazine*, September 1925. The answer was in the opening sentence: "Of course it should."

[4] Elton Mayo, *The Human Problems of an Industrial Civilization* (Macmillan, New York, 1933), Elton Mayo, *The Social Problems of an Industrial Civilization* (Routledge & Kegan Paul, London, 1949), hereafter referred to as Mayo, *Human Problems* and Mayo, *Social Problems*.

number of popular accounts have described the experiments as his personal conception and direct responsibility, but Mayo never claimed to be more than a member of the "Harvard research group" associated with them, despite the fact that for more than twenty years he was its most senior member and its principal and most effective spokesman.[1] Again, the Hawthorne Experiments, and even Mayo's recruitment to Harvard are sometimes represented as direct consequences of the setting-up of the Harvard Fatigue Laboratory under L. J. Henderson; in fact both the experiments and Mayo's appointment began before the Laboratory itself was established in 1927. Finally, the group working with Mayo was generally known as the "Department of Industrial Research", although it was not a formally constituted department of the university; nor was the research carried out by members of the group exclusively industrial.

Given the confusion that appears to persist over the precise organization of the studies and of Mayo's role in them, it is useful to try to establish an order of events, according to the more reliable accounts of the Hawthorne studies. The Hawthorne works of the Western Electric Co. was located in Cicero on the West side of Chicago. It was the largest of the Western Electric factories, with some 29,000 employees. At Hawthorne the principal manufactures were telephones and telephone equipment for the American Telephone and Telegraph Company. The Company enjoyed a reputation for advanced personnel and welfare policies, and had welcomed a research study promoted by the National Research Council into the relationship of illumination to individual efficiency. This work lasted from 1924 to 1927 and led to a series of inconclusive and puzzling results which upset firmly-held beliefs about the favourable effects of improved lighting on productivity. As a result the Hawthorne Experiments were instituted by the Western Electric Management themselves, initially with an academic consultant from the

---

[1] The official accounts are to be found in F. Roethlisberger and W. J. Dickson, *Management and the Worker* (Harvard University Press, Cambridge, Mass., 1939), and T. North Whitehead, *The Industrial Worker* (Oxford University Press, London, 1938). For a review of the popular accounts and criticisms of Mayo, see Landsberger, op. cit., especially pp. 28–47. L. Baritz, *The Servants of Power* (Wesleyan University Press, Conn., 1960) is a vigorous critique of Mayo (and of applied social science in general) which includes rather more detail than is customary in works of this type. At the same time, it would be difficult to class it as a balanced appraisal. See "A Note on Mayo's Critics", below, p. xxxix.

Massachusetts Institute of Technology already associated with the company, Dr C. E. Turner.[1]

The purpose was to record all the conditions—physiological and social, as well as industrial and engineering changes—that might be relevant to workers' performance.[2] The Relay Test Assembly Room was set up in April 1927. Mayo heard about the progress of the studies in the following winter and in April 1928 accepted an invitation from the Western Electric Management to "observe the test room and to make suggestions".[3] He was therefore not involved in the design of the first of the experiments. He did however establish a close relationship with Western Electric executives and much in the subsequent scope and continuity of the programme appears to have depended on Mayo as an essential link between researchers and company.[4]

Mayo enlarged the perspectives of the studies by introducing a number of academics to Hawthorne, notably the social anthropologist W. Lloyd Warner: this resulted in the setting up of the Bank Wiring Room study, one of the classics of small group research and still a point of departure for studies of restrictive practices on the shop floor.[5]

Mayo took a special interest in the employee-interviewing programme which was designed to throw light on the development of workers' attitudes and on the influence of attitudes on output. Eventually more than 86,000 comments were analysed,

[1] Mayo himself wrote: "Special mention must be made of those officers of the Western Electric Company whose intelligent insight designed and adapted the experiment, whose courage and persistence carried it through." Foreword to T. North Whitehead, op. cit. p. viii. Some detailed information about the immediate background to the start of the Experiments in April 1927 is given in Baritz, op. cit., pp. 78–83.

[2] Cf. Mayo, *Social Problems*, p. 62 of this volume.

[3] Baritz, op. cit., p. 90. It was not the case that Mayo had only one contact with the senior Western Electric management, as the account by Baritz suggests. He was certainly in touch with George A. Pennock, a superintendent at Hawthorne, who had attended a talk given by Mayo at the National Industrial Conference Board, and had told Mayo about the studies on that occasion.

[4] "One of his closest colleagues recalled that, instead of taking the Hawthorne executives to their country club for lunch, Mayo took them for a bowl of onion soup at one of the several lunchrooms on Cicero Avenue . . . the relationship between Mayo and his Harvard colleagues and the Western Electric executives began well and apparently continued amicable. . . ." Baritz, op. cit., p. 91.

[5] See Roethlisberger and Dickson, op. cit., pp. 377–568; Landsberger, op. cit.; D. F. Roy, "Efficiency and the Fix", *American Journal of Sociology*, Vol. 60, No. 3, 1954, pp. 255–66; T. Lupton, *On the Shop Floor* (Pergamon, Oxford, 1963); A. Carey, "The Hawthorne Studies: A Radical Criticism", *American Sociological Review*, Vol. 32, No. 3, 1967, pp. 403–16; A. J. M. Sykes, "Economic Interest and the Hawthorne Researches", *Human Relations*, Vol. 18, No. 3, August 1965, pp. 253–65. For an indication of Warner's contribution to the Studies as a whole, see Roethlisberger and Dickson, op. cit., p. 389.

made on 80 topics in some 10,000 interviews. This programme, which began in 1929 and lasted for two and a half years, was a direct expression of Mayo's concern to develop what he termed "clinical sociology" and the exercise of "social skills".

Mayo remained in contact with Hawthorne and the Western Electric for the rest of his time at Harvard but it was by no means his major preoccupation. To appreciate the breadth of his interests and his influence, it is necessary to take note of the close relationship he enjoyed with L. J. Henderson.

Henderson and the Fatigue Laboratory

L. J. Henderson (1878–1942) was a biochemist of international distinction, among other things the author of a fundamental work on the physiology of the blood. He was a powerful figure in Harvard where he spent virtually the whole of his academic life. He was a particularly close friend both of President A. L. Lowell and of Dean Wallace B. Donham of the Business School. Henderson and Mayo took to one another at once. They were about the same age; their interests were congenial; they were also apparently similar in outlook and in the stimulus they provided to colleagues and students.[1]

When Mayo arrived at Harvard, Dean Donham had begun to reorganize and expand the Business School. The Fatigue Laboratory was established in 1927 under Donham's sponsorship, with Henderson as its director. Financial support was made available by the Rockefeller Foundations for a programme of the laboratory designated as "research in industrial hazards".[2]

The initial focus of the laboratory's work was on normal human physiology; both Henderson and Mayo were concerned to widen this to include environmental factors affecting the individual's adjustment to mental and physical stress. In its Annual Report for 1930, the Rockefeller Foundation recorded that Henderson and Mayo had been concerned, since 1925, with "the psychological factors which control human behaviour (in order to form a basis for understanding problems) in business administration, and particularly in the labor field."[3]

[1] S. M. and E. C. Horvath, *The Harvard Fatigue Laboratory: Its History and Contributions* (Prentice-Hall, New Jersey, 1973), pp. 18–24. The Horvaths' study is an important source for an understanding of this period.
[2] Ibid., p. 21.
[3] *The Rockefeller Foundation Annual Report* (New York, 1930), p. 617 (quoted in Horvath and Horvath, op. cit., p. 21).

The precise organization of the Laboratory, including the respective responsibilities of Henderson and Mayo, is difficult to reconstruct. There were two distinct entities which received and spent the Rockefeller grant. One was the Fatigue Laboratory, under Henderson; the other was the group under Mayo sometimes called the Department of Industrial Research. In an appendix to the *Social Problems of an Industrial Civilization*, Professor George F. F. Lombard (one of Mayo's later collaborators) sets out a list of the researches conducted under Mayo's auspices.[1] It is a formidable catalogue, including a number of what are now familiar and obligatory references in social science, e.g. William Foote Whyte's *Street Corner Society*, Arensberg and Kimball's *Family and Community in Ireland*, Allison Davis's *Deep South*.

Support for this work came from a variety of sources, but it was the Rockefeller Foundation which made the whole enterprise possible.[2]

The informality of the arrangements for the funding and direction of the Fatigue Laboratory shows how close the understanding was between Henderson and Mayo. Undoubtedly Mayo benefited from his ready acceptance by one of the most influential members of the University.[3] His rapport with Henderson conferred manifest advantages on a newcomer seeking to make his way in the Harvard of the inter-war years. At the same time, it was not without certain risks which may account for at least some of the hostility subsequently directed towards Mayo himself.

Henderson was a man of forceful opinions who left no doubt as to his views on social as well as on scientific matters. Chester Barnard (1886–1961), the most important writer on management during the period and a frequent visitor to Harvard,

[1] See Appendix II of this volume, p. 132.

[2] The Horvaths estimate that the Fatigue Laboratory received some 645,000 dollars from the Foundation between 1927 and 1942. There are no detailed accounts of the amounts spent; or, as they say, "actually retained by Mayo and Henderson". Professor Lombard attempted, for the Horvaths' study, a reconstruction of the Fatigue Laboratory budget from which it emerges that Mayo and Henderson sometimes made grant applications jointly, sometimes separately. He describes Mayo and Henderson as "frugal researchers. It was not unusual for one of them to have unexpended funds in his research accounts at the end of the period of a grant. When this happened, he insisted that the balances be returned to the Foundation." Horvath and Horvath, op. cit., pp. 21–3.

[3] The best accounts of Henderson's career and interests, from the social science aspects, are to be found in Bernard Barber (ed.), *L. J. Henderson on the Social System* (University of Chicago Press, Chicago and London, 1970) and Cynthia Eagle Russett, *The Concept of Equilibrium in American Social Thought* (Yale University Press, New Haven and London, 1966).

described him as "intellectually quite arrogant. . . . He didn't suffer fools gladly, but he was highly respected by scientists."[1] Henderson was the moving spirit behind the Society of Fellows, an elitist institution within the University designed to encourage the work of younger researchers "of exceptional talent and independence in any field of science and scholarship".[2]

Three of the Junior Fellows, George Homans, William F. Whyte and Conrad Arensberg, worked with Mayo. Homans acknowledged his intellectual debt to both Mayo and Henderson, but wrote vividly of Henderson's more flamboyant characteristics. "His beard was red but his politics were vigorously conservative. . . . His method in discussion is feebly imitated by the pile-driver."[3] Mayo was judged "a considerably more modest man than Henderson".[4]

In the 1930s Henderson's talents were harnessed to an enthusiastic presentation of the ideas of the Italian social scientist Vilfredo Pareto (1848–1923), whom he placed in the company of Galileo and Machiavelli. Henderson was particularly attracted by Pareto's incorporation of the concept of system into social science and by the related possibilities inherent in the idea of equilibrium.[5] Henderson's career in the physical and life sciences had developed against the stimulus of new ideas of system and equilibrium, in which the analytical methods of physical chemistry had been recognized as applicable to the study of living things. Henderson's own early work on acid-base equilibria in the blood was part of this movement, the crowning point of which was the theory of W. B. Cannon, another of Henderson's Harvard intimates, of *homeostasis*, or equilibrium in the body.

Henderson saw Pareto's work as the means by which sociology could be added to the continum of the natural sciences. But this was not to take the form of a slavish application of natural science to social science, an enterprise for which Henderson

[1] William B. Wolf, *Conversations with Chester I. Barnard* (Cornell University Press, Ithaca, New York, 1973), p. 2.

[2] Barber (ed.), op. cit., p. 7.

[3] Crane Brinton (ed.), *The Society of Fellows* (Harvard University Press, Cambridge, Mass., 1959), p. 3.

[4] Horvath and Horvath, op. cit., p. 19.

[5] The summary which follows is based mainly on Barber, op. cit. and Russett, op. cit. See also L. J. Henderson, *Pareto's General Sociology: a Physiologist's Interpretation* (Harvard University Press, Cambridge, Mass., 1935); George C. Homans and Charles P. Curtis Jun., *An Introduction to Pareto, His Sociology* (Alfred A. Knopf, New York, 1934); Raymond Aron, *Main Currents in Sociological Thought*, Vol. 2 (Penguin Books, Harmondsworth, 1970).

expressed some distaste, as indeed did Mayo. Rather, Pareto's theory of the social system was to be regarded as "an application of the logical method that has been found useful in all physical sciences when complex situations involving many variables in a state of mutual dependence are described".[1]

Pareto had turned to sociology from a distinguished career in economics, when he became convinced that the frontiers of that discipline needed to be redrawn on a narrower basis. Scientific economics should focus on logical action in society, e.g. where the relation between means and ends in real life corresponds to the relationship as seen by the individual actor, and where the action is determined by reasoning. In contrast to this "logical conduct" Pareto observed that men's actions in real life could more often be classed as "non-logical" or non-rational. This side of human behaviour was to be dealt with by a scientifically-based sociology and psychology, which would complement the areas covered by a properly-demarcated economics.

Henderson fully accepted Pareto's distinction between logical and non-logical conduct. He had long taken a stance against positivism and excessive rationality in science generally. Pareto's emphasis on the importance of values and emotions in social behaviour fitted in closely with Henderson's existing views. He was particularly enthusiastic about Pareto's concept of the "residues" (Pareto's term for manifestations of the basic drives and sentiments out of which human motivation arises). Henderson argued that these "are of the first importance in the social system and . . . their importance is in no way diminished, but rather increased, by their independence of logic".[2]

Throughout the 1930s Henderson advanced and defended these ideas pugnaciously.[3] His conceptual approach clarified and sharpened Pareto's scheme and exerted a powerful influence on other social scientists at Harvard.[4] Talcott Parsons and George Homans acknowledged the strength of this influence, as did Barnard: others exposed to Henderson's ideas included the historians Bernard de Voto and Crane Brinton, the poet Conrad

[1] L. J. Henderson, "Pareto's Science of Society", in Barber, op. cit., p. 184.

[2] Barber, op. cit., p. 98.

[3] Chester Barnard commented: (Henderson) "became captivated right away because Pareto's got a lot of physics and chemistry and that kind of approach. . . . That's what got Henderson excited about it. Then he got into some disputes with other people about it. . . . He got himself into a polemic position where he was fighting everybody all of the time on behalf of Pareto." William B. Wolf, op. cit., pp. 17–18.

[4] Russett, op. cit., p. 118 and pp. 141–2.

Aiken and the anthropologists Elliot Chapple and Conrad Arensberg. The last two were subsequently to play an important part in the revival of social interactionist theories.[1]

Throughout the greater part of Mayo's time at Harvard, Henderson's ideas and interventions were crucial elements in the state of the social sciences there. His effect appears to have been no less profound on those who refused his lead as on those who followed it. In this intellectual ferment it was the work of Talcott Parsons which became the focus of a decisive shift in the character of sociology in the United States.[2] It is clear now that this shift should be seen as having political as well as academic dimensions.

The source was Henderson's enthusiasm for Pareto and his abundant scepticism about "intellectuals" and politicians. Some of those who took part in his Pareto seminar have acknowledged that an interest in the Italian writer was consistent with a politically conservative, anti-Marxist position. Crane Brinton remarked, "at Harvard, in the thirties there was certainly, led by Henderson, what the Communists or fellow travellers or even just mild American-style liberals in the University used to call 'the Pareto cult'."[3] At the same time Pareto was widely known as the "Marx of the Bourgeoisie"; Gouldner adds "when he was not . . . simply termed a fascist".[4] Henderson was well aware of this view of the "Pareto circle" and in 1935 had com-

[1] Ibid., pp. 138–52. How much of a methodological impetus came from Henderson is questionable. Whyte, whose *Street Corner Society* is a notable example of the interactionist approach, says he was most influenced by Arensberg and Chapple themselves. Henderson's intellectual influence seems to have been strongest in the acceptance of the social system as a frame of reference, coupled with the theory of equilibrium applied to the relations of individual members. Cf. Barber, op. cit., p. 50. See also Conrad M. Arensberg and G. Tootell in Mirra Komarovsky (ed.), *Common Frontiers of the Social Sciences* (Free Press, Chicago, 1957), pp. 310–37. Chapple, Arensberg and Whyte were all subsequently involved in industrial research: a major study of Arensberg's (with Douglas MacGregor) utilizing interactionist methods and a "social system" approach was used by Homans in his subsequent disentanglement from the Pareto-Henderson formulation he had faithfully reproduced in the mid-1930s. George C. Homans, *The Human Group* (Routledge & Kegan Paul, London, 1950); *Sentiments and Activities* (Routledge & Kegan Paul, London, 1961), pp. 1–49.

[2] Gouldner, writing of "Parsonsianism' at Harvard, says: "Its emergence there tokened a regional and cultural shift in the centre of gravity of academic sociology in the United States. Alvin W. Gouldner, *The Coming Crisis of Western Sociology* (Heinemann, London, 1971), p. 145.

[3] Quoted in ibid., p. 149. An account of the circle is given in Barbara Heyl, "The Harvard 'Pareto Circle' ", *Journal of the History of Behavioural Sciences*, IV, No. 4, October 1968, pp. 316–34.

[4] Pareto's endorsement by Mussolini in the last year of his life clouded his reputation among many social scientists from the rise of Fascism until after the end of the Second World War. For more details and a more sympathetic view, see Aron, op. cit., pp. 171–5.

mented with characteristic pungency (and in an appropriate Paretian form): "I hope it will now be clear that the prevalent description of Pareto as the Karl Marx of the bourgeoisie or of fascism is nothing more than a derivation."[1]

It is difficult to judge how far Mayo shared Henderson's zeal for Pareto. He was a member of the seminar but according to Homans, "Mayo was never a full-fledged Paretan".[2] There is a reference to the circulation of elites in the *Human Problems*, and some discussion of "non-logical social action", but the authorities mentioned in the latter case are social anthropologists (among them Malinowski, whose friendship with Mayo dated from his fieldwork in Australia before the First World War).[3] Mayo's intellectual contacts were far broader than this account of his close rapport with Henderson might suggest. His work with Roethlisberger, Homans and Whyte, or with clinical colleagues in psychiatry would be at least as significant features in any comprehensive evaluation of his ideas and their development. None the less, it is clear that any appraisal of the criticism subsequently directed against Mayo's work ought properly to take note of the strength and the nature of the feelings directed against Henderson and those associated with him.

The "Mayo Group"

Mayo was by now a well-established member of the Business School, with a growing reputation among a variety of audiences both in the United States and in Europe. He shared with Henderson a great liking for France: but his most frequent trips abroad were to England where his daughters were at school. He often spoke at summer conferences in Britain, particularly those held under the auspices of the Industrial Welfare Society and the National Institute of Industrial Psychology. He continued to focus his attention on the individual worker and the factors governing his response to the requirements of industrial production. But the experience of Hawthorne had posed new

---

[1] Barber (ed.), op. cit., p. 189. This essay, "Pareto's Science of Society", originally appeared in the *Saturday Review of Literature* in May 1935. "Derivations", in Pareto's usage, were the forms of reasoning in which non-logical conduct is clothed.

[2] Heyl, op. cit., p. 322.

[3] *Human Problems*, pp. 166–70. Mayo's comments on Pareto ignore the latter's primary emphasis on the process of "circulation" and focus instead on Mayo's own preoccupation with "quality" i.e. the training of administrators of exceptional capacity. The anthropologists referred to are Malinowski, Radcliffe Brown and Mayo's colleague Lloyd Warner (p. 172).

questions about the social requirements of teamwork, the role of supervision and the pressures of technology both on the structure of society and at the plant and shop-floor levels.

There are signs of these developing interests in *The Human Problems of an Industrial Civilization*, published in 1933. Mayo was still writing from the standpoint of an investigator whose central preoccupation was to apply the equilibrium concept to the behaviour of the individual at work. He saw Cannon's condition of *homeostasis* "as the framework within which such phenomena as 'fatigue' or 'monotony' could be made more meaningful". At the same time, the explanation of "induced unbalance in the worker" needed to be advanced along several dimensions—psychological and sociological, as well as physiological.[1] Sociological questions now occupied more of his attention: indeed, it was Mayo himself who first suggested the idea of the Yankee City Studies (of Newburyport, Massachusetts) subsequently carried out by Lloyd Warner and others, in which the influence of technological change on community structure was a major theme.[2]

His main influence at this time appears to have been through his personal contacts with a wide range of researchers, both among colleagues and students. He kept up his clinical interests and his skill as a practitioner was recognized outside as well as inside the University. He was closely concerned with the problems of students whose personal difficulties interfered with their work; he was also active in mental health clinics in local hospitals. He took a leading role in the setting up of a permanent "personnel counselling" programme at Western Electric, which was to be one of his most controversial legacies.[3]

It was during this period that his qualities of intellectual stimulus and leadership found their fullest expression. Many of those who worked with him at the time—including Fritz Roethlisberger and T. North Whitehead who produced the full accounts of the Hawthorne Studies, George Homans, Lloyd Warner,

[1] Mayo, *Human Problems*, pp. 27–52.
[2] The first of these studies appeared in 1941: W. Lloyd Warner and P. S. Lunt, *The Social Life of a Modern Community* (Yale University Press, 1941).
[3] For accounts of the controversy, see Landsberger, op. cit., Baritz, op. cit., and Bendix, op. cit. See also Jeanne L. and Harold L. Wilensky, "Personnel Counselling: The Hawthorne Case", *American Journal of Sociology*, Vol. 58, 1952, pp. 265–80. The programme was appraised in a final collaboration between the authors of *Management and the Worker*. See W. J. Dickson and F. J. Roethlisberger, *Counselling in an Organisation: A Sequel to the Hawthorne Researches* (Harvard University Press, Cambridge, Mass., 1966).

William Foote Whyte—have testified to this. Roethlisberger later wrote:[1]

> Mayo . . . was a man of imagination, a stimulator of thought, a promoter of clinical research. . . . His chief products were the people that he influenced and helped to develop. . . . It was both Mayo's strength and his weakness that he never discriminated, in terms of professional, educational, academic, disciplinary or social background among the different people with whom he communicated. Regardless of backgrounds, he was interested in people who were curious and could work with ideas.

Roethlisberger also referred to Mayo's own "restless, curious, creative mind". By the late 1930s, it seems that Mayo was thinking of moving on from Harvard, preferably to England: one possibility was that he might work with the National Institute of Industrial Psychology, although he had reservations about that body's traditional approach. But the war ensured that he remained at Harvard until he retired in 1947.

The War and the Human Relations Movement

For Mayo, the war years were a period of great activity coupled with anxiety and stress. His health was not good and he was worried about his family. One of his daughters was in England throughout the war: the other was trapped in France in 1940 and eventually escaped to America. As the war came to an end, he was approaching retirement and still uncertain about what he should do.

His chief empirical work in the Second World War is described briefly in Chapter V of this volume. There were two principal studies, one in small metal-manufacturing plants expanding rapidly to meet the needs of war production; the other based on the aircraft plants in Southern California which in 1943–4 were growing at an unprecedented rate. The immediate stimulus in both cases was given by official concern about absenteeism and labour turnover and the belief that their "causes" needed to be identified. These investigations not only confirmed Mayo's view that first-hand study was essential for a proper understanding of worker behaviour: they also led him to conclude that the key to the human situation in industry was to be found in discovering the conditions of effective "teamwork".

[1] F. J. Roethlisberger, Introduction to Mayo, *Human Problems* (The Viking Press, New York, 1960).

With many colleagues away on war service, Mayo's own teaching and administrative responsibilities were considerably increased. At the same time, the urgency of war generated an active interest among government departments, top managers and union leaders in a number of ideas with which Mayo was closely identified. The most immediate effects were seen in the acceleration of plans for the training of supervisors, in particular under the Training Within Industry (TWI) programme. This programme dealt with elementary work study, methods of teaching, job instruction, safety and the importance of "human relations" in industry. It was widely adopted in the United States and at the end of the war, the Ministry of Labour sponsored its introduction to Britain. For many managers and supervisors it provided their first experience of adult training.[1]

Less immediate in its effects, but more significant from the point of view of Mayo's standing among social scientists was the emergence from wartime studies and experience of what came to be known as the "Human Relations School".

This school was interdisciplinary in its origins and is generally described as such in its approach, though its underlying concern with the dynamics of group behaviour make it more properly classed as social-psychological. The chief interests of its members in the industrial setting may be summarized as (i) the relations between productivity and "morale", (ii) the nature of co-operation within work groups and between work groups and supervisors (especially the effects of participation in decision-making), (iii) the significance of leadership, especially leadership "styles" and procedures in selecting and appraising leaders. The industrial setting for these purposes was normally the "plant", "enterprise" or "organization".

The intellectual underpinnings of this movement, which reached the peak of its influence in the 1950s, were provided by the work of the Mayo group and by studies developed from Kurt Lewin's classic wartime experiments with types of leadership in boys' clubs. In the decade following the war, numerous studies were conducted at Chicago and in particular at the Survey Research Centre at Michigan: these were directly concerned with the development of more precise measures of the morale of

[1] A pioneering analysis of the foreman's role had been carried out by Mayo's colleague Fritz Roethlisberger. F. J. Roethlisberger, "The Foreman: Master and Victim of Double Talk", *Harvard Business Review*, Vol. 23, 1945, pp. 283–98. See also K. E. Thurley and H. Wirdenius, *Supervision: a Reappraisal* (Heinemann, London, 1973).

employees and the relation between morale and performance (at managerial and supervisory as well as shop-floor or office level).[1]

Retirement in England

Mayo took little part in these developments. The *Social Problems* had been published in America in 1946. He was contemplating another book to complete his trilogy, to be called *The Political Problems of an Industrial Civilization*. In May 1947, shortly before his retirement from Harvard, he delivered two lectures eventually published by the Business School under that title: they appear as Appendix I of this volume.

Mayo published no further work on this theme. However, before retiring he completed a book based on his notes on the psychology of Pierre Janet, with whom he had enjoyed a long friendship. Janet had survived the war but died in his late eighties shortly before Mayo returned to Europe.

In the summer of 1947, Mayo left Harvard for the last time and went to England. He and his wife settled in a flat at Polesdon Lacey, a National Trust property in Surrey famous for its gardens and downland views.

There was talk of various projects, but Mayo was reluctant to commit himself to further work.[2] His health was failing and he died in a nursing home at Guildford on 1 September 1949. He was 68 years of age. His widow died in London in 1962.

TOWARDS AN ASSESSMENT OF MAYO

A proper assessment of Mayo's contribution has yet to be made. It is true that his name has not been forgotten; but this is due chiefly to the vehement controversy during the 1950s and early 1960s over the nature and purposes of social science research in industry. Interpretations of Mayo's work and influence were

---

[1] For general accounts of these studies, see Bernard Bass, *Leadership, Psychology and Organisational Behaviour* (Harper, New York, 1960); Rensis Likert, *New Patterns of Management* (McGraw-Hill, New York, 1961); Morris Viteles, *Motivation and Morale in Industry* (Staples Press, London, 1960). For a development in line with the tradition of the Mayo group see A. Zaleznik, C. R. Christensen and F. J. Roethlisberger, *The Motivation, Productivity and Satisfaction of Workers* (Harvard University Press, Cambridge, Mass., 1958).

[2] Some confusion still exists as to whether Mayo was involved in studies in England after his retirement. This arose because his daughter was then active in industrial research in Britain and writing under the name, Patricia Elton Mayo. Mayo himself addressed a few conferences and wrote to *The Times*, but he did not take part in any further investigations. The confusion spread to former colleagues in Harvard. See George Homans, "Some Corrections to 'The Perspectives of Elton Mayo'", *Review of Economics and Statistics*, Vol. 31, 1949, p. 321.

generally tailored to fit one side or the other of that argument and only very rarely attempted to judge the man and his contribution as a whole.

It is beyond the scope of this essay to do more than to offer observations on the lines that a comprehensive assessment might follow and to comment on some of the difficulties involved. *The Social Problems of an Industrial Civilization* is a convenient starting-point for the student, since it is the closest thing we have to a self-assessment by Mayo. Part I offers his interpretation of the critical problems of the age, against a background of his views on what the social sciences had to offer towards solutions of those problems. Part II summarizes his experience of industrial research and offers some tentative conclusions about the importance of social relations (especially the workgroup) in industry.

At this point, the reader should be warned how difficult it is to appraise Mayo on the basis of his published work. It has to be said that Mayo's writings do not always embody his own precepts about "systematic logic" and the need for social scientists "to begin work by a thorough painstaking acquaintance with the whole subject matter of their studies".[1]

Mayo disliked writing for publication and seems to have had no taste at all for the heavyweight treatise. He is said to have been happiest in discussion and in the direct presentation and exchange of ideas. That he was an unusually compelling lecturer seems to have been beyond question and much of his published work originated in lectures.[2] But it is rare to find in his writings a fully worked-out scheme, or a comprehensive or rigorously-constructed argument. There are plenty of ideas, but few are at all developed. At best there is an assemblage of research findings, idiosyncratic speculations and clinically-based insights which Mayo uses to block out a number of bold propositions. These propositions are focused on the individual and his socio-emotional needs in an industrial society, particularly on the need to adapt to a work-situation which is continually reshaped by technological change.

Mayo's View of Society

As has been said, *The Social Problems of an Industrial Civilization*

---

[1] *Social Problems*, p. 18.

[2] The *Human Problems* and *Democracy and Freedom* were based on lectures. The *Notes on the Psychology of Pierre Janet* convey directly the quality of Mayo's style as a speaker, including a certain dry humour. See *Janet*, pp. 3–4, 9–10, 81–2.

is the best single source for any judgment of Mayo based on his writings. In particular, the first two chapters, "The Seamy Side of Progress" and "The Rabble Hypothesis" are his most sustained pieces of writing. In them, he presents (i) his analysis of the consequences of industrialization for the life of the individual in the setting of group and community relations, (ii) his concept of "social skill" and the failure of the social sciences to develop knowledge and practice relevant to the needs of a changing society, and (iii) his celebrated critique of the inadequacies of classical economic theory as an explanation of the behaviour of the industrial worker.

These chapters neatly illustrate his strengths and his weaknesses as a writer in this field. The presentation is lively, with some striking turns of phrase, there is no shortage of ideas, which are taken freely from a wide range of sources. But the pace is often too brisk, the phrasing too dramatic, the grasp of sources too wide, almost indiscriminate. At the same time, the argument has considerable force, as a summary outline shows.

In "The Seamy Side of Progress" Mayo begins by outlining his version of the "unacceptable face of capitalism". Aesthetic protests about the environmental costs of industrialization have been matched by unheeded warnings (e.g. by Le Play and Durkheim) about its socially-disruptive effects, especially the collapse of traditional communities and social codes. Mayo notes two principal consequences: (i) an increase in the number of "unhappy individuals" and (ii) a "wariness or hostility" between social groups. Growing material standards are accompanied by a "destruction of individual significance in living". As Durkheim argues, established social contexts have all disappeared, except one—the political state. The organization of social life is necessarily left to the State—a task it cannot perform for the intimate daily life of its citizens. Industrial society therefore juxtaposes "an ineffective state authority" with "a disordered dust of individuals".

Mayo next contrasts the tremendous effort expended on technical and material progress and the failure of industrial societies to tackle the problems of co-operation. He describes the routines of collaboration in primitive society, not to recommend a return to them, but instead to point out their obsolescence in an industrial society characterized by continuous change. Modern industry is also a co-operative system, but it embodies a different principle of social organization—that of an *adaptive* society, as opposed to an *established* society.   Mayo then advocates the need for the systematic study and acquisition of "social skills" in order to meet the requirements of an adaptive society, i.e. where change and adaptability are prime requirements.   Previously apprenticeship provided a form of training in which technical and social skills developed side by side.   Mayo sees the disjunction between technical and social skills as a possible cause of increasing psychoneurosis in modern society.

In the rest of the chapter Mayo sets out his views on the nature of social skills and the conditions for their effective development and use.   This is impossible to summarize briefly, but three points should be noted: (i) skills are rooted in observation; logic and theory come later; (ii) the success of the natural sciences is due to their cautious pursuit of this rule; (iii) the social sciences have no usable skills at present.   Mayo offers an example of a "simple social skill that can be practised and that, as it develops, will offer insight and the equivalent of manipulative capacity to the student".   This is "the capacity of an individual to communicate his feelings and ideas to another, the capacity of groups to communicate effectively and intimately with one another".   Mayo then advances clinical examples, drawn from his own experience, to support his contention that the lack of social skill is "the outstanding defect that civilization is facing today".   He concludes by urging the development of such skills on the social sciences, particularly on sociology and psychology.

The full title of Chapter 2 is "The Rabble Hypothesis and its Corollary, The State Absolute".   Its principal feature is a vigorous critique of the "behavioural" assumptions of classical economic theory.   Mayo's chief aim is to demonstrate its inadequacy as a source of the social skills industrial society so badly needs.   The divorce between economic theory and the realities of economic practice demonstrates the irrelevance of classical doctrines to the scale and technical complexity of modern industry; and its indifference to the consequences of the success or failure of individual firms for the well-being of entire communities.   In an examination of economic theory, Mayo fastens on Ricardo to exemplify the shortcomings of its view of man and society.   Ricardo, he argues, "bases his studies and his logic upon three limiting concepts.   These are:

1. Natural society consists of a horde of unorganized individuals.

2. Every individual acts in a manner calculated to secure his self-preservation or self-interest.

3. Every individual thinks logically, to the best of his ability, in the service of this aim."

Mayo examines the grounds for each of these propositions and concludes that the first two hold good under certain limited conditions. He finds the third more questionable, indeed "positively misleading", and cites the Bank Wiring Room Study as contrary evidence.

All of this leads Mayo to doubt the applicability of economic theory to "normal" life. "Must we conclude", he asks, "that economics is a study of human behaviour in non-normal situations, or, alternatively, a study of non-normal behaviour in ordinary situations?" (The crux here is the definition of "normal" behaviour. Is it "logical", according to the postulates of economics or "non-logical", according to the postulates of sociology?) Mayo concludes that the "rabble hypothesis" (i.e. the view that mankind is a horde of unorganized individuals actuated by self-interest) is too narrow and pathological a view to serve as a basis for "industrial studies".

The rest of the chapter is devoted to the connexion between the rabble hypothesis and "the conviction of a need for a leviathan, a powerful state, which by the exercise of a unique authority shall impose order on the rabble". In considering theories of authority Mayo contrasts the views of writers like J. N. Figgis and Chester Barnard who display direct experience of "the world of affairs", with the exponents of the rabble hypothesis. He sees the latter as "remote" from it, describing them as "academics, writers, lawyers . . . students of law, government, philosophy. Very few, if any, have taken responsibility for the life, work and welfare of their brother humans." Barnard's discussion of authority shows that it depends vitally on the co-operation of others; therefore, "social understanding and social skill are involved equally with technical knowledge and capacity". In real life authority depends on co-operation, yet the dominance of the rabble hypothesis emphasizes the imposition of order. Dictatorship thus becomes possible.

After a critical discussion of Jenks's theory of the development of the State, Mayo moves to a final summing-up. While not denying the reality or the necessity of the State, he sees the rabble hypothesis and "a politics that postulates 'a community of individuals' ruled by a sovereign state" as harmful, in that they "foreclose on and discourage any investigation of the facts of social organization". He concludes: "The forms of democracy are not enough; the active development of social skill and insight must make these dry bones live."

Some Views of Mayo

The chief criticism of Mayo is that his solution to the problem of industrial civilization—co-operation—is at once too narrow and too open to a variety of interpretations to be of any signifi-cance.[1] Certainly the summary of "findings" from his industrial studies which Mayo offers at the end of Chapter V seems rather unexciting. Against this, it might be said that nowadays the need to take account of the reality of workgroups is widely under-stood; the limitations of traditional selection procedures and aptitude tests in relation to on-the-job requirements are generally recognized; and that management and supervisory (and for that matter trade-union) education now proceed on the assumption that first-hand study of industrial situations is a prime require-ment. In such respects, the insights and tentative conclusions of Mayo are now commonplaces among social scientists, managers and trade unionists.

None the less, Mayo's elliptical, sometimes off-hand style, provides abundant ammunition for his critics, who have made good use of the ambiguities, omissions and implicit assumptions of his work. Mayo's brusque approach was fortified by his conviction that the social sciences were at such a primitive stage of development that they had very little to contribute other than "to talk endlessly about alleged social problems".[2] They also lacked the basic intuitive skills grounded in "direct experience of fact and situation", which are achieved by the students in the natural sciences through the laboratory method.

His contrary view that "erudition" was by contrast "easily transmitted" probably accounts for the fact that Mayo is remark-ably casual about his own intellectual assumptions, particularly those bearing on the nature of society and of the political process. In the case of the latter, these assumptions are most fully laid down in his first book, *Democracy and Freedom*, which directly reflects Mayo's early experience as a philosopher and his interest

[1] See "A Note on Mayo's Critics", below, p. xxxix.
[2] *Social Problems*, p. 19.

in political behaviour.   In examining the problems of democratic government he reveals a close familiarity with a wide range of relevant sources, including Graham Wallas, G. D. H. Cole, the Webbs and Ostrogorski.   His chief conclusion is that modern society has undervalued existing social forms and put an altogether disproportionate emphasis on the State as the embodiment of authority and the means of social unity.

It is clear that Mayo is sceptical about the capacity of the State to promote "spontaneous co-operation", which he values; or its capacity to reduce conflict, especially class conflict, which in his view is actively promoted by party politics.[1]   Mayo's more extreme critics saw his mistrust of politicians and his sceptisicm about the power of formal procedures to resolve conflict as evidence of a total disbelief in politics and government. They coupled this with his discussion of the habitual social order of traditional societies and concluded that he had a preference for the social organization of the Middle Ages; or at best for pre-industrial America where "community" was still meaningful. His prescription for the ills of an industrial society, therefore, was simply an attempt "to make possible the re-creation of Agrarian Virtue, Agrarian Loyalty and the Agrarian Sense of Community in the twentieth century's world of skyscrapers and subways, of smoke and steam".[2]

Did Mayo really imply this?   The casual, sometimes arrogant way in which he expresses his ideas (coupled with a tendency to switch in argument from the Byzantium of Justinian to the Bell Telephone Company of Chester Barnard) make him an easier target than he deserves.   One must admit that there are gaps in his argument; that he is unmistakeably conservative in his respect for the strengths of traditional association; that he pays little direct attention to trade unions and collective bargaining and does not admit a constructive role for conflict; also that he is generally vague about what he means by co-operation, or just how the "active development of social skill and insight" will make the "dry bones" of democracy live.[3]

Against this, Mayo is a more subtle writer than his critics

---

[1] *Democracy and Freedom*, pp. 42–4. Mayo was arguing on the basis of the Australian experience in politics, which he saw as an extreme case of the generalization of industrial grievances into party political issues.

[2] Baritz, op. cit., pp. 111–12.

[3] *Social Problems*, p. 50.

suggest, as a careful reading of this volume will show. He antici-
pates some of the now familiar criticisms of his own position.
For example, on the question of his supposed preference for the
social order of the Middle Ages or the habitual co-operation of
traditional societies, he has this to say (in a comment on Le Play
and Durkheim):[1]

> These earlier studies tend naturally to look back at the life of
> simpler communities with regret; they tend inevitably to the
> conclusion that spontaneity of co-operation cannot be recovered
> except by reversion to the traditional. This, however, is a road we
> cannot travel in these days; for us there can be no easy return to
> simplicity.

Another of Mayo's problems as a writer is that he is altogether
too terse and impatient to follow through a line of argument,
especially when it involves considering alternative conclusions.
Also, as a practised speaker, he had a liking for the well-turned
phrase, the vivid assertion, the arresting declaration. Each of
these characteristics lands him in difficulties with his critics.
As an example of the first, in the *Social Problems* he takes from
Durkheim the notion of "anomie" (the absence of norms or the
collapse of norms) to underline his general argument about the
disintegration of traditional social forms in industrial society. He
presents it succinctly and in a way which suggests he was fully
familiar with Durkheim's analysis. But he altogether ignores
Durkheim's lifelong interest in the possibility that "corporations"
(professional organizations which would include employers as
well as employees) are the modern social groups likely to
foster the social integration of individuals. Logically this would
have been consistent with Kerr's view of the "all-absorbing
corporation of Elton Mayo", but Mayo shows no sign of having
even registered Durkheim's conclusion. Again, he frequently
refers to the need to educate first-class administrative talent, but
he nowhere develops what he means by an "administrator" or
considers the nature of the enterprises dependent on this talent.
In the *Social Problems* the term "élite" has disappeared altogether
and of Pareto there is no mention at all. His critics, however,

---

[1] Ibid., p. 8. Or again (p. 14) on the position of the industrial worker: "the remedy
cannot be a return to simple apprenticeship and the primitive establishment."

attribute to him closely-reasoned views on both anomie and élites.[1]

Mayo's relish for the striking phrase and arresting declaration is exemplified by the famous (or infamous) sentence: "If our social skills had advanced step by step with our technical skills, there would not have been another European war."[2]   Apart from being untestable, the proposition arouses expectations which Mayo's prospectus—or any conceivable improvement on it—is unable to satisfy.   All the same, the extravagance of the phrasing has obscured the fact that Mayo's concept of a "social skill" has more depth and content than the typical patent remedy of the "communication" field: grounded in his experience of clinical observation and practice, the concept is an important guide to Mayo's view of the possibilities (and limitations) of social science methods.[3]

These examples could be multiplied but the reader will find no difficulty in adding to them.   There is little profit in trying to decide what sort of books Mayo might have written had he been more attentive to the business of sociological scholarship and (inevitably) more guarded, abstruse and long-winded.   As a result some of his critics have made his work into much more of a piece—in particular, into more of a dogma—than the evidence really allows: against this, one must resist the temptation to treat Mayo's work as if it were *Edwin Drood* or Schubert's *Unfinished* and provide him with what might now seem a more appropriate set of conclusions.   In any case, after a quarter of a century, Mayo's idiosyncrasies and sociological ambiguities are among his principal attractions.   Few social scientists, after all, write so directly or with such self-assurance; fewer still write books which never exceed 150 pages.

THE SIGNIFICANCE OF MAYO'S CONTRIBUTION

An assessment of the significance of Mayo's contribution must

[1] Mayo's "chief intellectual forebears were two: Pareto and his preoccupation with non-logical action and the role of the elite, Durkheim and his persistent concern with the anomie of industrial society." Clark Kerr and Lloyd H. Fisher "Plant Sociology: The Elite and the Aborigines", in M. Komarovsky (ed.), op. cit., p. 287. Some felt that other critics had not gone far enough. "Of all the criticisms of Mayo, few indicate his careful acceptance and extension of Pareto's pro-elitist orientation, an orientation which led to the use of many of Pareto's ideas by Mussolini and others." Melvin J. Vincent and Jackson Mayers, *New Foundations for Industrial Sociology* (Van Nostrand, Princeton, 1959), p. 241.
[2] Mayo, *Social Problems*, p. 30.
[3] Ibid., pp. 18–30. Mayo, *Janet*, pp. 3–23. For a development of this point, see J. H. Smith, "Elton Mayo Revisited", *British Journal of Industrial Relations*, Vol. XII, No. 2, July 1974, pp. 282–91.

begin by acknowledging the impact of the general argument presented in the *Social Problems*. Mayo's emphasis on the contemporary failure (i) to study the social aspects of industrialization, and (ii) to develop social skills to match the technical skills of a rapidly changing society, drew attention to the possible contributions of sociology to industry and industrial management. His own gradual progression from a psychological/physiological approach to one with more of a sociological perspective was widely believed to demonstrate the desirability of this development. His subsequent critique of the shortcomings of economic theory as a basis for the explanation of behaviour in industry provided further confirmation. The first point to note, therefore, is that it was chiefly on the basis of Mayo's work that the case for the sociological study of industrial behaviour was advanced. It also paved the way for the introduction of sociology into business school courses and management education generally.

Another significant point is his leadership of the "Mayo Group" at Harvard and the stimulus he provided to a distinguished group of researchers who advanced the boundaries of investigation in a number of directions. Mayo's encouragement and advice was clearly of great importance during the 1930s and the war years. The effect of that leadership was still in evidence after his death.

The effect of Mayo and his reputation on other social scientists concerned with industry was and continues to be considerable. Although this is a complex subject, a number of observations may be made. What Mayo emphasized and what he disregarded became common points of departure for the growing number of "industrial sociologists" in the late 1940s and 1950s. Many of these were concerned to rectify Mayo's lack of attention to trade unions by pointing out that unions could satisfy the worker's need to belong; also that conflict could be viewed as a positive as well as a negative influence. Equally, Mayo's supposed myopia concerning what went on beyond the factory gates aroused the feelings of those sociologists who wanted to show that social-structural factors such as class affected the orientation and behaviour of workers on the shop floor, and that sociology as an academic discipline dealt with a far broader range of phenomena than work groups and the training of supervisors. Another point of view—perhaps now rather dated in the light of "commitment" and "crisis-bound sociology"—led to a rejection of Mayo as a sociologist on the grounds that his sympathies were too apparent. The reader who follows up the Note after this essay will see that there was plenty of grist to this particular mill: indeed he may wonder how in the 1950s industrial sociologists had time to do much else other than criticize Mayo.

Mayo's influence in the ten years or so after his death, it is clear, was no less pronounced than it had been during the peak of his Harvard career: indeed, it might be argued that it became greater. It has to be seen, however, in almost wholly negative terms, since the principal concern in that period was to investigate areas judged to have been neglected by Mayo. As studies were made of such questions as the influence of formal organization on behaviour, the social-structural sources of industrial conflict, the power of economic incentives, the constraints on group formation and "teamwork" imposed by technology and other factors, so the focus of industrial sociology shifted away from Mayo's preoccupation with group behaviour and the sources of co-operation. One might conclude that the age of Mayo was well and truly over.

Yet Mayo's name is still remembered—or perhaps one should say, his skeleton is still rattled. He is of course widely regarded as the archetypal "managerial sociologist", but this is hardly sufficient reason for continuing to mention him. Today there are many sociologists and social psychologists actively involved in industry of whom a sizeable proportion could be more unambiguously classed as "managerial" and whose work provides more thoroughgoing examples of bias towards management.

In all this there is a further curiosity. Mayo's ideas, both on politics and on the methods of social science, are distinctly more fashionable than they were in the years immediately following his death. Indeed his scepticism about the motives of politicians, his advocacy of decentralization in decision-making, his conviction that the need for consultation and co-operation takes priority over the mechanics of institutions, and his pessimism about the prospects for genuine democracy in an increasingly centralized state are wholly topical twenty-five years after his death. So too in the realm of sociological method is his emphasis on the need to explore, as part of the techniques of interviews, the meaning of a situation from the point of view of the other person; while his opinions on the social responsibilities of the investigator and the need to develop structures of knowledge rooted in first-hand observation would ensure him an invitation to any of the currently-fashionable conferences on "new directions" in sociology.

Despite all this, Mayo has not been rediscovered except in a mild form as a guru of "participatory democracy".[1] The explanation is simple enough. Without the old, familiar Mayo, industrial sociology would lose its most reliable landmark. A developing field of study needs a founder whose errors can be analysed and formally repudiated by his successors. Mayo might have been less readily disowned had he been a voluminous or more obscure writer, but he was not. His errors, prejudices and omissions are easy to identify, but so too are his capacities for generalization, his concern for the human condition and his flair for skilful illustration. That is, to those who bother to read what he has to say. As the reader of this volume will discover, there is much here that is fresh, worthwhile and of genuine intellectual interest.

A NOTE ON MAYO'S WRITINGS[2]

Mayo's first published work of consequence was *Democracy and Freedom* (p. xiii, n. 2), which should be read in conjunction with his contribution to Atkinson's symposium on Australia after the First World War (p. xiii, n. 1). These works provide the most coherent and developed account of Mayo's views of the State and of the nature of politics in industrial society. Mayo himself made little reference subsequently to this work, although the central assumptions embodied in *Democracy and Freedom* underpin the general argument of the *Social Problems*, published nearly thirty years later. The latter work is properly seen as Mayo's final commentary on the themes first explored in *Democracy and Freedom*.

Mayo's two other books, the *Human Problems* (p. xiv, n. 4) and his notes on *Janet* (p. xii, n. 1) fall into a different category. The *Human Problems* (originally delivered as the Lowell Lectures at Harvard) expresses Mayo's view of the limitations of traditional research into human behaviour in industry and his growing interest in a sociological perspective. It contains his fullest exposition of relevant studies, including some of the Hawthorne

---

[1] P. Blumberg, *Industrial Democracy: The Sociology of Participation* (Constable, London, 1968).

[2] N.B. References in brackets are to the footnotes in this essay where full details have been given. Publications not already referred to in the text are cited in this section as a continuation of the essay footnotes.

Experiments. This book probably conveys most accurately Mayo's quality as a scientific popularizer. The book on Janet is not well known, because it was published posthumously when Mayo's reputation was already declining. It contains a variety of examples drawn from Mayo's own work as a psychotherapist, as well as some autobiographical material, albeit rather sketchy. In it Mayo also reflects more extensively on questions of method. The appendix, "Frightened People" (originally published in the *Harvard Medical Alumni Bulletin* in January 1939) ranks as one of the earliest essays in the sociology of illness behaviour.

The rest of Mayo's published work falls into two main groups, each of which needs to be further subdivided, i.e.: (i) scientific: major/minor and (ii) popular: major/minor. However, such a detailed classification cannot yet be undertaken as there is as yet no full list of Mayo's publications: we must await the results of Dr Richard Trahair's enquiries in Australia for this.

Mayo's major scientific papers are based on his empirical work after arriving in the United States. His study of fatigue in a Philadelphia textile mill provided the basis for his first academic publication in the United States (p. xiv, n. 2).[1] His first references to the Hawthorne Studies appear to have been given in a paper called "Supervision and Morale" which was published in Britain as well as in the United States.[2]

Mayo published numerous short pieces on the Hawthorne Studies, including at least one radio talk (part of an educational series).[3] Some of these are repetitious and of interest chiefly as an indication of the demand for his services as a speaker. An important exception however is the joint paper with L. J. Henderson which was read before a symposium "The Environment and its Effects on Man" at the Harvard Tercentenary Celebration in 1936.[4] This paper is of interest for two reasons. First, it is a concrete example of collaboration between the two men. Second, the closing section shows the influence of Henderson's thinking in the manner in which attention is directed to the reality of the "spontaneous social system" in understanding the behaviour of workers.

---

[1] He used the same study for his first academic paper to be published in Britain, "Day Dreaming and Output in a Spinning Mill", *Journal of the National Institute of Industrial Psychology*, 1925, pp. 203–9.

[2] Published in the *Personnel Journal* (1930) and the *Journal of the N.I.I.P.* (1931).

[3] "The Problem of Working Together", *Psychology Series Lecture No. 27* (for National Broadcasting Company) (University of Chicago Press, 1932).

[4] L. J. Henderson and Elton Mayo, "The Effects of Social Environment", *Journal of Industrial Hygiene and Toxicology*, Vol. 18, 1936, pp. 401–16.

Mayo's wartime activities produced only one work of conse-quence to which he put his name as author. This was the study of aircraft workers with George Lombard, on *Teamwork and Labour Turnover*.[1] The emphasis placed in this study on the influence of supervision was to prove a powerful influence on subsequent research; the monograph also contains some anticipation of the need to classify work groups in terms of size and structure—a need which has yet to be properly explored empirically.

Mayo's popular articles for *Harper's* have already been men-tioned in this essay (p. xiv, n. 3). He had been involved in journa-lism in London after leaving Edinburgh and had a few pieces published at the time, including one in the *Pall Mall Gazette*. He wrote more after his return to Australia, including some fiction. Dr Trahair of La Trobe University, Melbourne, is assembling a comprehensive list of all Mayo's publications.

A NOTE ON MAYO'S CRITICS (AND A FEW SYMPATHIZERS)[2]

Mayo's critics have included some of the most distinguished post-war students of industrial society, e.g. Clark Kerr, Reinhard Bendix, Ralf Dahrendorf, C. Wright Mills As has been suggested, their indictments are weighty but sometimes not as attentive to Mayo's own writings as they might have been. In particular, there is a tendency to make Mayo into more of a mouthpiece for management interests (as opposed to labour) than the record warrants. Also, some writers attribute arguments and perspec-tives to Mayo that properly belong to those who worked with and followed him. Above all, as this essay has argued, Mayo's views are often given an ideological solidity and coherence which he did not seek and which his writings do not justify.

It is unfortunate that the basis on which much of this criticism is founded is the well-known article by Bendix and Fisher (p. ix, n. 2). This was the first serious critique of Mayo's perspectives; ironically, its publication in Harvard coincided with Mayo's death in England. Bendix and Fisher show familiarity with Mayo's work as a whole and appreciate the significance of the ideas presented in *Democracy and Freedom*. A few minor errors of

[1] *Teamwork and Labour Turnover in the Aircraft Industry of Southern California* (Harvard Business School, Division of Research, Business Research Studies No. 32, 1944).

[2] N.B. As in the note on Mayo's writings, the references in brackets are to the foot-notes in the main body of this essay. Some further references are given as a continua-tion of the essay footnotes.

fact or interpretation apart, their article remains the most convincing of its kind and must still command serious attention, as does Bendix's subsequent and more extensive appraisal of Mayo's influence in his *Work and Authority in Industry*.[1] Clark Kerr's article in *Fortune* (p. ix, n. 3) and his more general critique of the human relations school (with Fisher as co-author) in Komarovsky (ed.) (p. xxi, n. 4) may also be placed in this category, together with the article by H. L. Wilensky in a collection of papers on human relations research edited by Arensberg.[2]

Other major criticisms of Mayo published in the late 1940s and 1950s include an often-cited article by Harold L. Sheppard, two characteristically definitive papers by W. E. Moore and at least one full-blooded appraisal by C. Wright Mills.[3]   All these papers are important for an understanding of the intellectual context in which Mayo's ideas found acceptance or rejection.   A more comprehensive guide, which includes a list of the main reviews of Mayo's work as well as of *Management and the Worker* is given in Landsberger (p. x, n. 1).   After more than fifteen years, this monograph is still the most useful starting-point for anyone wishing to examine the character of the controversy centred on the Hawthorne Studies and Mayo's contribution to them.

Subsequent critical attention to Mayo's ideas has dwindled along with his reputation.   However, there is a section in Dahrendorf's influential *Class and Class Conflict in Industrial Society* which offers a more realistic appraisal than is customary of Mayo's ideas from the standpoint of sociological theory.[4]

Mayo's influence in the development of management thought in Britain has been assessed in an important book by Child.[5]   However, Child is unable to throw much light on Mayo's contacts in Britain during the 1930s—a subject deserving additional research.   Furthermore, the author gives too much weight to "Mayoism" as a dogma and overstates its influence in the

---

[1] R. Bendix, *Work and Authority in Industry* (John Wiley & Sons, New York, 1956), Ch. 5.

[2] Conrad Arensberg (ed.), *Research on Industrial Human Relations—A Critical Appraisal* (Harper, New York, 1957).

[3] Harold L. Sheppard, "The Social & Historical Philosophy of Elton Mayo", *Antioch Review*, Vol. 10, 1950, pp. 396–406. W. E. Moore, "Current Issues in Industrial Sociology", *American Sociological Review*, Vol. 12, 1947, pp. 651–7; "Industrial Sociology—Status and Prospects", *American Sociological Review*, Vol. 13, 1948, pp. 382–400. C. Wright Mills, "The Contributions of Sociology to Studies of Industrial Relations", *Proceedings*, Industrial Relations Research Association, Vol. 1, 1948, pp. 199–222.

[4] R. Dahrendorf, *Class and Class Conflict in Industrial Society* (Stanford University Press, 1959), pp. 109–14.

[5] J. Child, *British Management Thought* (Allen & Unwin, London, 1969).

development both of industrial social science research and of management education in the late 1940s and 1950s.[1] Having said that, Child's work is none the less of considerable importance for the serious student of Mayo's influence in Britain.

Apart from these two studies and Baritz's polemical but not very well judged assault (p. xv, n. 1) there has been little recent interest in Mayo or his ideas. The critical attack has concentrated on Hawthorne itself and in challenging the hitherto-unchallenged findings of the studies, as in the papers by Carey, Sykes and others on the validity of the Bank Wiring Room conclusions (p. xvi, n. 5). Developments in organization theory—in particular applications of the "systems" approach and the concept of equilibrium to organizational behaviour—have revived Mayo's fame to a certain extent, but in his now traditional function of the champion of consensus as against conflict.[2]

It would be wrong to leave the reader with the impression that all writing on Mayo is consistently hostile. The standard texts on industrial sociology and industrial social psychology continue to treat him as an important figure in the development of research and practice, although now more of an historical figure. At the same time, the current revival of interest in grass-roots participation in both the political and the industrial sphere has produced at least one work in which Blumberg sees Mayo's contribution as still worth examining (p. xxxvii, n. 2). It is unlikely that this will be the final example.

Finally, there is a fairly substantial body of sympathetic writings from those who worked directly with Mayo and who acknowledge their intellectual and other debts to him. Including as they do Roethlisberger, Homans and Whyte, these contributions are more than the usual pieties. Although some of these have already been mentioned, for convenience they are listed together overleaf.[3]

In reflecting on the circumstances which gave rise to the paradox of severe criticism and generous tributes attached to Mayo's name, it seems plausible to suggest isolation as the cause

[1] See J. H. Smith, *The University Teaching of the Social Sciences—Industrial Sociology* (UNESCO, Paris, 1961). See also the debate between V. L. Allen and J. H. Smith, "Management and the Universities", *Listener*, 13 July 1961; 20 July 1961, and F. Bechhofer, "Why Not Industrial Studies?" *New Society*, 2 April 1964.

[2] Examples include Sherman Krupp, *Pattern in Organization Analysis* (Holt, Rinehart & Winston, New York, 1961) and D. Silverman, *The Theory of Organization* (Heinemann, London, 1970). For a rather different view see C. Argyris, *The Applicability of Organizational Sociology* (Cambridge University Press, 1972).

of his vulnerability to attack and his treatment after his death. A contributory factor was Mayo's decisive break in mid-career when he left Australia for good. Although by then well-established in Australian academic life, his influence was limited to his own students and severely constrained by the lack of interest in the Social Sciences in his own country. Apart from generous but not always accurate obituaries such as Kyle's (p. xii, n. 2) little of Mayo's influence is to be noted in work published in Australia after his departure.

Isolation could also be regarded as a feature of his life at Harvard after his arrival in the United States. Certainly his membership of the Henderson camp restricted his influence and his standing among sociologists. His intellectual inclinations, in any case, were too open-ended to bind him to membership of any particular group: he often made it clear that he had no taste for moving with the herd. What is lacking in Mayo's own writings and in writing about him—both favourable and unfavourable—is any marked impression of the man's own personality and style. These questions deserve further examination before a comprehensive evaluation of his work and undoubted influence can be made.

J. H. SMITH
Professor of Sociology
University of Southampton

---

[3] The first of these was Homans's rejoinder to Bendix and Fisher; George C. Homans, "Some Corrections to the Perspectives of Elton Mayo", *Review of Economics and Statistics*, Vol. 31, 1949, pp. 319–21. Homans has paid regular and generous tribute to the influence of Mayo's teaching in his own work. Fritz Roethlisberger has left several memoirs of Mayo. See his *Man-in-Organization* (Harvard University Press, Cambridge, Mass., 1968), especially pp. 227–40; also (with W. J. Dickson) *Counselling in an Organization* (Harvard University Press, Cambridge, Mass., 1966). Like Homans, William Foote Whyte has fully acknowledged his debt to Mayo. See his *Street Corner Society* (University of Chicago Press, 1943), also *Organizational Behaviour: Theory and Application* (Richard D. Irwin and the Dorsey Press, Illinois, 1969).

FOREWORD

THIS is the second in a series of books by Professor Elton Mayo, now planned to be three in number. Jointly they will present selected aspects of over a quarter-century of clinical research in industry. This research has been carried on in an effort to get a better and more fundamental understanding of human relations—that most neglected of subjects—and how to improve them. These books present also Mayo's mature reflections based on long self-training and clinical experience with individuals in a great variety of social environments before he began the study of men and women in industry. As a result of his earlier work, when he turned his attention to industry he brought to his studies, ". . . first, intimate, habitual, intuitive familiarity with things; secondly, systematic knowledge of things; and thirdly, a useful way of thinking about things", which the late Lawrence J. Henderson considered the basic necessities for objective clinical study of a new field.

For about twenty years Mayo has been senior professor in the Department of Industrial Research in the Harvard Business School. The research conducted by this Department, by him and his co-workers in industry and in the School, has always been first-hand, clinical studies of concrete industrial situations. The history of this twenty-year programme has been a history of steadily increasing insight.

In his first comprehensive report on this industrial research, *The Human Problems of an Industrial Civilization*, published in 1933 (reprinted in 1946), Mayo broke new ground in methods of studying and securing better understanding of individual workers in relation to their industrial jobs and of ways to improve their sense of well-being on the job. This report was followed by more detailed accounts[1] of a five-year experiment conducted at and by the Western Electric Company, with the advice and collaboration of Mayo and his associates. All these accounts involved recognition of the importance of social groupings and of teamwork as well

[1] T. North Whitehead, of the Business School Faculty, in *The Industrial Worker*, (Cambridge, Mass., Harvard University Press, 1938), and F. J. Roethlisberger, of the Business School Faculty, and William J. Dickson, of the Western Electric Company, in *Management and the Worker* (Cambridge, Harvard University Press, 1939).

as of the individual worker; Whitehead's studies, based on a careful statistical analysis of unique records of the experiment kept by the Western Electric Company, threw strong light on the significance of the social factors which affected the experimental group. Roethlisberger and Dickson's book brought out the importance of the same factors. Nevertheless, the net result of the three reports, as they came to the interested reader, was emphasis on the individual, including of course emphasis on him in his social surroundings.

In the current report, published twelve years later, Mayo's emphasis changes, not to exclude the individual, but to stress the importance of groups and methods of understanding the behaviour of groups, whether formally organized and recognized by management or self-constituted, informal organizations. The significance and even the existence of the latter are generally overlooked by management and often even by workers themselves. The report brings to the fore the problem of securing group collaboration in the essential activities of industry. It also points out the increasing significance of this problem, which results from rapid technological progress and the ensuing frequent changes in the human associations of the worker while he is at work. This progressive destruction of old, technical skills receives inadequate attention by management. The difficulties are, of course, intensified by the progressive destruction of neighbourhood life and by the constant loosening of the stabilizing influences which surround us in what Mayo refers to as an *established* society. These again result in large part from the impact of applied science on the lives men lead in industry and of significant developments such as the automobile on their lives when they are not at work.

Here also Mayo gives us instances where industrial administrators have succeeded in making factory groups so stable in their attitudes of group co-operation that men in the groups explicitly recognized that the factory had become for them the stabilizing force around which they developed satisfying lives. This accomplishment was achieved in spite of technological changes within the plant and social chaos in the community outside. Thus Mayo shows us for the first time in the form of specific instances that it is within the power of industrial administrators to create within industry itself a partially effective substitute for the old stabilizing effect of the neighbourhood. Given stable employment, it might make of industry (as of the small town during most of our national life) a socially satisfying way of life as well as a way of making a living.

This seems a far cry from the existing warfare between labour and management and the growing hatreds and prejudices which distress us. Yet unless we can regain in this heterogeneous industrial civilization the capacity to live our daily lives in something like mutual understanding that provides for individual differences, unless we can learn how to adapt our civilization to constant change, we shall not maintain essential stability in the domestic scene, nor become an effective force for peace in the international field. Surely our current situation at home can hardly impress Mr. Stalin as an indication that we will be a lasting influence for peace abroad. We show few signs of having solved the problems of an *adaptive* civilization competent to deal with constant technological and social change.

Mayo has a job of study and interpretation yet to do. We need the more complete development of his tantalizing suggested study, *The Political Problems of an [Adaptive] Industrial Civilization.* When it comes, I hope it will involve not only the problems of a democratic state and effective collaboration within it, but more attention to similar problems which exist in securing collaboration in the huge aggregations of men and things inherent in mass production industries where high technological efficiency is struggling constantly against increasing social disintegration, both within and without the industries involved.

And there is an educational job to be done both within industry and in our schools and colleges, a job on which Mayo himself and his associates at the Harvard Business School under his leadership have already gone far to prove that important accomplishments are possible.

WALLACE B. DONHAM.

INTRODUCTORY

Dr. Wallace B. Donham
    Professor of Administration
        Harvard University

My dear Donham:

Here is the book you demanded before I should put off the responsibilities of office. It is not in any sense a complete account of the work done since you and I—you were then Dean of this Graduate School of Administration—agreed that a research study of human behaviour and human relations was eminently desirable. Such a study, if made without presuppositions other than those justified by biology or by the human aspect of clinical medicine, might, we believed, be more productive than a direct attack on labour relations. It is twenty years since our conversation in New York, and our venture began the next year—mid-1926—at Harvard with the support of the Laura Spelman Rockefeller Memorial, later The Rockefeller Foundation. Almost immediately we were joined by Lawrence Henderson, Arlie V. Bock, and D. B. Dill of the Fatigue Laboratory. In 1927, F. J. Roethlisberger began his valuable study, as yet unpublished, of the Harvard student and his difficulties. To include this work, the Western Electric study, and the many and various achievements of the Fatigue Laboratory—some still military secrets—has been impossible; I have been compelled to follow a single track, to trace the development of a single complex illumination of our studies, and to set down, as best I could, the importance that I believe this illumination possesses for our war-torn world.

The scene has changed tragically since we first talked of these matters in 1925. At that time the United States, or some of its would-be leaders, believed that a general level of prosperity had been established, that the problem of recurrent depressions had been conquered. Most of us believed, or at least hoped, that the League of Nations at Geneva had set to work seriously, and with humility, to substitute peace and wisdom for war and national self-assertion. The problems of industry did not seem to imply any covert threat to constitutional methods of reform. There was no expectation of a barbarian attack upon the foundations of civilization. In brief, society, here as elsewhere, was totally unprepared for the events that followed the fateful year of 1929.

And now, having passed through a major depression and the most terrible war humanity has known, we face a world pitifully changed—in Europe, cities reduced to rubble and utter human chaos; in Asia and the Pacific islands, an awakened and uncertain multitude totally unprepared for the heavy responsibilities that face them. In Eastern Europe, as in China, the peasant, thoroughly roused from his passivity and seeming content, is demanding a higher standard of material living. And, as ever in the primitive human, he believes that it is to be had for the asking, if the asking be sufficiently vociferous. A higher standard as something constantly re-created or earned is not within his comprehension; if it is not forthcoming, he will easily be persuaded that someone—American or plutodemocracy or capitalist—is deliberately withholding it from him.

There are those—perhaps radio commentators—who seem to imply, by their enthusiastic advocacy of "democracy", that some one of the many forms of representative government will act as a magic talisman—will aid a people, however lowly its civilization, to sort out and solve the problems of co-operation successively and systematically. Unfortunately for this theory, there are at least three limiting conditions that determine the applicability in a given instance of the forms of democratic government. These are:

First, there must be a sufficiently general standard of technical skill and literacy. Perhaps this qualification did not wholly apply to those periods of, for example, English history when the literate and scholarly caste was for the most part religious. In such times the political power exercised by the priestly class was very limited, at any rate in England; and the actually powerful and technically accomplished class, though perhaps more experienced in administration than the commonalty, was not generally literate. But in a modern and industrial society ultimate decisions, if they are to be reasonable and progressive, must vest in groups that possess both technical and social understanding. This requirement does not by any means exclude workers and their representatives from participation, although it might possibly exclude from active participation those sections of the legal profession that are sunk in outdated and verbal theories of sovereignty. In effect, this claim for a standard of effective skill and literacy merely announces the rather obvious fact that an *adaptive* society cannot be controlled by any but *adaptive* persons. And this again implies a need for greatly improved concepts of training and education, and equally improved methods. Personal adaptability is not achieved except by experience and education. Routine training sufficed for an "established" society; it cannot fulfil the requirements of a world created by modern science and technology.

Second, representative government does not work satisfactorily for the general good in a society that exhibits extreme differences in the material standards of living of its various social groups. This prerequisite is especially true when the more lowly classes work very hard for a maintenance that is actually insufficient for their organic and social needs. History abounds in instances: the France of the later eighteenth century or England of the early nineteenth. Wisdom dictates a sufficiently high standard of material living throughout a society as a prerequisite of democratic institutions. England recognized this need during the war when she assured to every child, whatever its social or financial status, an adequate supply of the necessaries of life.

Third, representative government cannot be effectively exercised by a society internally divided by group hostilities and hatreds. There is grave danger that sheer ignorance of administrative methods in the political and industrial leaders of the democracies may give rise to increasing disabilities of co-operation. Stanley Casson points out[1] that *stasis*—the inability of functional groups to co-operate and a consequent mutual hostility —has been the historic destroyer of great civilizations.

During a minimum period of fifteen years, Russia has struggled to lift the primitive population of a vast geographical area in eastern Europe and northern Asia to a level of technical skill and cultural literacy that could not have been accomplished by so-called democratic methods in many generations. On the verge of considerable success in achievement of the arts of peace, she was attacked by barbarian German hordes and her chief triumphs ruthlessly destroyed. With the considerable material aid of the United States and England, Russia rallied to defeat and drive out the invader; and with the military aid of her allies, she has fully played her part in the destruction of the German in his own country—a country that Hitler said could never be subjugated by any combination of powers. It seems evident that in this achieve-

[1] *Progress and Catastrophe* (New York, Harper & Brothers, 1937), p. 205.

ment she has secured the spontaneous and wholehearted co-operation of her varied groups of peoples; and this result cannot be
wholly credited to the national emergency, although the emergency was obviously extreme. Naturally enough, therefore, it is
Russia that manifests unease at loose talk of "democratic methods";
it is the Russian who realizes most clearly the importance of the
three limiting conditions named. And differences at the San
Francisco Conference were based upon the observation of completely different types of social situation. In England and the
United States, the level of technical skill and general literacy is
high; it is based upon nearly two hundred years of scientific and
technical development, upon a century of discursive reading by
the general population. In Russia this is not so; her hold upon
technical skill and literacy must be regarded by her as still
tenuous. Whether Russia, as she develops the arts of peace, can
also develop at equal step toward democracy and popular control
must remain for the present an open question.

But what is the real implication of the word *democracy* about
which the Anglo-Saxon civilizations discourse so endlessly? The
difference between English-speaking democracy and all other
forms of government is important and profound. All other forms
of government are monophasic; democracy alone is polyphasic.
Other forms of government, from imperial Rome to the debased
fascism of Mussolini, could be represented in an engineering blue-
print—authority concentrated at the top, lesser authorities functioning down the scale only by permission or a delegation of
authority from the top. "The great *Leviathan* of Hobbes, the
plenitudo potestatis of the canonists, the *arcana imperii*, the sovereignty
of Austin, are all names of the same thing—the unlimited and
illimitable power of the law-giver in the State, deduced from the
notion of its unity. It makes no difference whether it is the State
or the Church that is being considered." [1]

In the democracies there is no such final concentration of
authority at the top; theoretically the locus of authority moves
from place to place according to the demand of the situation.
Democratic forms of government are immeasurably superior to
all other forms, from monarchy to communism. Whereas all
other forms are medieval and rigid—authority central, whether
termed King or the Law—the democratic form approximates

[1] John Neville Figgis, *Churches in the Modern State* (London, Longmans, Green &
Co., 1913), p. 79.

very nearly to the norm of human and social development. During a national emergency—depression, war, pestilence, flood, famine —the central authority must assume powers, for the time being, as arbitrary as those of a tyrant. But when the emergency passes, the central control is relaxed and the locus of authority again passes to the peripheral organizations; for it is always in the informal groups at the working bench and elsewhere that spontaneity of co-operation originates. The central and peripheral authorities thus supplement and complete each other—logical and purposive control from above, spontaneous and co-operative control from below. Historically speaking, the great democracies represent a quest for wisdom in control rather than authority, an attempt to set the locus of decision in any difficulty approximately where the situation demands that it be placed. So a wise administrator frames his policy, and even in modern industry one finds such administrators. Full expression by the groups affected is as important as a logical and purposive scheme framed by the few who possess high technical skill. For a society must secure the effective participation and co-operation of everyone in addition to the contrivance of technical advance.

Effective co-operation, then, is the problem we face in the middle period of the twentieth century. There is no "ism" that will help us to solution; we must be content to return to patient, pedestrian work at the wholly neglected problem of the determinants of spontaneous participation. The periodic elections of the democracies are but a primitive and crude sketch of a society in which the locus of control shall move in accordance with the dictates of wisdom and understanding. In these matters our political leaders, our scientific leaders, have failed us; we must try again.

Political leadership is not extensively discussed in this book, although Chapter II, "The Rabble Hypothesis", indicates defects in our political as in our economic thinking. It is, however, my hope that we may at some time publish a study of the political problems of an industrial civilization.

The application of scientific methods to the study of social situations, calls however for preliminary comment before it is possible to place on record the findings of clinical method in industry. Chapter I, "The Seamy Side of Progress", accordingly calls attention to the unbalance in systematic studies—the immense emphasis placed upon the technical and material, the abandonment of the human and social field (outside of medicine) to silly "isms" and haphazard guess.

And, if it were necessary, the atomic bomb arrives at this moment to call attention both to our achievement and to our failure. We have learned how to destroy scores of thousands of human beings in a moment of time: we do not know how systematically to set about the task of inducing various groups and nations to collaborate in the tasks of civilization.

It is not the atomic bomb that will destroy civilization. But civilized society can destroy itself—finally, no doubt, with bombs —if it fails to understand intelligently and to control the aids and deterrents to co-operation.

Your own discussion of education for responsible living indicates the path that we must travel.

Yours most sincerely,

ELTON MAYO

October 1, 1945.

THE SOCIAL PROBLEMS OF AN INDUSTRIAL CIVILIZATION

(October 1st, 1945)

PART I: SCIENCE AND SOCIETY

CHAPTER I

THE SEAMY SIDE OF PROGRESS

I

THE Victorians were very sure of their progress—of its reality and beneficence for humanity. In the 1890's a small book was published, a "school reader", entitled *The Nineteenth Century;* it told with pride of man's triumphs over circumstance during a century, it implied that at last man was becoming master of his fate. And the sequel for us, fifty years afterward, has all the character of Greek tragedy on a scale hitherto unknown. Man inspired by small success to wanton presumption—ὕβρις—has called down upon himself the wrath of the gods. His fine intentions, his grandiose plans, have in thirty years been reduced to chaos; his magnificent buildings, to dust and rubble. And man himself has done it; by way of those advances in science that were to give him perfection, he has achieved mainly destruction, desolation, misery.

But there were contemporaries who saw that this same progress had its underside, its very seamy side. Artistic protests, for the most part ignored, were numerous. One of the most vigorous statements was made by Mr. H. G. Wells in his *New Machiavelli.* Writing in the year 1910 of the changes that progress had brought to the village of Bromstead—probably Bromley in Kent—he says:

> The whole of Bromstead as I remember it and as I saw it last— it is a year ago now—is a dull useless boiling-up of human activities, an immense clustering of futilities. It is as unfinished as ever; the builders' roads still run out and end in mid-field in their old fashion; the various enterprises jumble in the same hopeless contradiction, if anything intensified. Pretentious villas jostle slums, and sculleries gape towards the railway, their yards hung with tattered washing unashamed; and there seem to be more boards by the railway every time I pass, advertising pills and pickles, tonics and condiments, and such like solicitudes of a people with no natural health or appetite left in them. . . .

His general characterization of the change from a pleasant country village to slum and chaos runs as follows:

I suppose one might have persuaded oneself that all this was but the replacement of an ancient tranquillity, or at least an ancient balance, by a new order. Only to my eyes, quickened by my father's intimations, it was manifestly no order at all. It was a multitude of incoordinated fresh starts, each more sweeping and destructive than the last, and none of them ever worked out to a ripe and satisfactory completion. Each left a legacy of products— houses, humanity or what not—in its wake. It was a sort of progress that had bolted; it was change out of hand, and going at an unprecedented pace nowhere in particular.

As one runs by train into Pittsburgh or Philadelphia through country that still suggests pleasant rolling hills and woods with running streams, one can easily lapse into a similar vein of reflective thinking. And this is reinforced by the presence in trains and hotels of strange groups of men that one never meets elsewhere in this great country, except in trains or hotels. Cigar in corner of mouth, each talks incessantly of dollars. To the artist's eye, something was decidedly askew in the actual Victorian progress; and that something continues to this day. It is as though man himself is not expected to progress, but only his material surrounding, his bodily comfort; and the high gods exact as price turmoil, confusion, chaos—and, finally, internecine war.

Another artist, who was Prime Minister of England, was almost prophetic:

. . . amid arts forgotten, commerce annihilated, fragmentary literatures and populations destroyed, the European talks of progress, because by an ingenious application of some scientific acquirements he has established a society which has mistaken comfort for civilization[1].

But vision of the seamy side of progress was not confined to artists. One might say of recent history that each successive decade has brought a competent observer to warn us of our failure to study man, to consider the effect upon him of all this progress. Such warnings, Cassandra-like, have passed unheeded; it has taken major tragedy—catastrophe, indeed—to call our attention to the realities of the human scene.

Frédéric Le Play, for instance, was a French engineer whose

[1] Benjamin Disraeli, Earl of Beaconsfield, *Tancred*, quoted from John Neville Figgis, *Civilization at the Cross Roads* (London, Longmans, Green & Co., 1912), p. 17.

professional work, early in the nineteenth century, took him widely through the length and breadth of Europe. As early as the year 1829, he had come to doubt whether rapid technical and industrial development was altogether beneficial to the various European communities in which he worked. For twenty-five years, with this in mind, he made careful observations of the living conditions, broadly conceived, of the many diverse groups of workers with whom he was associated. These observations extend from the steppes of Eastern Europe to the Atlantic shores of France; they are recorded in six volumes published between the years 1855 and 1879. It is a fact significant of our continued disregard of the human-social problem that these volumes have never been translated into English and are probably known only to those academic students of society who are ill-equipped to assess their practical importance.[1]

His general finding is that in simpler communities, where the chief occupation is agriculture or fishing or some primary activity, there is a stability of the social order that has ceased to characterise highly developed industrial centres. In these simpler communities every individual understands the various economic activities and social functions, and, in greater or less degree, participates in them. The bonds of family and kinship (real or fictitious) operate to relate every person to every social occasion; the ability to cooperate effectively is at a high level. The situation is not simply that the society exercises a powerful compulsion on the individual; on the contrary, the social code and the desires of the individual are, for all practical purposes, identical. Every member of the group participates in social activities because it is his chief desire to do so.

Le Play's finding with respect to the modern and characteristically industrial community is entirely contrary. He finds in such communities extensive social disorganization: the authority of the social code is ignored, the ties of kinship are no longer binding, the capacity for peace and stability has definitely waned. In these communities, he says, individuals are unhappy; the desire for change—"novelty"—has become almost passionate, and this of itself leads to further disorganization. Indeed, Le Play feels that the outstanding character of an industrial community is a condition of extensive social disorganization in which effective

[1] For a development of this point, see Wallace Brett Donham, *Education for Responsible Living* (Cambridge, Mass., Harvard University Press, 1944), Chap. V.

communication between individuals and groups has failed, and the capacity for spontaneous and effective co-operation has consequently failed also. These observations were made by a trained engineer—himself a competent technician. His own country, France, and, for that matter, every industrial society chose to ignore his warnings.

Remarkably similar observations were made toward the end of the nineteenth century in France by Emile Durkheim, founder of the French school of sociology. In his study of suicide published in 1897, he showed that, in those parts of France where technical industry had developed rapidly, a dangerous social disunity had appeared that diminished the likelihood of all individual or group collaboration. He says that the difference between a modern and technically developed centre and the simple, ordered community is that in the small community the interests of the individual are subordinated, by his own eager desire, to the interests of the group. The individual member of this primitive society can clearly anticipate during infancy and adolescence the function that he will fulfil for the group when adult. This anticipation regulates his activity and thinking in the adolescent period and culminates in a communal function and a sense of satisfaction when he is fully grown. He knows that his activities are wanted by his society, and are necessary to its continued life. He is throughout his life *solidaire* with the group.

During the nineteenth century, the rapid development of science and industry put an end to the individual's feeling of identification with his group, of satisfaction in his work. Durkheim develops this in some detail: no longer is the individual *solidaire* with a geographical locality and with the people in it. He leaves the family for school and education. It is unimportant whether this involves geographical movement or no; the significant modern innovation is that the family tie is weakened and, more often than not, no new or developing group relation is substituted for it. An improved standard of general education is a wholly admirable achievement; but to improve such a standard at the cost of personal and group relationship is of doubtful value.

After this first disruption, Durkheim points out, yet another is customary; the individual is compelled to remove himself again from developing group associations in order to find work. The quest may not be immediately successful, and the social disruption grows. In extreme instances, we may find individuals who have lost all sense of social relationship or obligation—the melancholic, the suicide, the "lone wolf", or the criminal. Even in those instances where the quest for group relationship finally succeeds —fortunately still a majority, although diminishing—the individual is not equipped by experience immediately to understand the nature of social relationship. And his group consequently represents a lower level of unity and obligation to the common purpose than the primitive.

In a modern industrial society we consequently find two symptoms of social disruption.

First, the number of unhappy individuals increases. Forced back upon himself, with no immediate or real social duties, the individual becomes a prey to unhappy and obsessive personal preoccupations. Long ago, Bishop Butler said, ". . . a man may have all the self-love in the world and be miserable".

Second, the other symptom of disruption in a modern industrial society relates itself to that organization of groups at a lower level than the primitive of which I have already spoken. It is unfortunately completely characteristic of the industrial societies we know that various groups when formed are not eager to co-operate wholeheartedly with other groups. On the contrary, their attitude is usually that of wariness or hostility. It is by this road that a society sinks into a condition of *stasis*—a confused struggle of pressure groups, power blocs, which, Casson claims, heralds the approach of disaster.[1]

In the last part of his book, Durkheim concedes that the successive creation of larger economic units by the coalescence of smaller units has enabled civilization to give its citizens greater material comfort. But he echoes Le Play's insistence upon the compensating disadvantage; step by step with our economic progress there has been a destruction of individual significance in living for the majority of citizens. "What is in fact characteristic of our development is that it has successively destroyed all the established social contexts; one after another they have been banished either by the slow usury of time or by violent revolution, and in such fashion that nothing has been developed to replace them." [2] This is a clear statement of the issue the civilized world is facing now, a rapid industrial, mechanical, physicochemical

---

[1] Stanley Casson, *Progress and Catastrophe* (New York, Harper & Brothers, 1937).
[2] Emile Durkheim, *Le Suicide* (Paris, Librairie Felix Alcan, 1930), p. 446.

advance, so rapid that it has been destructive of all the historic social and personal relationships. And no compensating organization, or even study of actual social or personal relationships, has been developed that might have enabled us to face a period of rapid change with understanding and equanimity. Durkheim is of the opinion that the French Revolution operated to destroy the last traces of what he calls the secondary organization of society— that is to say, those effective routines of collaboration to which, far more than to any political agency, the survival of the historic societies has been due. He points out that a solitary factor of collective organization has survived the destruction of the essentials of French society. This is the political State. By the nature of things, he says, since social life must organize itself in some fashion, there becomes manifest a tendency for the State to absorb into itself all organizing activity of a social character. But the State cannot organize the intimate daily life of its citizens effectively. It is geographically remote from the majority, and its activity must be confined to something of the nature of general rules. The living reality of active, intimate collaboration between persons must forever lie outside the sphere of political control. The modern industrial society consequently moves always in the direction of an ineffective State authority facing "a disordered dust of individuals".[1] I shall return to this topic in Chapter II.

Let me comment again that neither the six volumes of Le Play nor Durkheim's volume on suicide have been translated into English. Their warnings have been ignored; their findings were too remote from the naive exuberance of physicochemical and technical development. Yet, if we look at the civilized world since the fateful year 1939, we cannot feel that this neglect was wise. These earlier studies tend naturally enough to look back at the life of simpler communities with regret; they tend inevitably to the conclusion that spontaneity of co-operation cannot be recovered except by reversion to the traditional. This, however, is a road we cannot travel in these days; for us there can be no easy return to simplicity.

But the implication of such opinion does not detract from the value of Le Play's or Durkheim's observations. The real importance of these studies is the clear demonstration that *collaboration in an industrial society cannot be left to chance*—neither in a political

[1] Ibid., p. 448.

nor in an industrial unit can such neglect lead to anything but disruption and catastrophe. Historically and traditionally our fathers worked for social co-operation—and achieved it. This is true also of any primitive society.[1] But we, for at least a century of the most amazing scientific and material progress, have abandoned the effort—by inadvertence, it is true—and we are now reaping the consequences.

Every social group, at whatever level of culture, must face and clearly state two perpetual and recurrent problems of administration. It must secure for its individual and group membership:

(1) The satisfaction of material and economic needs.
(2) The maintenance of spontaneous co-operation throughout the organization.

Our administrative methods are all pointed at the materially effective; none, at the maintenance of co-operation. The amazing technical successes of these war years show that we—our engineers —do know how to organize for material efficiency. But problems of absenteeism, labour turnover, "wildcat" strikes, show that we do not know how to ensure spontaneity of co-operation; that is, teamwork. Indeed, had not the emergency of war been compelling and of personal concern to every least worker, it is questionable whether the technicians could have achieved their manifest success. And, now that the urgency is diminished, the outlook for continued co-operation is not good. There is no active administrator of the present who does not fear that peace may see a return of social chaos.

The problem of co-operation, to which I shall address myself in all that follows, is far more difficult of solution with us than in a simple or primitive community. And most certainly we shall not solve it by ignoring it altogether. In a simple society, the extent of change from year to year, or even from century to century, is relatively small. Traditional methods are therefore brought to a high degree of perfection; almost from birth disciplined collaboration is drilled into the individual. But any study of such simple societies, whether by anthropologists or sociologists, possesses small relevance to the problems that so sorely beset us now. In these days of rapid and continuous change, the whole conception of social organization and social discipline must be radically revised. And, in this, the so-called "radicals"

[1] F. J. Roethlisberger, *Management and Morale* (Cambridge, Mass., Harvard University Press, 1942), Chap. IV.

are of small aid, being not radical but reactionary: they would require us to return to a form of social organization that has been made obsolete by technical advance.

II

Two writers have recently emphasized the fact that an industry, or, for that matter, the larger society, is a co-operative system. The one book is a highly technical treatise on organization;[1] the other is, in a sense, a popular version of some findings of the Western Electric Company's Hawthorne experiments.[2] But both alike realize clearly that the change from the village or small town type of social economy to the city or industrial centre type has occurred without attracting the attention of intelligent management. And the consequence of this failure to take due account of a fundamental and important change is not merely that village Bromsteads proliferate outwards, becoming dirtier and more chaotic with the passing years. It is a consequence also that the human capacity for eager collaboration continuously and rapidly deteriorates, so that we develop, within a nation or as between nations, not only toward chaos but also toward anarchy. An eminent contemporary historian states the issue thus:

The growing complication of modern mechanized civilization, especially in the more highly industrialized countries, demands a correspondingly higher degree of organization. This organization cannot be limited to the material elements in the complex, it extends inevitably to society itself and through society to the ethical and psychological life of the individual. Hence the historical trend has been from politics to sociology. Problems which were a century ago regarded as purely political became economic in the second half of the nineteenth century and during the present century have become sociological and psychological ones. But public opinion as yet is not fully aware of this change. Society is adapting itself as it were unconsciously and instinctively to the new conditions, and much of the tension and unrest of the present time is due to the inadequacy of our inherited stock of social traditions to cope with the realities of the situation, and the difficulty of squaring the already emergent

[1] Chester I. Barnard, *The Functions of the Executive* (Cambridge, Mass., Harvard University Press, 1938).
[2] F. J. Roethlisberger, *Management and Morale*.

system of social organization with political theories and social doctrines to which we still consciously adhere, but which are to a great extent irrelevant to the modern situation.[1]

One can simplify this statement by adding that observation of modern industry during twenty-five years justifies the assertion that there is an unrealized difference between two principles of social organization—the one, that of an *established* society; the other, that of an *adaptive* society. With the organization of an established society, we are all familiar; it has been bred into the blood and bone of every one of us—even if the process, in Dawson's phrase, has been "unconscious and instinctive". The established society finds illustration, at a low level, in the rigid and systematic ritual procedures of the Australian blackfellow,[2] in the *Kula* system of the Trobrianders,[3] in the Andaman Islanders.[4] It was also, at a somewhat higher level, the essential feature of the social organization of Victorian England, of the early industries of New England, or of the small Australian city of the 1880's. The advantages of an established society are many; and the majority of liberal, or even revolutionary, movements of our time take origin in a strong desire to return from present uncertainty to established certainty —a desire that is in fact reactionary and opposed to the spirit of the age. In the small town of sixty years ago, the choice of occupation offered a young man was small; he might follow his father's trade of blacksmith or carpenter or he might try to advance a step—bank clerk, teacher, or clergyman. His choice was usually made, or made for him, before he entered his teens, and thereafter his way of life was determined by what he was to be.

Even those who entered factory or business—both small scale, as measured by the present, but both rapidly coming to maturity in the nineteenth century—did so under these conditions. The boy was thus apprenticed in some fashion to his life work and his trade, and began to acquire simultaneously technical capacity and the art of communication with his fellows. In the usual case this group changed but little during his apprenticeship. Thus through practice at his trade with the same group of persons, he learned to manipulate the objects with which he worked and to understand

[1] Christopher Dawson, *Beyond Politics* (London, Sheed & Ward, 1939), pp. 35–36.
[2] W. Lloyd Warner, *A Black Civilization* (New York and London, Harper & Brothers, 1937).
[3] Bronislaw Malinowski, *Argonauts of the Western Pacific* (London, George Routledge & Sons, Ltd., 1932).
[4] Alfred R. Radcliffe-Brown, *The Andaman Islanders* (Cambridge University Press, 1933).

the attitudes and ideas of his companions. Both of these are of immense importance to successful living. Dr. Pierre Janet, in fifty years of patient, pedestrian, clinical research, has shown that sanity is an achievement and that the achievement implies for the individual a balanced relation between technical and social skills. Technical skill manifests itself as a capacity to manipulate things in the service of human purposes. Social skill shows itself as a capacity to receive communications from others, and to respond to the attitudes and ideas of others in such fashion as to promote congenial participation in a common task. The established society by its apprenticeship system developed technical and social skills simultaneously in the individual; psychoneurosis, the consequence of insufficient social discipline and practice, seems to have been less prevalent in successful established societies. In these days, education has gone over—often extravagantly—to the development of technical skills and the appropriate scientific bases for such skills. This would be excellent were it not for the fact that the universities have failed to develop an equivalent study of, and instruction in, social skill. Students are taught logical and lucid expression; they are not taught that social skill begins in the art of provoking, and receiving, communications from others. The attitudes and ideas thus communicated, by no means wholly logical, will serve to form the basis of a wider and more effective understanding.

Little of the old establishment survives in modern industry: the emphasis is upon change and adaptability; the rate of change mounts to an increasing tempo. *We have in fact passed beyond that stage of human organization in which effective communication and collaboration were secured by established routines of relationship.* For this change, physicochemical and technical development are responsible. It is no longer possible for an industrial society to assume that the technical processes of manufacture will exist unchanged for long in any type of work. On the contrary, every industry is constantly seeking to change, not only its methods, but the very materials it uses; this development has been stimulated by the war. In the established societies of no more than a century ago, it was possible to assume a sufficient continuity of industrial processes, and therefore apprenticeship to a trade was the best method of acquiring skill, both technical and social. The technical skill required by industry in these days has developed in two directions. On the one hand, a much higher type of skill is required—that, namely, which is based upon adequate scientific and engineering know-ledge and is consequently adaptable or even creative. On the other hand, the skill required of the machine-hand has drifted downwards; he has become more of a machine tender and less of a mechanic. Now this is not the place to discuss whether the latter change is altogether desirable, however admirable the former. But it is altogether proper to point out that no equivalent effort to develop social or collaborative skill has yet appeared to compensate or balance the technical development.

The skills acquired by the individual during apprenticeship were, we have already said, of two kinds: on the one hand, mechanical and technical; on the other, social. Furthermore, these skills were in balance in respect of the situations he encountered. What was demanded of him technically did not require social skills of the order necessary to adjust to constantly changing work associates. Stability of techniques went hand in hand with stability in companionship.

Put in ordinary language, the apprentice learned to be a good workman, and he also learned to "get on with" his fellows and associates. This second acquisition was clearly understood to be an essential part of his training; many colloquial phrases existed to describe it, such as, for example, "getting the edges rubbed off", "learning to take the fences", and so on—homely similes that recognized the value for society of such experience. Unfortunately this important social discipline was never clearly specified as a necessary part of the individual's education, and consequently, when the tempo of technical change was accelerated, no one posed a question as to the consequence for individuals and society of a failure to maintain and develop social skill. In the universities, we have explicit and excellent instruction in the physicochemical sciences and engineering: but we have provided no instruction or experience to replace or develop the social aspect of the apprenticeship system. It is no longer true that every individual will have a continuity of daily association with others that will allow him slowly to acquire a skill of communication and of working with them. It is more than probable that, in any part of the modern industrial scheme, an individual's personal associates will constantly change. We live in a constant flux of personal associations, as of technical procedures. And it may well be that many individuals do not sufficiently continue association anywhere with anyone to develop, as formerly, a social skill. It was in situations such as this that Durkheim discovered personal dis-satisfaction, planlessness, and even despair. And it was here also that Le Play found deterioration in the sense of social obligation, a decay alike of the group life and of capacity for active collabora-tion in a common venture.

But the remedy cannot be a return to simple apprenticeship and the primitive establishment. It is certain that the passage from an established to an adaptive society is one we have to make; we have put our hands to the plough and cannot turn back. We have undertaken to transform an economy of scarcity into an economy of abundance, and the technicians are showing us the way. We are committed to the development of a high human adaptability that has not characterized any known human society in the past, and it is our present failure in this respect that finds reflection in the social chaos which is destroying civilized society. Can this present failure be translated into future success? The way forward is not clear, but certain starting points can be dis-cerned: we are in need of social skills, skills that will be effective in specific situations. When a man has developed a skill, it means that the adjustment of his whole organism, acting as a unit and governed by his thinking and nervous system, is adequate to a particular point in the situation which he is handling. No verbal statements however accurate can act as substitute.

III

Now a skill differs from general knowledge in that it is mani-fested at a particular point as a manipulative dexterity acquired by experience in the handling of things or people, or complexes of either, or both. And a study is not a science unless it is capable of demonstrating a particular skill of this kind. The first really important training of a student of physics, chemistry, or medicine is in the clinic and laboratory; it is thus that he develops intuitive familiarity with the materials of his study and manipulative capacity with respect to these materials. Only upon the basis of skill thus acquired can he build a systematic logic and slowly acquire the further insight that a developed science gives him. The chemist must be equipped to handle material substances in skilled fashion; the physician must be able to assess the condition of organic functions and also to assess in a more general way the condition of the individual patient he studies.

A simple distinction made by William James in 1890 has all the significance now that it had then; one can only suppose that its very simplicity has led the universities to brush it aside as obvious, which is true, or as of small account, which is not true. James pointed out that almost every civilized language except English has two commonplace words for knowledge—*connaître* and *savoir*—γνῶναι and εἰδέναι, *knowledge-of-acquaintance* and *knowledge-about*.[1] This distinction, simple as it is, nevertheless is exceedingly important; *knowledge-of-acquaintance* comes from direct experience of fact and situation, *knowledge-about* is the product of reflective and abstract thinking. "Knowledge derived from experience is hard to transmit, except by example, imitation, and trial and error, whereas erudition (*knowledge-about*) is easily put into symbols—words, graphs, maps. Now this means that skills, although transmissible to other persons, are only slowly so and are never truly articulate. Erudition is highly articulate and can be not only readily transmitted but can be accumulated and preserved."[2] The very fact that erudition (logic and systematic knowledge) can be so easily transmitted to others tends to prejudice university instruction in the social sciences heavily in its favour. Physics, chemistry, physiology have learned that far more than this must be given to a student. They have therefore developed laboratories in which students may acquire manipulative skill and be judged competent in terms of actual performance. In such studies the student is required to relate his logical *knowledge-about* to his own direct acquaintance with the facts, his own capacity for skilled and manipulative performance. James's distinction between the two kinds of knowledge implies that a well-balanced person needs, within limits, technical dexterity in handling things, and social dexterity in handling people; these are both derived from knowledge-of-acquaintance. In addition to this, he must have developed clinical or practical knowledge which enables him to assess a whole situation at a glance. He also needs, if he is to be a scientist, logical knowledge which is analytical, abstract, systematic—in a word, the erudition of which Dr. Alan Gregg speaks; but it must be an erudition which derives from and relates itself to the observed facts of the student's special studies.

Speaking historically, I think it can be asserted that a science

---

[1] William James, *The Principles of Psychology* (London, Macmillan and Co., Limited, 1890), Vol. I, p. 221.
[2] From a letter written by Dr. Alan Gregg (November 13, 1942).

has generally come into being as a product of well-developed technical skill in a given area of activity. Someone, some skilled worker, has in a reflective moment attempted to make explicit the assumptions that are implicit in the skill itself. This marks the beginning of logico-experimental method. The assumptions once made explicit can be logically developed; the development leads to experimental changes of practice and so to the beginning of a science. The point to be remarked is that scientific abstractions are not drawn from thin air or uncontrolled reflection: they are from the beginning rooted deeply in a pre-existent skill.

At this point, a comment taken from the lectures of a colleague, the late Lawrence Henderson, eminent in chemistry, seems apposite:

> . . . In the complex business of living, as in medicine, *both* theory and practice are necessary conditions of understanding, and the method of Hippocrates is the only method that has ever succeeded widely and generally. The first element of that method is hard, persistent, intelligent, responsible, unremitting labour in the sick room, not in the library: the complete adaptation of the doctor to his task, an adaptation that is far from being merely intellectual. The second element of that method is accurate observation of things and events, selection, guided by judgment born of familiarity and experience, of the salient and recurrent phenomena, and their classification and methodical exploitation. The third element of that method is the judicious construction of a theory—not a philosophical theory, nor a grand effort of the imagination, nor a quasi-religious dogma, but a modest pedestrian affair . . . a useful walking-stick to help on the way. . . . All this may be summed up in a word: The physician must have, first, intimate, habitual, intuitive familiarity with things; secondly, systematic knowledge of things; and thirdly, an effective way of thinking about things.[1]

Science is rooted deep in skill and can only expand by the experimental and systematic development of an achieved skill. The successful sciences consequently are all of humble origin— the cautious development of lowly skills until the point of logical and experimental expansion is clearly gained. Science did not begin with elaborate and overwhelming systems, and thence proceed to study of the facts. Its characteristic pedestrian, step-by-step advance from lowly beginnings has the merit of consolidating

---

[1] Lawrence J. Henderson, *Sociology 23, Introductory Lectures* (three lectures given in course Sociology 23 at Harvard College, privately distributed, 2nd ed., revised in October, 1938), p. 6; also in *Fatigue of Workers*, report of National Research Council (New York, Reinhold Publishing Corporation, 1941), pp. 12–13.

its gains; later advances do not ever completely vitiate earlier careful observations.

Scientific method, then, has two parts, represented in medicine by the clinic and the laboratory. The two are interdependent, the one unfruitful without the other. The characteristic of the clinic is careful and patient attention to a complex situation any part of which may suddenly discover unanticipated importance; that of the laboratory is experiment and logical construction. In the nineteenth century the former of these was termed *observation* and much was made of its necessity. In recent years the emphasis has passed to logical or mathematical construction after careful experiment. This would be admirable were it not for the fact that the need for selection before experiment seems frequently to be forgotten. It is not any laboratory experiment plus mathematical construction that leads to scientific advancement. Among the most notable discoveries of recent years are radar and penicillin. Both of these began in the observation by a careful worker of a phenomenon irrelevant to his immediate preoccupation—the one a wireless operator at sea, the other a laboratory biologist. And in both instances, the observation aroused the curiosity and imagination of the scientist—to the lasting benefit of humanity and civilization. It is probably wise that the emphasis for students should fall upon the systematic setup of an experiment and logico-mathematical construction. But the origin of science in first-hand observation may not be forgotten without consequence in experimental futility, illustrations of which may be seen all about us. Observation—skill—experiment and logic—these must be regarded as the three stages of advancement. The first two are slow and far from dramatic; but they are necessary to the third. "The second-handedness of the learned world is the secret of its mediocrity. . . . The main importance of Francis Bacon's influence does not lie in any peculiar theory of inductive reasoning . . . but in the revolt against second-hand information of which he was a leader."[1]

In the course of centuries, the sciences have by this slow and steady method erected an imposing structure of knowledge, knowledge which is related at all points to the appropriate skills. The problems that they study, the methods that they use, are to some extent understood by those in charge of administrative

[1] Alfred North Whitehead, *Aims of Education & Other Essays* (London, Williams and Norgate, 1929), p. 79.

activities. No chemist, for instance, is asked to provide at short notice a scheme for the reorganization of government, of industry, or of society. He is asked to examine specific possibilities, such as that of improving the tanning of leather or of manufacturing synthetic rubber. He is not even asked to consider what consequential changes in industrial organization will follow from his discoveries; the cobbler sticks to his last. And the chemist himself, although as a fallible human being he may have the wildest dreams of social reorganization, yet knows that these dreams bear no relation to his skill and must be kept apart from it. Many years ago a Labour Premier of Queensland said in conversation that, when a workman became "class-conscious", the change seemed to deteriorate his skill and his interest in it.

IV

When one turns from the successful sciences—chemistry, physics, physiology—to the unsuccessful sciences—sociology, psychology, political science—one cannot fail to be struck by the extent of the failure of the latter to communicate to students a skill that is directly useful in human situations. Since the student body of to-day will provide the administrators of to-morrow, this failure is a grave defect. Chemistry and physics are thoroughly conversant with the materials of their study; they work in skilled fashion upon such materials every day. Economics and psychology cannot be said to be entirely innocent of skills, but such skills as they communicate seem to be at least partly dictated by a desire to give impressive imitations of physical science rather than by a determination to begin work by a thorough, painstaking acquaintance with the whole subject matter of their studies. Indeed, a newspaper quotes a psychologist of some note as having said that he knew less about human beings than any headwaiter. If this were true—and it probably was not—it would be an ignominious confession of incompetence. Nevertheless the comment of a colleague is eminently just; namely, that in the area of social skill there seems to be a wide gulf between those who exercise it—the actual administrators—and those who talk about it.[1] The fact that the United States has developed a successful series of tests for technical skills does not provide any extenuation for psychology. Within its narrow limits, this is useful and, indeed, excellent. But

[1] F. J. Roethlisberger, *Management and Morale*, p. 138.

the general effect is to concentrate attention on technical problems and to blind us to the importance of the problems of human
co-operation—social skill. This blindness has unquestionably contributed to the advent of calamity.

The so-called social sciences encourage students to talk endlessly about alleged social problems. They do not seem to equip
students with a single social skill that is usable in ordinary human
situations. Sociology is highly developed, but mainly as an
exercise in the acquisition of scholarship. Students are taught to
write books about each other's books. Of the psychology of normal
adaptation, little is said, and, of sociology in the living instance,
sociology of the intimate, nothing at all. Indeed, in respect of
those social personal studies that are becoming more important
year by year, no continuous and direct contact with the social
facts is contrived for the student. He learns from books, spending
endless hours in libraries; he reconsiders ancient formulæ, uncontrolled by the steady development of experimental skill; the
equivalent of the clinic, or indeed of the laboratory, is still to seek.

The successful sciences are of humble birth; each had its lowly
origin in a simple skill. Some centuries of hard and unremitting
labour have enabled chemistry and physics to achieve structures
of knowledge that are most imposing. In doing this, they have not
strayed into other paths, no matter how entrancing the prospect.
The social sciences are impressed by this achievement, there is no
doubt of that; but the unfortunate effect has been to encourage
too much jerry-building of imposing façades in the social area.
The pedestrian step-by-step development of a simple unquestionable skill, if it exists, is concealed by these elaborate fronts. It is
kindness to suppose that the pretentious façades are perhaps only
camouflage and that somewhere behind them real work is
going on.

The result is that those graduates of brilliant achievement who
lead the procession out of the universities are not well equipped
for the task of bringing order into social chaos. Their standard of
intellectual achievement is high; their knowledge-of-acquaintance
of actual human situations is exceedingly low. They dwell apart
from humanity in certain cities of the mind—remote, intellectual,
preoccupied with highly articulate thinking. They have developed
capacity for dealing with complex logic, they have not acquired
any skill in handling complicated facts. And such a student of
society is encouraged to develop an elaborate social philosophy

and to ignore his need of simple social skills. Discursive and uncontrolled reasoning is preferred to observation. Yet patient observation is what the world most needs, observation that holds its logical tools in abeyant readiness.

The social skills students develop at universities, in athletics or clubs or other activities, are not closely related to their studies. The two are more often considered as in opposition; the one to be achieved at the expense of the other. Consequently, the development of a student's social skills may be restricted to association with fellow students in activities at least by implication frowned upon by many university authorities. This social restriction may prevent the development of whole-hearted participation with others in the general educational aims of the institution. Association of student and student without full participation in the broad purposes of the university develops a lower order of social skill than that which the apprentice learns at his trade. It leads often to social group exclusiveness and discrimination. This artificial and narrow experience has limited use in later life, for maturity demands a highly developed, and continuously developing, social skill. In these respects the environment of a small college may be more helpful to students than that of a large university. But nowhere have scientific studies developed training in social skills adequate to the rapidly changing needs of an industrial civilization.

Now I have no doubt much work that will some day be found useful is being done in the social sciences—economics, psychology, sociology—but at present it would seem that the various special inquiries are not related to each other, nor to any general scheme or thesis. I believe that the reason for this is that these studies are trying, like Pallas Athene, to leap into existence full panoplied and are trying to evade the necessary periods of infancy and growth. It is, no doubt, in consequence of this attempt that they have neglected the pedestrian development of a simple social skill.

At this point one should ask for an example of a simple social skill that can thus be practised and that, as it develops, will offer insight and the equivalent of manipulative capacity to the student. I believe that social study should begin with careful observation of what may be described as communication: that is, the capacity of an individual to communicate his feelings and ideas to another, the capacity of groups to communicate effectively and intimately with each other. This problem is, beyond all reasonable doubt, the outstanding defect that civilization is facing to-day.[1] The studies of Pierre Janet, of which I shall have more to say in the sequel, lead to observation of the fact that those individuals usually described as psychoneurotic (though apparently free from any organic pathology) are unable to communicate easily and intimately with other persons. And beyond this highly individual problem, our international troubles are unquestionably due to the fact that effective communication between different national groups was not accomplished even at Geneva. League of Nations discussions were conducted in generalized terms which sometimes seemed to lead to intellectual understanding and agreement. But in no instance was this understanding based upon an intimate acquaintance of either side with the actual situation of the other. Indeed, it is questionable whether any attempt was made to gain such understanding. On the contrary, an effort was often made to "find a formula", a logical statement which should conceal the fact that neither side had any insight into the actual situation of the other. Within the various nations also as our industrial civilization has developed, there has been an increasing difficulty of direct communication between specialized groups. The outstanding instance of this defect is the group of acute issues between managements and workers.

V

The consequences for society of the unbalance between the development of technical and of social skill have been disastrous. *If our social skills had advanced step by step with our technical skills, there would not have been another European war:* this is my recurrent theme. For the moment, however, I must return to consideration of the effect upon students, the group from which to-morrow's administrators will be drawn, of the type of social education I have been describing. It was indeed the appearance in universities of students brilliantly able but unhappy and ineffective that first called attention to the more general problem. Certain subjects seem to possess a fatal attraction for these unhappy individuals—philosophy, literature, sociology, law, economics, and—God save us all— government. Such students may be poorly equipped in respect of manipulative technical skills, but this is not the proper basis of

[1] See Chap. IV, infra, for detailed discussion of the importance of "listening" as the basis of communication.

diagnosis; they are always almost devoid of social skill, and this is diagnostic. The personal histories are monotonously iterative of circumstance that prevented active experience in early life of diverse social groups and different social situations. In a word, they have little or no knowledge-of-acquaintance of social life, and it is only in such experience that skill in communication can have origin. The number of such persons increases in all countries that are urban and industrialized: the phenomenon is not peculiarly American. Pierre Janet, for example, describes the French counterpart. After commenting that the disability affects, for the most part, persons of native ability and at least some education, he continues:

> They can ordinarily comport themselves like other people, chatter or complain of their disabilities to intimate friends; but directly action becomes important and by consequence involves the manipulation of reality, they cease to be able to do anything and tend to withdraw more and more from their avocation, the struggle with other people, external living and social relationships. Indeed their lives are highly specialized and utterly meaningless—without active relationship either to things or to people . . . such minor interests as they retain are always given to those matters that are farthest from material actuality: sometimes they are psychologists; before all things philosophy is the object of their devotion; they become terrible metaphysicians. The spectacle of these unfortunates makes one ask sadly whether philosophical speculation is no more than a malady of the human mind.[1]

Elsewhere Janet remarks that their difficulties are chiefly with, first, decision and action, and second, association with other people. And their only conception of a remedy is to indulge in metaphysical discussions that "last all night and get nowhere". Since such persons are for practical purposes devoid of both manipulative and social skills, they have no method of determining the respective values of alternate logical possibilities. *Argument, however rational, that is unrelated to a developing point of contact with the external world remains—however logical—a confusion of indeterminate possibilities.* Some of these persons—able, unhappy, rebellious—rank as scholars. If, at any point in their training, there had been insistence upon a simple skill, especially a social skill, the whole elaborate logical structure of their thinking would have revealed its slim foundations. But the scholars of a university are

[1] Pierre Janet, *Les Névroses* (Paris, Ernest Flammarion, 1915), p. 357.

ill equipped to detect amongst their more enthusiastic students those whose very enthusiasm is a symptom of unbalanced development. Indeed, scholarship departments, by reason of their over-valuation of discursive reasoning and their undervaluation of actual skills, do much to exaggerate the individual disability and little, if anything, to remedy it.

Janet's description, however, is of the extreme instance, and such cases, though possibly more numerous than in former times, are—fortunately—comparatively rare. Such an individual is by sheer mishap devoid of both types of skill. He has not developed the normal complement of manipulative or technical skills: he consequently fails in decision and action because no sufficient practical acquaintance with things aids him to decide between merely logical alternatives of action. He is also defective in the ordinary simple social skills: consequently those human associations that for most of us add a happy satisfaction to the day's routines are for him crises demanding energy and effort. This personal defect induces in him reluctance at the prospect of the most ordinary human occasions, misplaced overactivity when such occasions arise, and overwhelming fatigue afterwards.

A far more common instance in universities and elsewhere is that of the person whose manipulative skills are sufficiently developed but whose social skills are practically non-existent. Thirty years ago, I was one of the university members of a joint committee, appointed to organize the classwork of a local Workers' Educational Association in Australia. In this capacity I had occasion frequently to speak before the meetings of various trade unions to ask for their support of the movement to extend the facilities of adult education. As a general rule this support was freely accorded, though not without vigorous discussion in which extremist members would accuse the university of bourgeois sympathies and other social malefaction. Usually the more moderate and responsible union members sat in the front rows; the back rows were the haunt of those who represented the irre-concilable extreme Left. Before long it became evident that six men were the nucleus of all the most savage opposition. In the course of many years, I came to know these six men well. The extreme party changed its name many times during these years —Socialist, I.W.W., Bolshevist, Communist—but whatever the change of name or doctrine, it was always the same six who led the opposition at union meetings or spoke from soap boxes in the public parks. The fact that I came to know them personally made no difference to their platform attitude to me or to the university: but on other occasions they would talk freely to me in private. This enabled me to place on record many observations, the general tenor of which may be summarized as follows:

1. These men had no friends except at the propagandist level. They seemed incapable of easy relationship with other people; on the contrary, the need to achieve such relationship was for them an emergency demanding energetic effort.

2. They had no capacity for conversation. In talk with me they alternated between self-history and oratory which reproduced the compelling topic—revolution and the destruction of society.

3. All action, like social relationship, was for them emergency action. Any idea of routine participation in collaborative effort, or of the "ordinary" in living, was conspicuously absent from their thinking. Everything, no matter how insignificant, was treated as crisis, and was undertaken with immense and unreasoned "drive".

4. They regarded the world as a hostile place. Every belief and action implied that society existed not to give but to deny them opportunity. Furthermore, they believed that hostility to be active, not merely inert; they regarded everyone, even their immediate associates, as potentially part of the enemy forces arrayed against them.

In every instance the personal history was one of social privation—a childhood devoid of normal and happy association in work and play with other children. This privation seemed to be the source of the inability to achieve "ordinary" human relationships, of the consequent conviction that the world was hostile, and of the reaction by attack upon the supposed enemy. One of the six drifted into the hands of a medical colleague with whom I was accustomed to work on problems of adaptation. Thus was established a clinical relation of confidence in his physician. He discovered that his medical adviser was not at all interested in his political theories but was very much interested in the intimate details of his personal history. He made a good recovery and discovered, to his astonishment, that his former political views had vanished. He had been a mechanic, unable to keep his job although a good workman. After recovery he took a clerical job and held it; his attitude was no longer revolutionary.

These instances are still perhaps extreme, but they begin to approximate more closely to the general problem. The observations I have recorded in summary were made before and during the First World War. At that time none of us had conceived the possibility of such a person as the German Führer leading a general destructive attack upon society and civilization. Yet, if one turns the pages slowly of the first chapter in Stephen H. Roberts's book, *The House That Hitler Built*,[1] one cannot fail to be interested by the close similarity of attitude and history that is there described. I am not building upon this apparent similarity, except to the extent of suggesting that it is well to beware of, and provide assistance for, such cases: the price of neglect is heavy.

Acquaintance with a certain number of these more extreme cases is useful and indeed necessary if one is to be able to recognize without fail the symptoms of social maladjustment in a specified situation—personal or group. Janet says of his patients that all, without exception, regard the world about them—especially the social world—as a hostile place, "*Ce monde hostile*".[2] There seems to be, however, a difference in type of response: two-thirds, approximately, of the total number take the attitude "This world is dangerous, I must be careful"; the remaining third is rebellious, their attitude is "The world is hostile, let me attack it". Both attitudes are of course found in all instances, but one or the other will be predominantly characteristic.

Dr. J. S. Plant in his extensive studies of socially maladjusted children in New Jersey asserts that the attitude of these unfortunate youngsters to their surroundings varies between "panic" and "rebellion".[3] There is in this statement a high coincidence with the findings of Janet: for a social deprivation of some kind is an essential part of the personal history. And indeed this is a commonplace for those who try to help students in difficulty with their work or for those who make intimate studies of industrial situations. The student who declares that he cannot keep his attention on his work (his official record may seem to lend support to his statement) frequently, in private conversation, reveals that he is in terror of being asked to demonstrate before the class. If the occasion should arise, he is convinced that the lecturer and the remainder of the class are hostile, waiting with uncharitable amusement for him to blunder into absurdity. And, as consequence of this unhappy preoccupation, he often fulfils the bitter

[1] New York, Harper & Brothers, 1938.
[2] Pierre Janet, *Les Obsessions* (Paris, Librairie Felix Alcan, 1919), p. 636.
[3] James Stuart Plant, *Personality and the Cultural Pattern* (New York, The Commonwealth Fund, 1937).

expectation exactly and is convinced. In at least an approximate fifty per cent of such cases, the student is easily adequate to the technical task set him, and if freed from his preoccupation, will go on to take a good degree. His limitation is due to social unskill, and his seeming incapacity to sustain attention is due to the inter-ference of preoccupations arising from his social inadequacies—to a perpetual overthinking of social situations—and fear of action. The personal histories of these students are of at least two kinds: First, those who by reason of family circumstance have not had the range and variety of personal friendships outside the family that are necessary for the development of skill in living. Second, those who have developed a considerable social skill in a small community and perhaps a local college, and by reason of success in this sphere have been promoted to graduate work in a larger and more metropolitan university. The glamour of the uni-versity's historic name has perhaps already inspired an unadmit-ted panic in such a student; the subsequent discovery that his previously developed social skills are of small use in the new situation throws him back into self-centred preoccupation. These latter cases are often quite easy to help; indeed sometimes one interview will suffice. There is a foundation of social knowledge-of-acquaintance and skill to build upon; encouragement to bring into use a skill he actually possesses may become manifest in a sudden recovery of confidence. There are many such cases: in a certain sense, the disability is primarily in the situation rather than in the individual; a too sudden and too complete change of surroundings, especially when one is young and insufficiently experienced or older and somewhat "set" in work routines, is apt to be seriously disturbing.

Variants of this last situation are extremely common in the industry of our time; and it is unfortunate that adversity of cir-cumstance usually affects individuals and groups no longer young enough to show the remarkable resilience of youth in recovery. Some years ago, a supervisor of factory work involving consider-able technical skill was promoted from his departmental work in a mid-western city to be general supervisor of such work in perhaps a score of similar plants in the East. Previously he had lived only in the Mid-west, but he took up his work on the eastern seaboard with the same vigour and competence that he had always shown. For a time all went well, then came the industrial depression of the early thirties, in consequence of which the company was forced to close down many plants, or otherwise to restrict their operations. Little by little the sphere of operation of the general supervisor contracted until finally he was merely supervisor of a single department in a single factory, a job identical with that in which he had formerly shown such competence. But the original competence had apparently vanished; he bullyragged his men, who cordially detested him, he became critical of the East as compared with the Mid-west, he attributed his diminished status not to circumstance or to the general depression but, alternatively, to conspiracy against him or to his own foolishness in "coming East". Put in other words, his reflective thinking, originally factual and effective, had completely "run off the rails". He was overthinking his situation and attributing his ills to a hostile world just as a Janet patient might have done. Now situations of this kind in industry can be remedied, and, to my knowledge, have been remedied by a skilled interviewer. Such an interviewer is trained to *listen with attention and without comment*[1] (especially without criticism or emotion) to all that such an unfortunate has to say, and to give his whole attention to the effort of understanding what is said from the point of view of the speaker. This is a very simple skill, but it can have the most astonishing effects in industrial situations. We have seen many individuals, apparently prey to obsession, after a few such interviews, or many, according to need, return to work with the declaration that they have "talked it off". And in some instances the capacity for sane judgment of the situation seems to be wholly restored.

Another type of industrial situation, characteristic of our time, is in urgent need of careful observation. Scientific advance and changes of business organization are constantly reflected in changes of industrial method that may abolish trades or avocations which have been a means of livelihood for generations in a family. The "head rollers" in the tin mills of western Pennsylvania were brought in, many of them, originally from Wales. For years in Pennsylvania they prospered, owned the houses they lived in, and became persons of some weight and prestige in their communities. Quite suddenly, after the depression of ten years ago, the method of manufacturing tin plate was radically changed, and these men, many of them in later middle age, found themselves without an avocation and without means of continuing to support themselves and their families in the way of life to which they had

[1] See Chap. IV, infra.

become accustomed. This was for them a personal calamity of the first magnitude; as former pillars of society they did not lapse easily into revolutionary attitudes. And they drifted downwards toward unemployment as their savings became exhausted, and toward profound personal depression. Their attitude to themselves and to society might be described as a complete loss of confidence. In some degree this echoes that aspect of the European situation which led the German people to hail Hitler as deliverer.

In stating these facts, I must not be supposed to be arguing for the placing of any limitation upon scientific advance, technical improvement, or, in general, change in industrial methods. On the contrary, I am entirely for technical advancement and the rapid general betterment of standards of living. But, if our technical skills are to make sudden and radical changes in methods of working, we must develop social skills that can balance these moves by effecting social changes in methods of living to meet the altered situation. We cannot live and prosper with one foot in the twentieth century and the other in the eighteenth. *In the last hundred years, civilized society has completely changed its postulates.* Whereas human society in the eighteenth century, and for that matter the nineteenth, trained its adolescents to economic and social service by some form of apprenticeship, in these days the slow acquisition of both technical skill and capacity for collaboration by the process of "living into" a prescribed set of traditional routines is no longer appropriate to the modern world. Knowledge-of-acquaintance, with its derivatives of technical and social skill, is as important as ever it was. But, whereas in an established society the emphasis is upon established skills, the emphasis for us is upon adaptable skills. Those of us who began life in the Victorian era will remember the importance then attached to "established society"; for the present and the future, if we survive at all, the "adaptive society" will be the ideal.

The head rollers of Pennsylvania have been caught between the upper and the nether millstone. Trained for an established society, they are living in a society that places a higher value upon adaptability. This fact need not be interpreted to mean that their situation is hopeless. Indeed, the urgency of the war need has led to study of the means by which the country can multiply, and speedily, the number of skilled workers in this or that industry where the existing supply is obviously inadequate. And, whether we look at developments here or in other lands, we find that, immediately intelligent attention at the top of an organization has been given to training within industry, the workers have loyally and capably responded to the urgent need. And this applies not only to men; during the war, in England and here, girls formerly in beauty parlours, in restaurants, in domestic service, were successful in jobs that were thought to require a long and masculine apprenticeship. It is true that this result cannot be effectively accomplished without what I have called intelligent attention at the top. But it is worthy of remark that, in respect of the acquisition of new technical skill, the workers of the community have never let us down. The advent of the typewriter, the automobile, the aeroplane, has not revealed wide incapacity to learn a new technical skill anywhere in the population. The problem of the adaptation of, for example, superseded tin mill workers in our changing society is not insoluble; indeed changes induced by the war suggest that it may not even be so difficult as it might seem on first inspection. But there will be no solution and there will be increasing discontent until the social consequences of this major change in the structure of our society are clearly stated and responsibly in the charge of those who have sufficient skill and understanding.

VI

Now it is evident that our high administrators have, in these days, accepted responsibility for training workers in new technical skills; it is equally evident that no one has accepted responsibility for training them in new (adaptive) social skills. In the universities the acceptance of responsibility, and especially social responsibility, apparently presents a terrifying prospect to certain of the more timid academics. Yet it is doubtful whether any group that disclaimed responsibility ever achieved a skill worthy of the name. The physician accepts responsibility for his patient, the chemist accepts responsibility for the success or failure of the methods he devises. And so through the long list of scientific endeavours, although the percentage of failure may be higher than that of success, we find that the acceptance of responsibility of one or other kind is the invariable accompaniment of the development of usable skill. What is sometimes called skill in the use of words, in argument, in the development of uncontrolled logics is not analogous: studies of this type have gone through the same weary cycle of disputation and the quotation of authorities for a thousand years; there has been little, if any, development of them in terms of actualities of life. Current texts on politics still quote Aristotle, Plato, Machiavelli, Hobbes, and the books of other authors. What chemist finds need of quoting Thales and the alchemists? His claims are based on his own skill and his capacity for experimental demonstration. In sociology and political science there does not seem to be any equivalent capacity for the direct demonstration of a usable skill in a particular situation at a given time. And I do not think there can be until these studies take responsibility for what happens in particular human situations—individual or group. A good bridge player does not merely conduct post-mortem discussions of the play in a hand of contract; he takes responsibility for playing it. The former will help a beginner if, but only if, he attempts the latter. Sociology will be the Cinderella of the sciences until such time as she dons the crystal slippers and walks into adventure.

But there is none that can afford to be disdainful of poor Cinderella, least of all the prince or politician. The achievements of physical science, of chemistry, of medicine, in the last century have been very great; but the very dimension of these achievements has thrown society out of balance. And, until such time as sociology and psychology can, out of lowly and pedestrian skills, develop the beginning of understanding, until then we shall continue to find technical advance provocative of social chaos and anarchy.

If our social skills (that is, our ability to secure co-operation between people) had advanced step by step with our technical skills, there would not have been another European war.

CHAPTER II

THE RABBLE HYPOTHESIS
AND ITS COROLLARY, THE STATE ABSOLUTE

I

FOR nearly two centuries economic study has been supposed to provide the social skills requisite for the effective handling of civilized human activities. And in some areas its more concrete studies have unquestionably fulfilled this demand. For example, questions of cost accounting, marketing, and the large-scale organization of industry in its formal aspect have been handled with considerable and growing skill. But in these affairs there has developed economic practice of a valuable kind far removed from classical economic theory. E. H. Carr has said that in recent years the "chronic divorce" between economic theory and practice has become more marked than ever.[1] And he pictures economic theory "limping bewildered and protesting" in the train of economic practice. Chester Barnard, himself an executive of great experience, finds that effective leadership in industry, that is, successful administration, "has to be based on intuitions that are correct, notwithstanding doctrines that deny their correctness".[2]

This divorce suggests a question as to the original clinical or practical adequacy of economic theory to the facts it studied. Science begins in the clinic and is effectively developed in the laboratory. In the clinic one uses relatively simple logics to examine complicated fact; in the laboratory clinically developed skill has suggested the isolation of certain aspects of the complex fact for separate study and, when successful, this may result in the development of highly complicated logic. The one method informs and develops the other—simple logic and complex fact, simplified fact and complex logic. But, even when the laboratory has come to aid the clinician with highly developed techniques of

---

[1] Edward Hallett Carr, *Conditions of Peace* (New York, The Macmillan Company, 1942), p. 79.
[2] Chester I. Barnard, *The Functions of the Executive*, Preface, p. xi.

31

examination, it is nevertheless the clinician who has finally to piece together the various scraps of detailed information thus obtained and, guided both by scientific training and by experience, to determine the diagnosis and treatment *in the particular instance*—i.e., the patient. Economics, like other human studies, would seem to have been over-eager to arrive at laboratory methods and to have ignored the need for continuous detailed study of all the various aspects of actual industrial situations. Yet this clinic-laboratory relationship is the essential of scientific method.

One has to realize, with respect to common economic practice and its relation to social and political urgencies, that the actual industrial situation has changed immensely since the early part of the nineteenth century. Carr, in the book I have already quoted, asserts that in the days of the classical economists the industrial system was made up chiefly of small industries and businesses. His implication is that the whole theory of competition and the value of competition was based upon such an actual society. A former colleague, the late Philip Cabot, was accustomed to talk of his early life in New England as having been lived in such a society. He used to declare that the mills and industries of New England fifty or sixty years ago were essentially small organizations. They employed perhaps a few hundred people, and the life of any such business was rarely more than two generations of proprietorship or at most three. Cabot attributed this to the fact that the organizing ability of a father did not usually survive two generations of success. He pointed out, however, that the cessation of such a business did not create a problem for the community in which it was situated. By the time that a particular organization ceased to operate, some local rival had developed and was prepared to employ the skilled workmen, if indeed it had not already done so. Consequently there was no local community problem of widespread unemployment following a shutdown. In these days, the general situation is altogether different. During the economic depression of the early thirties, many manufacturing organizations accustomed to employ thirty or forty thousand people found themselves faced with a much diminished demand for products. Instances can be quoted where the roster of employees fell to ten thousand or even less. And this did not mean a stony disregard of human welfare: in many cases a company struggled for years to retain as many of its employees as it could without facing economic disaster itself. But in the then existing situation such attempts were doomed to failure; and in certain industrialized areas, within a period of months, many thousands of workers were inevitably "released". A situation such as this cannot compare with the characteristic nineteenth-century situation of which Carr and Cabot speak.[1] The so-called release of twenty or thirty thousand persons in two or three suburbs of a large city inevitably becomes a community problem of the first magnitude. And a problem of this kind cannot be left to "individualism" or "enlightened self-interest"; that nineteenth-century track is closed. Cabot was accustomed to say that, instead of expecting the life of a particular business to come to an end in two or three generations, we have, by improving industrial organization, conferred upon such businesses a "species of immortal life" which must be maintained by the community at its peril.

All this indicates that a primary assumption of nineteenth-century economic theory is no longer tenable. Even one hundred years ago, it was probably easy to believe in the essential relevance and propriety of the principle that the pursuit of individual interest is the basis of economic organization. But, although this assumption is still voiced by economic and political theorists, it is perfectly clear that business and political practice are based nowadays upon a vitally different conception of human society. This divergence between theory and practice is perhaps the source of at least part of the confusion that prevails in politico-economic discussions of the present. Whereas the economic theorist of the university still assumes individual interest as a sufficient basis for theory and the development of economic insight, the administrator with actual experience of handling human affairs bases his action upon a contrary, but empirically derived, assumption. This leads to endless confusion, not only in the public mind, but also in the writings of economists themselves. The practical economist stands on firmer ground but is troubled by a lack of clinical experience and by an uneasy allegiance to economic theory.

Economic theory as at present understood may be said to have begun originally with the physiocrats, especially with the publication by François Quesnay, physician to Louis XV, in 1758, of his

---

[1] Detailed consideration of the depressions of 1837, 1873, and 1893 is not relevant to this discussion. But, no doubt, a competent historian could show that the widespread unemployment in these periods was not unrelated to the already increasing pace of technical advance.

Tableau Economique. Charles Gide declares that a group of eminent men soon became the disciples of Quesnay and adopted the name of *physiocrats* or economists.[1] Quesnay introduced two new ideas into economic study. First, the superiority of agriculture over commerce and industry: this idea soon fell into disregard. And, second, the conception of a "natural and essential order of human societies". This is the basic conception of the physiocrats, the idea that man must learn to live according to nature, especially according to human nature, and that governments and authorities generally must give up the idea of devising endless laws and regulations. They must learn to let things alone—*laisser faire*. The ideas of the physiocrats were strongly developed by the so-called liberal school of economists, sometimes known as the Manchester School, in England. For a long time the physiocratic phrase, *laisser faire, laisser passer*, served as its motto. Gide gives the principles of this liberal school as three:

(1) Human societies are governed by natural laws *which we could not alter, even if we wished*, since they are not of our own making. Moreover, *we have not the least interest in modifying them, even if we could;* for they are good, or, at any rate, the best possible. The part of the economist is confined to discovering the action of these natural laws, while the duty of individuals and of governments is to strive to regulate their conduct by them.

(2) These laws are in no wise opposed to human liberty; on the contrary, they are the expression of relations which arise *spontaneously* among men living in society, wherever these men are left to themselves and are free to act *according to their own interests*. When this is the case, a *harmony* is established among these individual interests which are apparently antagonistic; this harmony is precisely the natural order of things, and is far superior to any artificial arrangement that could be devised.

(3) The part of the legislator, if he wishes to insure social order and progress, must therefore be limited to developing individual initiative as fully as possible, to removing whatever might interfere with such development, and to preventing individuals from meddling with one another. Therefore the *intervention of governments ought to be reduced* to that minimum which is indispensable to the security of each and of all—in a word, to the policy of "let alone".[2]

These principles give us in a few words the essential theoretic

---

[1] Charles Gide, *The Principles of Political Economy* (London, D. C. Heath and Company, 1909), English translation by C. W. A. Veditz, p. 9.

[2] Ibid., pp. 24–25. The italics are Gide's.

background of the economic and political thinking of the nineteenth century. There is much in this conception of human cooperative activity which is still important and still to be commended. A chief source of difficulty for the writers who expounded *laisser faire* lay in the restricted manner in which they developed to explicit statement the second of these principles, namely, "the relations which arise spontaneously among men living in society, wherever these men are left to themselves and are free to act according to their own interests".

E. H. Carr finds fault, and rightly, with the Manchester School's development of this principle; he considers that what he calls the profit motive was the next logical step this school formulated in its explicit statement of economic theory. But the idea of profit motive, used as Carr uses it, concedes too much to economics. The nineteenth century tried to base business organization generally on the presumption that some such motive dominated the human scene; in this, Carr was right. But, whereas Carr implies that to some extent this principle "worked" as the basis of industrial organization, we shall probably be nearer the facts if we consider that it failed completely.

The origin of the misapprehension upon which the whole of economic theory is based must be traced to David Ricardo. He it was who first tried explicitly to use this narrow conception of "the relations which spontaneously arise among men living in a society" as a sufficient abstraction for the development of a science. His personal history reveals the source of his narrow interpretation of this phrase.

Ricardo's father came to London from Holland in the latter part of the eighteenth century; there he opened a stockbroker's office. The young David entered this office at the age of fourteen years. When twenty-one, he married Miss Wilkinson and became a Christian. He had to leave his father's office after these changes, so he bought a country estate where he settled with the former Miss Wilkinson and, according to his biographer, "devoted himself to scientific pursuits", that is to say, to the writing of his *Principles of Political Economy and Taxation*.

It is easy to believe that the genius of David Ricardo manifested itself in discussions of finance, taxation, and economic rent. It is not easy to believe that the seven years between the ages of fourteen and twenty-one spent wholly in the atmosphere of stockbroking equipped him to understand the "relations which arise spontaneously among men living in society". Group life and group determination of individual behaviour are probably at their lowest expression in a stockbroker's office. Nevertheless advocates of his consequent theory as to the nature of human society persist to this day. Perhaps the clearest statement of the modern Ricardian position is to be found in an essay on *The Nature and Significance of Economic Science*.[1] Professor Robbins's circumscription of the topic is clear. "We (i.e., mankind) have been turned out of Paradise. We have neither eternal life nor unlimited means of gratification. Everywhere we turn, if we choose one thing we must relinquish others which, in different circumstances, we would wish not to have relinquished. Scarcity of means to satisfy given ends is an almost ubiquitous condition of human behaviour".[2] He continues: "Here, then, is the unity of subject of Economic Science, the forms assumed by human behaviour in disposing of scarce means." This is a perfectly legitimate abstraction, provided it is worked out with a becoming rigour of logic and experiment, provided the process of inquiry remains uncomplicated by confused irrelevancies—whatever their human importance. Moreover, this is in some degree the abstraction had in mind by Quesnay in his *Tableau Economique*, by Adam Smith in his *Wealth of Nations*, as well as by Ricardo in his *Principles*. The study of markets, of demand and supply, of prices, of production at the margin, and of economic rent, is indispensable and will remain so to the extent to which "the forms assumed by human behaviour in disposing of scarce means" remains one of the characters of society. The contribution of the economist to any theory of social equilibrium is thus valuable, and economics has developed many special skills for the advantage of those who practise them. The general confusion arises not merely in economic abstraction but also in the lack of other social studies necessary to any general concept of social equilibrium. The claim of the economist is not that the world is "peopled only by egotists or pleasure-machines. . . . The fundamental concept of economic analysis is the idea of scales of relative valuations".[3]

Under what conditions, then, are the postulates of economics satisfied? If we return to Ricardo, I think it may be said that he bases his studies and his logic upon three limiting concepts. These are:

---

[1] Lionel Robbins (London, Macmillan and Co., Limited, 1932).
[2] Ibid., p. 15.
[3] Ibid., p. 87.

1. Natural society consists of a horde of unorganized individuals.
2. Every individual acts in a manner calculated to secure his self-preservation or self-interest.
3. Every individual thinks logically, to the best of his ability, in the service of this aim.

1. *Natural society as a horde.*

In Ricardo's time, the influence of Hobbes, and beyond Hobbes that of Rousseau and the theory of a social contract, were still very strong. This theory, which still finds expression in unexpected places, regarded the life of natural man as "solitary, poor, nasty, brutish and short". The exchange of this type of natural living for social living involved, it was thought, the deliberate limitation of natural desires but secured for man as compensation all the advantages of co-operative activity. After Ricardo's time, this doctrine was roundly condemned by T. H. Green as an intellectualist fiction parading as description of primitive society.[1] More recently the field studies of modern anthropology have made the theory untenable. But for Ricardo and his contemporaries there was every reason for the presupposition and little against it.

Moreover, in certain situations of which Ricardo was aware, the description does apply now and at all times. If extreme emergency shatters the routines of co-operation in a specific social group, if no leader appears providentially to devise co-operative means of meeting the crisis, then the society will disintegrate temporarily into a horde of individuals each seeking desperately the means of self-preservation. This perhaps exaggerates that aspect of human affairs with which economics is specifically concerned. But scarcity of a necessary commodity is emergency or crisis—perhaps the most usual, perhaps the most serious—so that the findings of modern anthropology cannot lead us to discard Ricardo wholly and out of hand.

2. *The individual and motives of self-preservation.*

Clearly then the presupposition of scarcity lends support to the conception of competition for limited means of subsistence—especially perhaps in markets that are impersonal and in foreign trade and the exchanges. *If there is no leadership and no social organization* to order the distribution of necessary commodities, the principles discovered by the logic of economics will apply. The disorganization of a specific society and the lack of organiza-

---

[1] Thomas Hill Green, *Lectures on the Principles of Political Obligation* (London, Longmans, Green & Co., 1911), pp. 121 ff.

tion between societies are thus indicated as exceedingly important human problems by the findings of the economists. These are problems that nowadays are thrust urgently upon our attention.

3. *Every individual thinks logically in the service of this aim.*

This is, of course, fallacy if it be interpreted to mean that the thinking of every individual is continuously logical, according to his capacity. But it is not wholly fallacy, for as a postulate it is true within the narrow limits of the validity originally claimed for it. That is to say, the thinking of an individual is never so continuously logical as when he is faced with an emergency or crisis in which his customary routines are clearly useless. The human value of capacity for systematic thinking, considered as a natural fact, is chiefly an emergency value.

The statements of academic psychology often seem to imply that logical thinking is a continuous function of the mature person—that the sufficiently normal infant develops from syncretism and non-logic to logic and skilled performance. Such a description seems to be supported by much of the work of Piaget, of Claparède, and, with respect to the primitive, by Lévy-Bruhl. If one examines the facts with care, either in industry or in clinic, one finds immediately that this implication, so flattering to the civilized adult, possesses only a modicum of truth. Indeed, one may go further and say that it is positively misleading. This may be illustrated from a variety of industrial investigations.

The final phase of the first series of experiments at Hawthorne has been described under the title of the Bank Wiring Observation Room.[1] Payment to workers was made in terms of a group incentive plan; but this plan completely failed of effect. Work done was in accord with the group's conception of a day's work; this was exceeded by only one individual who was cordially disliked. Nor was output in accord with the capacity of individuals as predicted by certain tests. "The lowest producer in the room ranked first in intelligence and third in dexterity; the highest producer in the room was seventh in dexterity and lowest in intelligence."[2]

These observations are not unique; exactly the same phenomenon is recorded by Mathewson in his extensive industrial studies.[3] Golden and Ruttenberg discuss the situation at length and claim

[1] F. J. Roethlisberger and William J. Dickson, *Management and the Worker* (Cambridge, Mass., Harvard University Press, 1939), Part IV.

[2] F. J. Roethlisberger, *Management and Morale*, p. 82.

[3] Stanley B. Mathewson, *Restriction of Output among Unorganized Workers* (New York, Viking Press, 1931).

that unionism offers remedies for this—according to their statement—inevitable condition of "unorganized" industry.[1] It is at
least evident that the economists' presupposition of individual
self-preservation as motive and logic as instrument is not characteristic of the industrial facts ordinarily encountered. The desire
to stand well with one's fellows, the so-called human instinct of
association, easily outweighs the merely individual interest and
the logical reasoning upon which so many spurious principles of
management are based.

Indeed, certain facts offered for consideration in the preceding
chapter also support this claim. It was pointed out that only
students who have failed to develop the ordinary skills of human
association overthink their personal situations to the point of trying to resolve every successive moment by logical thinking rather
than by social routine where possible. For these individuals their
very lack of acquaintance with group routines transforms every
ordinary social situation into emergency and crisis. So the economists' essential contention that the function of logic is to meet
crises holds true here. It is unfortunate for economic theory that
it applies chiefly to persons of less, rather than greater, normality
of social relationship. *Must we conclude that economics is a study of
human behaviour in non-normal situations, or, alternatively, a study of non-
normal human behaviour in ordinary situations?* This is a question not
lightly to be dismissed. Nor can the use of the word normal in
this context be misunderstood; its meaning is simple and the
reference obvious. If one observes either industrial workers or
university students with sufficient care and continuity, one finds
that the proportionate number actuated by motives of *self-interest
logically elaborated* is exceedingly small. They have relapsed upon
self-interest when social association has failed them. This would
seem to imply that economics, strictly defined, is not merely study
of the forms assumed by human behaviour in disposing of scarce
means—another condition must be fulfilled, the condition,
namely, that the situation is socially disorganized.

This would make it seem that extensive social disorganization or
lack of organization, international and intranational, must be
postulated before the so-called laws of economics apply. In other
words, our studies of economic fact are upside down; we have, as
it were, an extensive pathology, but no physiology, an elaborate

[1] Clinton S. Golden and Harold J. Ruttenberg, *The Dynamics of Industrial Democracy*
(New York and London, Harper & Brothers, 1942).

study of abnormal social determinants, none of the normal. I think that the later chapters of Robbins's essay illustrate this fact. In his chapter on economic generalizations and their relation to reality, he points out that the *a priori* deductions of economics do not justify the assertion that "caviare is an economic good and a carrion a disutility".[1] He considers that, from a purely scientific economic viewpoint, these matters are determined by "individual valuations" on the one hand and on the other by "the technical facts of the given situation". Both of these conditions, he decides, are "outside the sphere of economic uniformity".

But this is too hasty—without doubt his assertion is true of the theory he is discussing, but the evidence of fact is against the conception that merely individual valuations are actual determinants, except for those who adopt Ricardo's assumption that mankind is a horde of unorganized individuals actuated by self-interest. All the essay proves is that the "proper area" of economic study, though it has something of the importance he claims for it, is nevertheless too restricted by hypothesis to be used as sufficient basis for industrial studies or for so-called economic planning. In other words, the pathology of disorganization requires supplementation by direct observation of organization. And, until such inquiries are better developed, all assertions that "there is no reason to suppose that uniformities are to be discovered"[2] in human valuations must be regarded, not as observation of social fact, but as inference from the hypothesis that mankind is an unorganized rabble. Now it may be that the variables are many and the mutual dependence exceedingly complex; but the rabble hypothesis will not bear a moment's inspection.

II

For many centuries the rabble hypothesis, in one or other form, has bedevilled all our thinking on matters involving law, government, or economics. From this theory is evolved the conviction of need for a Leviathan, a powerful State, which by the exercise of a unique authority shall impose order on the rabble. So that in these days many of our liberals and our lawyers have come to enunciating doctrines that are only with difficulty distinguished from the pronouncements of a Hitler or a Mussolini. Indeed, the

---

[1] Lionel Robbins, *The Nature and Significance of Economic Science*, p. 98.
[2] Ibid., p. 99.

major difference seems not to be logical, but rather of the nature of a humane assurance that the liberal concept of state administration will permit greater freedom of speech and action than the National Socialism of Germany.

Historians know that this theory really stretches back to the Byzantium of Justinian, to Pope Innocent IV, to the Middle Ages.

. . . The dangers of anarchy under feudalism made the mass of men blind to the dangers of autocracy. . . .

. . . The great *Leviathan* of Hobbes, the *plenitudo potestatis* of the canonists, the *arcana imperii*, the sovereignty of Austin, are all names of the same thing—the unlimited and illimitable power of the lawgiver in the State, deduced from the notion of its unity. It makes no difference whether it is the State or the Church that is being considered. . . .

But this as a factual description of organized society is completely spurious.

. . . What we actually see in the world is not on the one hand the State, and on the other a mass of unrelated individuals, but a vast complex of gathered unions, in which alone we find individuals, families, clubs, trade unions, colleges, professions and so forth. . . .

. . . It would appear a more reasonable maxim to get a theory of law and government not by laying down an abstract doctrine of unity but by observing the facts of life as it is lived, and trying to set down the actual features of civil society. What do we find as a fact? Not, surely, a sand-heap of individuals, all equal and undifferentiated, unrelated except to the State, but an ascending hierarchy of groups, family, school, town, county, union, church, etc. . . .

. . . For in truth the notion of isolated individuality is the shadow of a dream. . . . In the real world, the isolated individual does not exist; he begins always as a member of something and . . . his personality can develop only in society, and in some way or other he always embodies some social institution. I do not mean to deny the distinctness of individual life, but this distinction can function only inside a society.[1]

Figgis was not only a competent historian: he was also a member of a religious community that worked amongst the people without reward. His historical knowledge gave him vision; his daily work, actual experience of that of which he talked and wrote. In all his writings one finds a deeply humane concern for certain tendencies of the modern world before 1914; it may in-

[1] John Neville Figgis, *Churches in the Modern State*, all the above quotations from Lecture II.

deed be claimed for him that he foretold the troubled times we
have lived through since that fateful year. But one finds also
evidence of his possession of simple but effective social skills,
informed by unusual erudition, that enabled him to put his
knowledge at the service of other people in the daily round. Those
passages that I have quoted show that he is talking of the actual
society about him and not of a Ricardian postulate of doubtful
value. He is concerned with fact and not with inference from a
questionable assumption.

A contrary claim must be made for exponents of the rabble
hypothesis. They seem to be, almost exclusively, persons remote
from the active world of affairs—academics, writers, lawyers.
This is still true; those who support most keenly the Ricardian
view, who mistake its postulates for facts of observation, are
students of law, government, philosophy. Very few, if any, have
taken responsibility for the life, work, and welfare of their brother
humans. They have small knowledge-of-acquaintance of various
social situations, a negligible equipment of social skill, and are
consequently able to ignore the facts of human organization, and
the extreme importance of these facts for him who would direct
the work and thought of others. There is a recent book which is
not in this category, probably the most important work on government and administration published in several generations. It is
not surprising that this difficult but interesting study has been
ignored by political science schools.

Mr. Chester Barnard is president of the New Jersey Bell Telephone Company: since he has worked his way upwards in the
company, he has proved, not only his knowledge-of-acquaintance
of the facts of human co-operative systems, but also his skill in
handling the many and diverse problems of human organization.
His book[1] shows that he is also endowed with unusual capacity
for reflective and logical thinking. More nearly than any of the
other authors of whom I have written, he fulfils the three Henderson requirements of leadership in such a field of inquiry:

> . . . he must have first intimate, habitual, intuitive familiarity
> with things; secondly, systematic knowledge of things; and, thirdly,
> an effective way of thinking about things. . . .[2]

Barnard prefaces his book with a short account of his attempt to
discover, by extensive reading, an adequate statement of the uni-

---

[1] *The Functions of the Executive.*
[2] Lawrence J. Henderson, see previous chapter.

versal characteristics of human organization: and he records his disappointment. He could discover no treatise that discussed organization as he had come to know it in his daily administrative work. More than this, such treatises as were supposed to discuss the topic seemed to be entirely ignorant of the actualities of executive practice.

. . . Always, it seemed to me, the social scientists—from whatever side they approached—just reached the edge of organization as I experienced it, and retreated. Rarely did they seem to me to sense the processes of co-ordination and decision that underlie a large part at least of the phenomena they described. . . .

And beyond this again these writers apparently did not even recognize the extreme importance of organization as the principal structural aspect of society itself.

. . . Mores, folkways, political structures, institutions, attitudes, motives, propensities, instincts, were discussed *in extenso;* but the bridge between the generalizations of social study on the one hand and the action of masses to which they related on the other was not included. . . .[1]

Barnard then points out that the long history of thought concerning the nature of the state and of the church has obstructed intelligent inquiry into the facts of formally organized human co-operation. Legists, canonists, historians, political scientists have for centuries been preoccupied with the question of the origin and nature of authority. An eminent contemporary historian asserts that European civilization was a product of *imperium* (the Roman Empire) and *ecclesia* (the Church) in action upon *gentes*, the Franks, Saxons, Celts, and other tribal organizations.[2] Whether we look at Justinian—representing imperial Byzantium and Rome—or at Innocent IV, we find the two equally assured that the source and base of any formal organization is the supreme authority. Any human organization for a human purpose— municipality, university, business institution, army—is supposed to derive what authority it has from a superior and unitary authority; its "personality", on the view of these authorities, is fictional and derivative. This, Barnard points out, as Figgis had before him, is still the legal theory, and, as such, it is not only inconsistent with the democratic theory that government is based on spontaneous co-operation but also has the effect of preventing

[1] Chester I. Barnard, op. cit., Preface, pp. viii–ix.
[2] Christopher Dawson, *The Making of Europe* (London, Sheed & Ward, 1932), p. 67.

inquiry into, and the development of understanding of, the essential facts of social organization. On the other hand, legalist theories of the state "utterly failed, even when spun out into their endless applications in judicial decisions, to explain the most elementary experience of organized effort".[1] The historic controversy over the source and nature of authority has operated to give legists and canonists illusions of knowledge and thus actually to discourage investigation.

Next to the question of authority as source of learned confusion, Barnard places "the exaggeration of the economic phases of human behaviour which the early formulation of economic theory made far too convenient". Adam Smith and his successors have, by their theories, greatly diminished the "interest in the specific social processes within which economic factors are merely one phase"; these writers, he claims, have "greatly overemphasized" economic interests.[2] This is conjoined with a false emphasis upon the importance of "intellectual, as compared with emotional and physiological, processes" in the determination of behaviour. Consequently in the current thought of many, man is still an " 'economic' man carrying a few non-economic appendages". His own experience in an organization, Barnard points out, has been quite otherwise:

> . . . though I early found out how to behave effectively in organizations, not until I had much later relegated economic theory and economic interests to a secondary—though indispensable—place did I begin to understand organizations or human behaviour in them. . . .[3]

Once again it is evident that knowledge-of-acquaintance and the intuitions that result from intimate and sustained familiarity are more trustworthy than elaborate logics uncontrolled by developed skill and responsibility.

Nowhere is the difference between knowledge of the facts and inference from words more apparent than in Barnard's discussion of authority as it is actually exercised in an organization. Gone are the thunders and lightnings on the secret top of Horeb or of Sinai, gone also philosophical discussions of unity and indivisibility. Authority is a convenient fiction which "is used because from the standpoint of logical construction it merely explains

---

[1] Chester I. Barnard, op. cit., Preface, p. ix.
[2] Ibid., Preface, p. x.
[3] Ibid., Preface, p. xi.

overt acts".[1] The person who exercises so-called authority is placed at an important point in the line of communication—from below upwards, from above down, if one thinks in terms of an organization chart. It is his business to facilitate a balanced relation between various parts of the organization, so that the avowed purpose for which the whole exists may be conveniently and continuously fulfilled. If he is unsuccessful in this, he will have no actual authority in the organization—however important may be his title. An "approximate definition" of authority is that it "is the character of a communication (order) in a formal organization by virtue of which it is accepted by a contributor or 'member' of the organization as governing the action he contributes . . . under this definition the decision as to whether an order has authority or not lies with the persons to whom it is addressed, and does not reside in 'persons of authority' or those who issue these orders".[2] Barnard is careful to specify a "zone of indifference": not all the communications of a day are critical for the sustenance of authority. But this apart, it remains true that "the efficiency of organization" depends upon "the degree to which individuals assent to orders".[3] "Thus authority depends upon a co-operative personal attitude of individuals on the one hand; and the system of communication in the organization on the other."[4] Authority therefore in actual exercise demands a capacity for vision and wise guidance that must be re-achieved daily: since the co-operation of others is a vital element in it, social understanding and social skill are involved equally with technical knowledge and capacity. Under the influence of economic theory, we have a system of education that trains young men in technical understanding and technical skill; we do nothing whatever to develop social insight or to impart social skill. Indeed we provide an education that operates to hinder the development of such skills.

And the general public, business leaders, and politicians are left with the implication that mankind is an unorganized rabble upon which order must be imposed. It was this delusion that encouraged Hitler's dreams of grandeur.

[1] Ibid., p. 170.   [2] Ibid., p. 163.   [3] Ibid., p. 169.   [4] Ibid., p. 175.

III

Christopher Dawson, in a book briefly alluded to above, ascribes the making of European civilization to the formative influence of the Roman State and the medieval Church upon the human material of tribally organized Europe—the so-called barbarians. This influence was by no means one-way; indeed he claims that the powerful currents of nineteenth-century nationalism were due to a belated recognition by writers of the fact that the final acceptance or rejection of elements of the higher culture had continuously vested in the European peoples. As between the higher culture and these peoples, authority and its exercise had always been an issue. "The essence of barbaric society is that it rests on the principle of kinship rather than on that of citizenship or that of the absolute authority of the state."[1] The social organization of the Celts or of the Germanic peoples was tribal, "based on kinship groups, such as the sept or clan". This organization, although it ranks as primitive, "possesses virtues which many more advanced types of society may envy". Such societies know no loyalties outside their own group; the desire of every individual member to co-operate in communal activities is spontaneous and complete. The tradition of the Roman State is explicit and logical, it rests upon the authority of the *imperium:* the tradition of the *gentes* is non-logical and not expressed, it rests upon the co-operative attitude of every member of the tribe.

Jenks, writing in 1897, tries to show that, as civilization develops, the state is compelled to take over the organizing function of the clan. "Before the State comes the Clan. But the relations between the two stages are often misunderstood."[2] And he proceeds to show that the State cannot be regarded as a mere enlargement of the Clan. He remarks that "there is no . . . identity of principles between the State and the Clan. The success of the State means the destruction of the Clan".[3] The change to a new principle of social organization is dictated in the first instance, he says, by military necessity, that is to say, by emergency. "The armies which swarm into the Roman Empire, the armies which invade Britain, are leagues of clans."[4] In the three centuries which have succeeded the era of Tacitus, the most famous of the

---

[1] Christopher Dawson, *The Making of Europe*, p. 68.
[2] Edward Jenks, *Law and Politics in the Middle Ages* (London, John Murray, 1913), 2d ed., p. 71.
[3] Ibid., p. 72.   [4] Ibid., p. 73.

old clans have disappeared or have been swallowed up in larger organizations. The new groups bear names that are military and descriptive—the Frank, a warrior, the Saxon, a swordsman, the Alamann, a stranger. "The new organism is not a mere enlargement of the old; it is based on entirely different principles."[1] The leader is no longer an hereditary chief, he is chosen for his military prowess: social organization is no longer based on kinship but on proved efficiency. But "the principle of selection for personal merit has wider results than the overthrow of a Clan nobility. It is responsible for what is, perhaps, the most vital difference between the Clan and the State".[2] And Jenks is thus led to enunciate the vital difference: "The Clan is a community of groups; the State is a community of individuals."[3] This statement is frequently repeated throughout his book; it may indeed be said that from it he develops his central theme—the necessary mutual hostility of state and clan.

Jenks's thesis has the merit of clear statement which adds to the engrossing interest of his topic. "The struggle between the State and the Clan is really the key to the internal politics of the Middle Ages; and its existence contributes to medieval history that curious dualism, with its inconsistencies and its oddities, which is to many students the chief charm of the period."[4] The State begins its existence as a union of warrior tribes, united by the spur of military necessity. Once this union is established, some form of internal order and system becomes necessary, so the State progressively takes over the tasks of "keeper of internal peace, dispenser of Justice, administrator of the affairs of the land".[5] Its progress to recognition by all as the supreme authority does not, however, continue unchecked. In feudal times, and especially among the post-Carolingian Franks, the social organization is disrupted; it becomes a collection of fiefs, the internal organization in each territorial division strongly resembling the earlier tribal system. "In the years of anarchy, the Clan had gained on the State."[6] But the "inherent military weakness" and inefficiency of the Clan in the face of heathen invasion leads to the restoration of the state and to its reinforcement as against clan organization. So Jenks develops his thesis of the rival principles of social organization as culminating in the final victory of the state.

[1] Ibid., p. 74, [2] Ibid., p. 77. [3] Ibid.
[4] Ibid., p. 312. [5] Ibid., p. 91. [6] Ibid., p. 84.

The struggle between State and Clan is long and bitter; and at first it looks as though the State were going to fail. The epoch of feudalism marks the end of the first campaign; and, on the whole, the Fief, which is evidently a compromise between State and Clan, seems to have more of the Clan than of the State in its composition. . . . With the revival of the State, however, in the tenth and eleventh centuries, the struggle is recommenced; and in the long run, as we have seen, the State is victorious all along the line. [1]

It was no doubt easy for Jenks, writing in 1897 and in Victorian England, to consider the issue finally and satisfactorily determined. At that time, in spite of the warnings of Le Play and Durkheim, there did not seem to be any considerable cloud upon the horizon. In addition to which, Jenks, in spite of his unquestionable competence as a historian, had the lawyer's tendency to be satisfied with an articulate and logical explanation, to substitute such explanation for the facts. In the half century that has elapsed since he wrote, we have learned that the problem of social organization is not so easily disposed of; Figgis and Dawson, Le Play and Durkheim, have taught us to look more carefully, more critically, at the facts of European history.

But Jenks is not without a qualm. In his summary he says, "No doubt that, as far as efficiency, pure and simple, is concerned, the principles of the State are sounder than the principles of the Clan". But "gentile (gens =the Clan) ideas spring from instincts deep-rooted in humanity, and they cannot be entirely neglected". [2] Which consideration leads him to conclude that "if gentile ideas do not make for efficiency, at least they make for stability". [3] Actually, and despite all of the Jenks argument, the problem for civilization is not that of rivalry between state and clan, between efficiency and stability, but the inclusion of the two in a complex social pattern. This is in fact the theme of Barnard's book: intelligent understanding and active co-operation are alike vital to civilized order and activity.

IV

When Barnard says of any particular organization that it must be *effective* (accomplish the "objective of the system") and also *efficient* (satisfy individual motives), [4] he is enunciating a principle that may be applied widely to any society as a whole. The social organization of any group must secure for its members, first, the

---

[1] Ibid., pp. 310–311.   [2] Ibid., p. 311.   [3] Ibid., p. 312.
[4] Chester I. Barnard, op. cit., p. 56.

satisfaction of their material needs, and second, the active co-operation of others in the fulfilment of many and diverse social functions. These are not ranked here as first and second in order of importance; both are important and must be simultaneously effected. But an inspection of primitive cultures might lead one to suppose that, of the two, the latter—the need to co-operate con-tinuously—is more vital to the communal life. For the rituals of any primitive tribe are almost wholly devoted to the promotion of co-operative harmony, to discipline that enhances the certainty of unity in work; the tribe apparently assumes implicitly that, if co-operation be assured, the material needs of the group will inevitably be satisfied.

Now there cannot be co-operation without organization. Any industrial organization is at once a way of working—which must be technically expert and effective—and also a way of living for many people—a co-operative system which must be efficient, satisfactory as a way of living. Our civilization has been immense-ly successful in respect of material and technical accomplishment, an utter failure as a co-operative system. Not only have we failed to secure continuous co-operation within the nation or as between nations; we have also committed ourselves to doubtful theories, at best of limited application, that seem to regard this failure as a civilized achievement. We have an economics that postulates a disorganized rabble of individuals competing for scarce goods: and a politics that postulates a "community of individuals" ruled by a sovereign State. Both these theories foreclose on and dis-courage any investigation of the facts of social organization. Both commit us to the competitive and destructive anarchy that has so far characterized the twentieth century. Now it is certain that economic studies have had many uses, and it may be that the time given to political science in universities has not been wholly wasted; but, for so long as these topics are allowed to be a substi-tute for direct investigation of the facts, the total effect will be crippling for society.

"Now the State did not create the family, nor did it create the Churches; nor even in any real sense can it be said to have created the club or the trade union; nor in the Middle Ages the guild or the religious order, hardly even the universities or the colleges within the universities: they have all arisen out of the natural associative instincts of mankind. . . ."[1] Figgis continues: "What I have tried . . . to make clear is this: that we are divided

[1] John Neville Figgis, *Churches in the Modern State*, p. 47.

from our adversaries by questions of principle, not of detail; that the principle is concerned . . . with the very nature of the corporate life of men and therefore with the true nature of the State. . . ."[1] He goes on to claim that, for so long as "the doctrine of State omnipotence remains unconquered", free institutions cannot develop freely.   For the true function of State organization is to provide a "framework under which the perennial social instincts of men can develop".[2] And he repudiates as a "scientific monstrosity" the idea of an "omnipotent State facing an equally unreal aggregate of unrelated individuals".

This conception of an all-powerful State and a rabble of unrelated individuals is implied by economic theory, expressly stated by law and political science. It has given us a Mussolini and a Hitler, and has confused the whole course of democratic politics.

The Axis powers have pressed these theories of law and politics beyond their ultimate logical conclusion to actual application. Perhaps this will give pause to academic expositions of the sovereign State and induce reflection, perhaps even some investigation of the actual human facts. The democracies have succeeded in developing toward a co-operative commonweal—if, indeed, they have succeeded—because of the unexpressed but actual resistance of democratic peoples to tyrants, divine right, and the State Absolute.   Time and again in history our ancestors have refused to give allegiance to authority imposed from above and have cast their vote for free expression from below as the sole source of genuine leadership. This has maintained the possibility of progressive development and has kept democracy upon the pilgrims' way undisturbed by the lures or byways of political theory. Parliamentary representation and periodic elections are a partial safeguard of this development—but only partial. Not yet, even in the democracies, are we rid of the danger of political tyranny.   Mr. Harold Butler reports a mountain guide's sage observation, "We have overthrown the power of the aristocracy and the power of the Church. Now we shall have to overthrow the power of the politicians, and that will be a hard fight."[3] The forms of democracy are not enough; the active development of social skill and insight must make these dry bones live. But discussion of this topic must be postponed until my last chapter.

[1] Ibid., pp. 49–50.   [2] Ibid., p. 51.
[3] Harold Butler, *The Lost Peace* (New York, Harcourt, Brace and Company, 1942), p. 89.

CHAPTER III

The First Inquiry

Economic theory in its human aspect is woefully insufficient; indeed it is absurd. Humanity is not adequately described as a horde of individuals, each actuated by self-interest, each fighting his neighbour ror the scarce material of survival. Realization that such theories completely falsify the normal human scene drives us back to study of particular human situations. *Knowledge-of-acquaintance* of the actual event, intimate understanding of the complexity of human relationships, must precede the formulation of alternatives to current economic abstractions. This is the clinical method, the necessary preliminary to laboratory investigation. Only when clinically tested by successful treatment can a diagnosis be safely developed toward logical elaboration and laboratory experiment.

The first inquiry we undertook ran headlong into illustration of the insufficiency of the assumption that individual self-interest actually operates as adequate incentive. Rather more than twenty years ago we were asked to discover, if possible, the causes of a high labour turnover in the mule-spinning department of a textile mill near Philadelphia.[1] The general labour situation elsewhere in the plant seemed highly satisfactory; the employers were unusually enlightened and humane; the work was exceedingly well organized in respect of operations and the company was generally regarded as an extremely successful venture. But the president and his director of personnel were much troubled by the situation in the mule-spinning department. Whereas the general labour turnover in other departments was estimated to be approximately 5% or 6% per annum, in the spinning department the turnover was estimated at approximately 250%. That is to say, about 100 men had to be taken on every year in order to keep about 40

---

[1] For a more detailed account of this inquiry, see Elton Mayo, "Revery and Industrial Fatigue," *Personnel Journal*, Vol. III, No. 8, December, 1924, pp. 273–281.

working. And the difficulty tended to be most acute when the factory was busily employed and most in need of men.

Several firms of efficiency engineers had been consulted; these firms had instituted altogether four financial incentive schemes. And these schemes had been a total failure; labour turnover had not dropped one point, nor had production improved: it was almost as a last resort that the firm consulted a university. Although other plants in the vicinity had apparently drifted into acceptance of low morale amongst mule spinners as inevitable, the president of this company refused to believe that the situation was beyond remedy.

On a first inspection the conditions of work in the department did not seem to differ in any general respect from conditions elsewhere in the mill. For some time Saturday work had been discontinued throughout the plant, so that the work week was of 50 hours—five days of 10 hours, two shifts of 5 hours each separated by a 45-minute lunch interval. The mule-spinner attendant was known as a piecer; his work involved walking up and down a long alley, perhaps 30 yards or more, on either side of which a machine head was operating spinning frames. These frames moved back and forth stretching yarn taken from the carding machines, twisting it, and rolling it up on cops. The number of frames operated by a machine head varied from 10 to 14. All had to be closely watched; threads constantly broke and had to be pieced together. The number of piecers in an alley, usually two or three, varied according to the kind of yarn being spun. To an observer the work looked monotonous—walking up and down an alley twisting together broken threads. The only variation in work occurred when a machine head was stopped in order to doff or to replace some spools.

Dr. S. D. Ludlum, professor of neuropsychiatry in the graduate school of medicine in the University of Pennsylvania, was of immense aid to us at this stage as later in the study. He arranged that a registered nurse, one of our group, should be able to relate her small clinic for minor troubles in the plant direct to the Polyclinic Hospital in Philadelphia. Serious cases she referred to the hospital clinicians; minor injuries, a cut or splinter, she could deal with herself. This arrangement seemed to do away with any need for further explanation. Workers gratefully accepted the services of the nurse and, in some instances, the further clinical aid of the hospital. These services were real and understandable.

From the first the mule spinners formed a large part of the nurse's regular callers—and either when at work or in the clinic talked to her and to us quite freely. It was of course clearly understood that nothing said to any of us was ever repeated to anyone in the plant.

As the men began to talk to us, the picture of the situation developed quite differently from that obtained at first inspection. We discovered that almost every piecer suffered from foot trouble of one or another kind for which he apparently knew no effective remedy. Many also claimed neuritis in various localities of arms, shoulders, or legs. But above and beyond all this, the striking fact was the uniformly pessimistic nature of the preoccupations of these workers while at work. To this there seemed no exception: their own opinion of their work was low, even lower than the estimate of mule spinning held by other workers in the plant. We discovered also that the job was essentially solitary: there might be three workers in an alley, but the amount of communication between them in a day was almost nil. One might be piecing threads together here; another, 20 yards away. And the doffing process when it took place involved rapid work with a minimum of communication. Some of the men were young—in the twenties, others were in the fifties—all alike claimed that they were too fatigued to enjoy social evenings after work. Occasionally a worker would flare out into apparently unreasonable anger and incontinently leave his job.

The whole group was characterized by a species of strongly held loyalty to the company president. He had been a colonel in the regular United States Army and had seen active service both before and during the First World War. Many of the workers had been in the trenches in France under his immediate command and had the highest opinion of him; they had come with him from his regiment to the textile mill. Perhaps for this reason their pessimistic moods showed no anger against "The Colonel" or "the company". For the most part the individual seemed to be almost melancholic about himself; this mood alternated with spurts of rage against some immediate supervisor.

After some discussion the management permitted us to experiment with rest periods—two of 10 minutes' length in the morning and two again in the afternoon. We arranged these rests so that the work period should be divided thus: 2 hours' work, 10 minutes' rest; $1\frac{1}{2}$ hours' work, 10 minutes' rest; and a final work period of 1 hour and 10 minutes, the actual uninterrupted work period thus diminished in morning and afternoon. In these rest periods the workers were permitted to lie down; we instructed them in the best methods of securing the maximum of muscular relaxation. We encouraged them to sleep for 10 minutes and most of them were able to do so.

We began with one team of piecers, about one-third of the total number, and the results were encouraging from the outset. The men themselves were pleased and interested; they speedily adopted the method of rest we advised. The effect was immediate—symptoms of melancholy preoccupation almost wholly disappeared, the labour turnover came to an end, production was maintained, and the morale generally improved. Such immediate effects could not be attributed to the mere elimination of physical fatigue. This was confirmed by the fact that an almost equivalent improvement showed itself in the work of the other two-thirds of the piecers. These men had discussed the experiment at lunch time with their fellows and were confident that "The Colonel" would extend the system to them if it were found satisfactory. And in the October of that year, 1923, this expectation was fulfilled; the management, pleased with the improved condition of the men and the work, decided to extend the rest period system to include the entire personnel of the spinning department. This made it possible for us to do what we could not do before—to measure the effect of the rest periods upon the productivity of the department.

Until October, 1923, the spinning department had never earned a bonus under one of the incentive systems introduced; in October and for the months recorded thereafter, with one interesting exception, the spinners consistently earned a bonus in addition to their wages. I have elsewhere described the bonus plan[1] and shall not repeat this detail here. Enough to say that, if the production of the department in any month exceeded 75% of a carefully calculated possibility, every spinner was paid an excess percentage of his flat-rate wage equivalent to the average excess percentage of production over 75%. Thus a monthly man-hour efficiency of 80% meant a 5% bonus on his monthly wage to every employee in the department. As said above, no fraction of bonus had ever been earned by the department. We were unable to get figures showing the average productivity of the department before October, 1923, when the experiment proper began; but it

[1] Elton Mayo, "Revery and Industrial Fatigue," loc. cit.

was generally admitted by executives and supervisors that production had never been above an approximate 70%.

The period from October, 1923, to mid-February, 1924, inclusive, showed a surprising change. The mental and physical condition of the men continued to improve, and, whereas the financial incentive of the bonus had not operated to stimulate production while they felt fatigued, they were now pleased by the fact that under conditions of work that seemed much easier they were earning bonuses as never before. The system was not, however, altogether satisfactory at this time. The immediate supervisors had never liked the sight of workers lying asleep on sacks while the mules were running; it occurred to one of them that the men should be made to "earn" their rest periods. That is to say, a task was set and, if finished within a given time, the men had their rest. For the most part, the workers had three or four rests every day and the innovation worked well enough. For example, the monthly average of productivity ran as follows:

		Efficiency	*Bonus*
October,	1923	$79\frac{1}{2}\%$	$4\frac{1}{2}\%$
November,	,,	$78\frac{3}{4}$	$3\frac{3}{4}$
December,	,,	82	7
January,	1924	$78\frac{3}{4}$	$3\frac{3}{4}$
February,	,,	$80\frac{1}{4}$	$5\frac{1}{4}$

This, for workers who had never before earned a bonus, meant much.

This general condition continued until Friday, February 15, when in response to a heavy demand for goods the supervisor who had introduced the idea of earned rest periods ordered the whole system abandoned. Within five days production fell to a point lower than it had been for months. And on February 22, we found that the old pessimistic preoccupations had returned in full force, thus coinciding almost exactly with the drop in production. The executive officer in charge ordered the resumption of the rest period system on Monday, February 25; this was done, but the idea of earned rest periods was also reinstated even more strongly than before. At this point, the workers gave every symptom of profound discouragement; they professed a belief that the system would be discontinued before long. In spite of this, the daily record for March showed definite improvement, but the general average for the month was back at the old point, 70%.

At this point the president of the company, "The Colonel", took charge. His military service had taught him two important things—one, to care for his men, and, two, not to be afraid of making decisions. He called a conference in his office to discuss the remarkable diminution from 80% to 70% in the department's productive efficiency. We were able to point out that in March there had been a recrudescence of absenteeism, an ill that had notably diminished in the October to February period. This meant that the men were taking their rest periods in the form of "missed" days, a proceeding that did not greatly remedy their condition and that produced chaos in the plant. We put it therefore that the question was not whether a certain proportion of their working time was to be given up to rest. We pointed out that they took the rest, whether it was given them or not. We were asking that a less proportion should be thus allotted, but that it should be done systematically. Furthermore, we were able to claim that the whole rest period system had never had a fair trial. In other words, it had not been possible for a worker to know as he entered the factory in the morning that he was assured of his four rests in the day.

In order to test our claim, the president ordered that during the month of April the spinning mules should be shut down for 10 minutes at a time four times a day and that all hands from the floor supervisor down should rest as they had been instructed to do. There was some difficulty in securing the requisite amount of floor space for approximately 40 men to lie down by their machines and in securing sufficient sacking to provide for their comfort. With the exception of the president himself, there were few who believed that this drastic alteration of method could result in increased production. The men themselves believed that 40 minutes lost by 40 men per day during a whole month could not be recovered. They pointed out that the machines could not be "speeded up" and that there was no other way of recovering the lost time. In spite of this general belief, the returns for April showed an improvement on March.[1] The March production-efficiency figure had been 70%, the April figure was $77\frac{1}{2}$%. This, while it represented a $7\frac{1}{2}$% gain in the company's rating, was actually a 10% gain. The men had had their rests, the pessimism had again disappeared; simultaneously, their morale had much improved, absenteeism had diminished, and every worker had earned a $2\frac{1}{2}$%

[1] Ibid.

bonus on his wages. In the month of May and thereafter, the president ordered a return to the system of alternating rest periods, with this important difference that each group of three men in an alley was to determine for itself the method of alternation, the understanding being that every worker was to have four such rest periods daily and regularly. In the month of May, the average efficiency of man-hour production was $80\frac{1}{4}\%$. In June it reached the then record high figure of 85%. During the following three months the department maintained its improved capacity: July, 82%; August, $83\frac{1}{2}\%$; September, $86\frac{1}{2}\%$.

It is interesting to observe the difference that an absolute certainty of a minimum number of rest periods made. The months from April to September differed from the preceding months in this respect and they revealed a steady progress. Mondays and Fridays were no longer the worst days in the week. The irregularity reported in May was due to the fact that the spinning mules were constantly "running away from the cards", that is, outdistancing the carding machines which supplied them with spooled yarn. By June, the company had put in two new carding machines, and June was as steadily above 85% as March was below 75%.

The investigation began with a question as to the causes of a very high labour turnover. In the 12 months of experiment there was no labour turnover at all. This does not mean that no worker left the factory—during a period of trade slackness, some were laid off, one at least moved his place of residence and found work elsewhere, another was found to be phthisical and sent to the country. But the former problem of a highly emotional labour turnover ceased to exist. The factory began to hold its mule spinners and no longer had difficulty in maintaining a full complement in times of rushed work. The attitude of management to the innovation was revealed in the fact that the company purchased army cots for the workers to rest upon. When these cots proved unequal to the wear and tear, management installed a bed and mattress at the end of each alley as provision for the workers' adequate rest. And the workers developed the habit of sleeping for the last three rest periods of the day, the late morning rest and both afternoon rests. Experience seemed to show that the benefit was directly proportionate to the completeness of the relaxation—hence the beds. Several years later, the president of the company said publicly that from this time the labour turnover sank to an approximate 5% or 6% per annum and stayed there until the mules were taken out and ring spinning substituted.

At the time when we completed our part in this work, we were sure that we had not wholly discovered the causes of the high labour turnover. We could not even attribute the change to the mere introduction of rest periods; inevitably many other changes had been simultaneously introduced. For example, we had listened carefully and with full attention to anything a worker wished to say, whatever the character of his comment. In addition to this, we—supported by the president—had demonstrated an interest in what was said by the introduction of experimental changes, by instruction in the best methods of relaxation. The Colonel also had demonstrated unmistakably a sincere interest in his workers' welfare; he had lived up to his Army reputation. The supervisor who instituted the earning of rest periods was swept aside by the president and the company—thereby "placing" the company's attitude in the minds of its workers.

But, in addition to this—and we did not see this clearly at the time—the president had effected another important change. He had helped to transform a horde of "solitaries" into a social group. In May, 1924, he placed the control of rest periods squarely in the hands of the workers in an alley with no one to say them nay. This led to consultation, not only between individuals, but between alleys throughout the group—and to a feeling of responsibility directly to the president. And the general social changes effected were astonishing—even in relationships outside the factory. One worker told us with great surprise that he had begun taking his wife to "movies" in the evenings, a thing he had not done for years. Another, equally to his surprise, gave up a habit of spending alcoholic weekends on bootleg liquor. In general the change was complex, and the difficulty of assigning the part played in it by various aspects of the experiment impossible to resolve. We should have liked to experiment further, but this desire —probably wisely in the circumstances—was disallowed. Thus the inquiry left us with many questions unanswered, but it pointed a direction for further studies, the results of which later proved helpful in reinterpreting the data of this first investigation.

But we had moved onwards. The efficiency experts had not consulted the workers; they regarded workers' statements as exaggerated or due to misconception of the facts and therefore to be ignored. Yet to ignore an important symptom—whatever its character—on supposedly moral grounds is preposterous. The "expert" assumptions of rabble hypothesis and individual self-interest as a basis for diagnosis led nowhere. On the other hand, careful and pedestrian consideration of the workers' situation taken as part of a clinical diagnosis led us to results so surprising that we could at the time only partly explain them.

CHAPTER IV

HAWTHORNE AND THE WESTERN ELECTRIC COMPANY: SOME FURTHER COMMENTS ON THE INTERVIEW EXPERIMENT

THE cases selected for discussion in these chapters must not be supposed to be a report of all the work done by the Industrial Research Department of Harvard University.[1] Any such conception would be very far from the truth; at some future time my colleagues will present reports of many other studies that will vie in interest with those here described. The selection of a case has been based upon the extent to which the experience developed our insight into, or understanding of, a particular industrial situation; those inquiries are presented that seem notably to have helped the department to move forward in its thinking. And, of these, the most signal instance is probably the five years and more spent in active collaboration with officers of the Western Electric Company at Hawthorne. In Philadelphia we had been fortunate in finding as president of a company an Army colonel who was not afraid of a crucial experiment, and, having experimented, was also not afraid to act on the result—even though his action seemed to the workers to be in their favour. Furthermore, he deemed it proper to give the workers control of their rest periods, thereby securing for him and his company an eager and spontaneous loyalty. We were equally fortunate in finding at Hawthorne a group of engineers who ranked as first-rate in matters of applied science or of organized industrial operation, but who wished to find out why human co-operation could not be as exactly and as accurately determined by the administrative organization.

I shall make no attempt to describe at length that which has been already and fully described. The interested public is well acquainted with *Management and the Worker*, the official account of the whole range of experiments, by my colleagues F. J. Roethlisberger of Harvard University and William J. Dickson of the Western Electric Company. The same public has not yet discovered *The Industrial Worker*,[2] by another colleague, T. North

---

[1] A brief description of the studies of the Department, together with a list of the publications resulting from them, may be found in Appendix II.

[2] Cambridge, Mass., Harvard University Press, 1938, 2 vols.

Whitehead. This is unfortunate, for the beginning of an answer to many problems significant for administration in the next decade is recorded in its pages. I refer to the problems involved in the making and adaptive re-making of working teams, the importance of which for collaboration in post-war years is still too little realized. Assuming that readers who wish to do so can consult these books, I have confined my remarks here to some comments upon the general development of the series of experiments.

A highly competent group of Western Electric engineers refused to accept defeat when experiments to demonstrate the effect of illumination on work seemed to lead nowhere. The conditions of scientific experiment had apparently been fulfilled—experimental room, control room; changes introduced one at a time; all other conditions held steady. And the results were perplexing: Roethlisberger gives two instances—lighting improved in the experimental room, production went up; but it rose also in the control room. The opposite of this: lighting diminished from 10 to 3 foot-candles in the experimental room and production again went up; simultaneously in the control room, with illumination constant, production also rose.[1] Many other experiments, and all inconclusive; yet it had seemed so easy to determine the effect of illumination on work.

In matters of mechanics or chemistry the modern engineer knows how to set about the improvement of process or the redress of error. But the determination of optimum working conditions for the human being is left largely to dogma and tradition, guess, or quasi-philosophical argument. In modern large-scale industry the three persistent problems of management are:

1. The application of science and technical skill to some material good or product.
2. The systematic ordering of operations.
3. The organization of teamwork—that is, of sustained co-operation.

The last must take account of the need for continual reorganization of teamwork as operating conditions are changed in an *adaptive* society.

The first of these holds enormous prestige and interest and is the subject of continuous experiment. The second is well developed in practice. The third, by comparison with the other two, is almost wholly neglected. Yet it remains true that if these three

[1] *Management and Morale*, pp. 9-10.

are out of balance, the organization as a whole will not be successful. The first two operate to make an industry *effective*, in Chester Barnard's phrase,[1] the third, to make it *efficient*. For the larger and more complex the institution, the more dependent is it upon the whole-hearted co-operation of every member of the group.

This was not altogether the attitude of Mr. G. A. Pennock and his colleagues when they set up the experimental "test room". But the illumination fiasco had made them alert to the need that very careful records should be kept of everything that happened in the room in addition to the obvious engineering and industrial devices.[2] Their observations therefore included not only records of industrial and engineering changes but also records of physiological or medical changes, and, in a sense, of social and anthropological. This last took the form of a "log" that gave as full an account as possible of the actual events of every day, a record that proved most useful to Whitehead when he was re-measuring the recording tapes and re-calculating the changes in productive output. He was able to relate eccentricities of the output curve to the actual situation at a given time—that is to say, to the events of a specific day or week.

First Phase—The Test Room

The facts are by now well known. Briefly restated, the test room began its inquiry by, first, attempting to secure the active collaboration of the workers. This took some time but was gradually successful, especially after the retirement of the original first and second workers and after the new worker at the second bench had assumed informal leadership of the group. From this point on, the evidence presented by Whitehead or Roethlisberger and Dickson seems to show that the individual workers became a team, whole-heartedly committed to the project. Second, the conditions of work were changed one at a time: rest periods of different numbers and length, shorter working day, shorter working week, food with soup or coffee in the morning break. And the results seemed satisfactory: slowly at first, but later with increasing certainty, the output record (used as an index of well-being) mounted. Simultaneously the girls claimed that they felt less fatigued, felt that they were not making any special effort. Whether these claims were

---

[1] Op. cit., p. 56.

[2] For a full account of the experimental setup, see F. J. Roethlisberger and William J. Dickson, *Management and the Worker*, and T. North Whitehead, *The Industrial Worker*, Vol. I.

accurate or no, they at least indicated increased contentment with the general situation in the test room by comparison with the department outside. At every point in the programme, the workers had been consulted with respect to proposed changes; they had arrived at the point of free expression of ideas and feelings to management. And it had been arranged thus that the twelfth experimental change should be a return to the original conditions of work—no rest periods, no mid-morning lunch, no shortened day or week. It had also been arranged that, after 12 weeks of this, the group should return to the conditions of Period 7, a 15-minute mid-morning break with lunch and a 10-minute mid-afternoon rest. The story is now well known: in Period 12 the daily and weekly output rose to a point higher than at any other time (the hourly rate adjusted itself downward by a small fraction), and in the whole 12 weeks "there was no downward trend". In the following period, the return to the conditions of work as in the seventh experimental change, the output curve soared to even greater heights: this thirteenth period lasted for 31 weeks.

These periods, 12 and 13, made it evident that increments of production could not be related point for point to the experimental changes introduced. Some major change was taking place that was chiefly responsible for the index of improved conditions—the steadily increasing output. Period 12—but for minor qualifications, such as "personal time out"—ignored the nominal return to original conditions of work and the output curve continued its upward passage. Put in other words, there was no actual return to original conditions. This served to bring another fact to the attention of the observers. Periods 7, 10, and 13 had nominally the same working conditions, as above described—15-minute rest and lunch in mid-morning, 10-minute rest in the afternoon. But the average weekly output for each girl was:

Period 7—2,500 units
Period 10—2,800 units
Period 13—3,000 units

Periods 3 and 12 resembled each other also in that both required a full day's work without rest periods. But here also the difference of average weekly output for each girl was:

Period 3—less than 2,500 units
Period 12—more than 2,900 units

Here then was a situation comparable perhaps with the illumination experiment, certainly suggestive of the Philadelphia experience where improved conditions for one team of mule spinners were reflected in improved morale not only in the experimental team but in the two other teams who had received no such benefit.

This interesting, and indeed amusing, result has been so often discussed that I need make no mystery of it now. I have often heard my colleague Roethlisberger declare that the major experimental change was introduced when those in charge sought to hold the situation humanly steady (in the interest of critical changes to be introduced) by getting the co-operation of the workers. What actually happened was that six individuals became a team and the team gave itself wholeheartedly and spontaneously to co-operation in the experiment. The consequence was that they felt themselves to be participating freely and without afterthought, and were happy in the knowledge that they were working without coercion from above or limitation from below. They were themselves astonished at the consequence, for they felt that they were working under less pressure than ever before: and in this, their feelings and performance echoed that of the mule spinners.

Here then are two topics which deserve the closest attention of all those engaged in administrative work—the organization of working teams and the free participation of such teams in the task and purpose of the organization as it directly affects them in their daily round.

Second Phase—The Interview Programme

But such conclusions were not possible at the time: the major change, the question as to the exact difference between conditions of work in the test room and in the plant departments, remained something of a mystery. Officers of the company determined to "take another look" at departments outside the test room—this, with the idea that something quite important was there to be observed, something to which the experiment should have made them alert. So the interview programme was introduced.

It was speedily discovered that the question-and-answer type of interview was useless in the situation. Workers wished to talk, and to talk freely under the seal of professional confidence (which was never abused) to someone who seemed representative of the company or who seemed, by his very attitude, to carry authority. The experience itself was unusual; there are few people in this world who have had the experience of finding someone intelligent, attentive, and eager to listen without interruption to all that he or she has to say. But to arrive at this point it became necessary to train interviewers how to listen, how to avoid interruption or the giving of advice, how generally to avoid anything that might put an end to free expression in an individual instance. Some approximate rules to guide the interviewer in his work were therefore set down. These were, more or less, as follows:[1]

1. Give your whole attention to the person interviewed, and make it evident that you are doing so.
2. Listen—don't talk.
3. Never argue; never give advice.
4. Listen to:
   (a) What he wants to say.
   (b) What he does not want to say.
   (c) What he cannot say without help.
5. As you listen, plot out tentatively and for subsequent correction the pattern (personal) that is being set before you. To test this, from time to time summarize what has been said and present for comment (e.g., "Is this what you are telling me?"). Always do this with the greatest caution, that is, clarify but do not add or distort.
6. Remember that everything said must be considered a personal confidence and not divulged to anyone. (This does not prevent discussion of a situation between professional colleagues. Nor does it prevent some form of public report when due precaution has been taken.)

It must not be thought that this type of interviewing is easily learned. It is true that some persons, men and women alike, have a natural flair for the work, but, even with them, there tends to be an early period of discouragement, a feeling of futility, through which the experience and coaching of a senior interviewer must carry them. The important rules in the interview (important, that is, for the development of high skill) are two. First, Rule 4 that indicates the need to help the individual interviewed to articulate expression of an idea or attitude that he has not before expressed; and, second, Rule 5 which indicates the need from

[1] For a full discussion of this type of interview, see F. J. Roethlisberger and William J. Dickson, op. cit., Chap. XIII. For a more summary and perhaps less technical discussion, see George C. Homans, *Fatigue of Workers* (New York, Reinhold Publishing Corporation, 1941).

time to time to summarize what has been said and to present it for comment. Once equipped to do this effectively, interviewers develop very considerable skill. But, let me say again, this skill is not easily acquired. It demands of the interviewer a real capacity to follow the contours of another person's thinking, to understand the meaning for him of what he says.

I do not believe that any member of the research group or its associates had anticipated the immediate response that would be forthcoming to the introduction of such an interview programme. Such comments as "This is the best thing the Company has ever done", or "The Company should have done this long ago", were frequently heard. It was as if workers had been awaiting an opportunity for expressing freely and without afterthought their feelings on a great variety of modern situations, not by any means limited to the various departments of the plant. To find an intelligent person who was not only eager to listen but also anxious to help to expression ideas and feelings but dimly understood—this, for many thousand persons, was an experience without precedent in the modern world.

In a former statement I named two questions that inevitably presented themselves to the interviewing group in these early stages of the study:

(1) Is some experience which might be described as an experience of personal futility a common incident of industrial organization for work?

(2) Does life in a modern industrial city, in some unrealized way, predispose workers to obsessive response? [1]

And I said that these two questions "in some form" continued to preoccupy those in charge of the research until the conclusion of the study.

After twelve years of further study (not yet concluded), there are certain developments that demand attention. For example, I had not fully realized in 1932, when the above was written, how profoundly the social structure of civilization has been shaken by scientific, engineering, and industrial development. This radical change—the passage from an *established* to an *adaptive* social order—has brought into being a host of new and unanticipated problems for management and for the individual worker. The

[1] Elton Mayo, *The Human Problems of an Industrial Civilization* (New York, The Macmillan Company, 1933; reprinted by Division of Research, Harvard Business School, 1946), p. 114.

management problem appears at its acutest in the work of the supervisor. No longer does the supervisor work with a team of persons that he has known for many years or perhaps a lifetime; he is leader of a group of individuals that forms and disappears almost as he watches it. Now it is difficult, if not impossible, to relate oneself to a working group one by one; it is relatively easy to do so if they are already a fully constituted team. A communication from the supervisor, for example, in the latter instance has to be made to one person only with the appropriate instructions; the individual will pass it on and work it out with the team. In the former instance, it has to be repeated to every individual and may often be misunderstood.

But for the individual worker the problem is really much more serious. He has suffered a profound loss of security and certainty in his actual living and in the background of his thinking. For all of us the feeling of security and certainty derives always from assured membership of a group. If this is lost, no monetary gain, no job guarantee, can be sufficient compensation. Where groups change ceaselessly as jobs and mechanical processes change, the individual inevitably experiences a sense of void, of emptiness, where his fathers knew the joy of comradeship and security. And in such situation, his anxieties—many, no doubt, irrational or ill-founded—increase and he becomes more difficult both to fellow workers and to supervisor. The extreme of this is perhaps rarely encountered as yet, but increasingly we move in this direction as the tempo of industrial change is speeded by scientific and technical discovery.

In the first chapter of this book I have claimed that scientific method has a dual approach—represented in medicine by the clinic and the laboratory. In the clinic one studies the whole situation with two ends in view: first, to develop intimate knowledge of and skill in handling the facts, and, second, on the basis of such a skill to separate those aspects of the situation, that skill has shown to be closely related, for detailed laboratory study. When a study based upon laboratory method fails, or partially fails, because some essential factor has been unknowingly and arbitrarily excluded, the investigator, if he is wise, returns to clinical study of the entire situation to get some hint as to the nature of the excluded determinant. The members of the research division at Hawthorne, after the twelfth experimental period in the test room, were faced by just such a situation and knew it. The so-called interview programme represented for them a return from the laboratory to clinical study. And, as in all clinical study, there was no immediate and welcome revelation of a single discarded determinant: there was rather a slow progress from one observation to another, all of them important—but only gradually building up into a single complex finding. This slow development has been elsewhere described, in *Management and the Worker;* one can however attempt a succinct résumé of the various observations, more or less as they occurred.

Officers of the company had prepared a short statement, a few sentences, to be repeated to the individual interviewed before the conversation began. This statement was designed to assure the worker that nothing he said would be repeated to his supervisors or to any company official outside the interviewing group. In many instances, the worker waved this aside and began to talk freely and at once. What doubts there were seemed to be resident in the interviewers rather than in those interviewed. Many workers, I cannot say the majority for we have no statistics, seemed to have something "on their minds", in ordinary phrase, about which they wished to talk freely to a competent listener. And these topics were by no means confined to matters affecting the company. This was, I think, the first observation that emerged from the mass of interviews reported daily. The research group began to talk about the need for "*emotional release*" and the great advantage that accrued to the individual when he had "talked off" his problem. The topics varied greatly. One worker two years before had been sharply reprimanded by his supervisor for not working as usual: in interview he wished to explain that on the night preceding the day of the incident his wife and child had both died, apparently unexpectedly. At the time he was unable to explain; afterwards he had no opportunity to do so. He told the story dramatically and in great detail; there was no doubt whatever that telling it thus benefited him greatly. But this story naturally was exceptional; more often a worker would speak of his family and domestic situation, of his church, of his relations with other members of the working group—quite usually the topic of which he spoke presented itself to him as a problem difficult for him to resolve. This led to the next successive illumination for the inquiry. It became manifest that, whatever the problem, it was partly, and sometimes wholly, determined by the attitude of the individual worker. And this defect or distortion of attitude was consequent on his past experience or his present situation, or, more usually, on both at once. One woman worker, for example, discovered for herself during an interview that her dislike of a certain supervisor was based upon a fancied resemblance to a detested stepfather. Small wonder that the same supervisor had warned the interviewer that she was "difficult to handle". But the discovery by the worker that her dislike was wholly irrational eased the situation considerably.[1] This type of case led the interviewing group to study carefully each worker's *personal situation* and attitude. These two phrases "emotional release" and "personal situation" became convenient titles for the first phases of observation and seemed to resume for the interviewers the effective work that they were doing. It was at this point that a change began to show itself in the study and in the conception of the study.

The original interviewers, in these days, after sixteen years of industrial experience, are emphatic on the point that the first cases singled out for report were special cases—individuals—and not representative either of the working group or of the interviews generally. It is estimated that such cases did not number more than an approximate two per cent. of the twenty thousand persons originally interviewed. Probably this error of emphasis was inevitable and for two reasons: first, the dramatic changes that occur in such instances seemed good evidence of the efficacy of the method, and, second, this type of interviewing had to be insisted upon as *necessary to the training of a skilled interviewer*. This last still holds good; a skilled interviewer must have passed through the stage of careful and observant listening to what an individual says and to all that he says. This stage of an interviewing programme closely resembles the therapeutic method and its triumphs are apt to be therapeutic. And I do not believe that the study would have been equipped to advance further if it had failed to observe the great benefit of emotional release and the extent to which every individual's problems are conditioned by his personal history and situation. Indeed, even when one has advanced beyond the merely psychotherapeutic study of individuals to study of industrial groups, one has to beware of distortions similar in kind to those named; one has to know how to deal with such problems. The first phase of the interview programme cannot therefore be discarded; it still retains its original importance. But industrial studies must nevertheless move beyond the individual in need of therapy. And this is the

[1] F. J. Roethlisberger and William J. Dickson, op. cit., pp. 307–310.

more true when the change from established routines to adaptive changes of routine seems generally to carry a consequence of loss of security for many persons.

A change of attitude in the research group came gradually. The close study of individuals continued, but in combination with an equally close study of groups. An early incident did much to set the new pattern for inquiry. One of the earliest questions proposed before the original test room experiment began was a question as to the fatigue involved in this or that type of work. Later a foreman of high reputation, no doubt with this in mind, came to the research group, now for the most part engaged in interviewing, and asserted that the girls in his department worked hard all day at their machines and must be considerably fatigued by the evening; he wanted an inquiry. Now the interviewers had discovered that this working group claimed a habit of doing most of their work in the morning period and "taking things easy" during the afternoon. The foreman obviously realized nothing of this, and it was therefore fortunate that the two possibilities could be directly tested. The officer in charge of the research made a quiet arrangement with the engineers to measure during a period the amount of electric current used by the group to operate its machines; this quantity indicated the over-all amount of work being done. The results of this test wholly supported the statements made by the girls in interview: far more current was used in the morning period than during the afternoon. And the attention of the research group was, by this and other incidents, thus redirected to a fact already known to them, namely, that the working group as a whole actually determined the output of individual workers by reference to a standard, pre-determined but never clearly stated, that represented the group conception of a fair day's work. This standard was rarely, if ever, in accord with the standards of the efficiency engineers.

The final experiment, reported under the title of the Bank Wiring Observation Room, was set up to extend and confirm these observations.[1] Simultaneously it was realized that these facts did not in any way imply low working morale as suggested by such phrases as "restriction of output". On the contrary, the failure of free communication between management and workers in modern large-scale industry leads inevitably to the exercise of caution by the working group until such time as it knows clearly

[1] F. J. Roethlisberger and William J. Dickson, op. cit., Part IV, pp. 379 ff.

the range and meaning of changes imposed from above. The enthusiasm of the efficiency engineer for the organization of operations is excellent; his attempt to resume problems of co-operation under this heading is not. At the moment, he attempts to solve the many human difficulties involved in whole-hearted co-operation by organizing the organization of organization without any reference whatever to workers themselves. This procedure inevitably blocks communication and defeats his own admirable purpose.[1]

This observation, important as it is, was not however the leading point for the interviewers. The existence and influence of the group—those in active daily relationship with one another—became the important fact. The industrial interviewer must learn to distinguish and specify, as he listens to what a worker says, references to "personal" or group situations. More often than not, the special case, the individual who talks himself out of a gross distortion, is a solitary—one who has not "made the team". The usual interview, on the other hand, though not by any means free from distortion, is speaking as much for the working group as for the person. The influence of the communication in the interview, therefore, is not limited to the individual but extends to the group.

Two girl workers in a large industry were recently offered "upgrading"; to accept would mean leaving their group and taking a job in another department: they refused. Then representatives of the union put some pressure on them, claiming that, if they continued to refuse, the union organizers "might just as well give up" their efforts. With reluctance the girls reversed their decision and accepted the upgrading. Both girls at once needed the attention of an interviewer: they had liked the former group in which they had earned informal membership. Both felt adjustment to a new group and a novel situation as involving effort and private discontent. From both much was learned of the intimate organization and common practices of their groups, and their adjustments to their new groups were eased, thereby effectively helping to reconstitute the teamwork in those groups.

In another recent interview a girl of eighteen protested to an interviewer that her mother was continually urging her to ask Mr. X, her supervisor, for a "raise". She had refused, but her loyalty

---

[1] For further evidence on this point, see Stanley B. Mathewson, *Restriction of Output among Unorganized Workers*, and also Elton Mayo, *The Human Problems of an Industrial Civilization*, pp. 119–121.

to her mother and the pressure the latter exerted were affecting her work and her relations at work. She talked her situation out with an interviewer, and it became clear that to her a "raise" would mean departure from her daily companions and associates. Although not immediately relevant, it is interesting to note that, after explaining the situation at length to the interviewer, she was able to present her case dispassionately to her mother—without exaggeration or protest. The mother immediately understood and abandoned pressure for advancement, and the girl returned to effective work. This last instance illustrates one way in which the interview clears lines of communication of emotional blockage—within as without the plant. But this is not my immediate topic; my point is rather that the age-old human desire for persistence of human association will seriously complicate the development of an adaptive society if we cannot devise systematic methods of easing individuals from one group of associates into another.

But such an observation was not possible in the earliest inquiry. The important fact brought to the attention of the research division was that the ordinary conception of management-worker relation as existing between company officials, on the one hand, and an unspecified number of individuals, on the other, is utterly mistaken. Management, in any continuously successful plant, is not related to single workers but always to working groups. In every department that continues to operate, the workers have—whether aware of it or not—formed themselves into a group with appropriate customs, duties, routines, even rituals; and management succeeds (or fails) in proportion as it is accepted without reservation by the group as authority and leader. This, for example, occurred in the relay assembly test room at Hawthorne. Management, by consultation with the girl workers, by clear explanation of the proposed experiments and the reasons for them, by accepting the workers' verdict in special instances, unwittingly scored a success in two most important human matters—the girls became a self-governing team, and a team that co-operated whole-heartedly with management. The test room was responsible for many important findings—rest periods, hours of work, food, and the like: but the most important finding of all was unquestionably in the general area of teamwork and co-operation.

It was at this time that the research division published, for private circulation within the company, a monograph entitled "Complaints and Grievances". Careful description of many

varied situations within the interviewers' experience showed that
an articulate complaint only rarely, if ever, gave any logical clue
to the grievance in which it had origin; this applied at least as
strongly to groups as to individuals. Whereas economists and
industry generally *tend to concentrate upon the complaint and upon logical
inferences from its articulate statement* as an appropriate procedure,
the interviewing group had learned almost to ignore, except as
symptom, the—sometimes noisy—manifestation of discomfort and
to study the situation anew to gain knowledge of its source. Diagnosis rather than argument became the proper method of
procedure.

It is possible to quote an illustration from a recently published
book, *China Enters the Machine Age.*[1] When industries had to be
moved, during this war, from Shanghai and the Chinese coast to
Kunming in the interior of China, the actual operation of an
industry still depended for the most part on skilled workers who
were refugees from Shanghai and elsewhere. These skilled workers
knew their importance to the work and gained considerable prestige from it; nevertheless discontent was rife among them. Evidence of this was manifested by the continual, deliberate breaking
of crockery in the company mess hall and complaints about the
quality of the food provided. Yet this food was much better than
could have been obtained outside the plant—especially at the
prices charged. And in interview the individual workers admitted
freely that the food was good and could not rightly be made the
subject of complaint. But the relationship between the skilled
workers as a group and the *Chih Yuan*—the executive and supervisory officers—was exceedingly unsatisfactory.

Many of these officers—the *Chih Yuan*—have been trained in
the United States—enough at least to set a pattern for the whole
group. Now in America we have learned in actual practice to
accept the rabble hypothesis with reservations. But the logical
Chinese student of engineering or economics, knowing nothing of
these practical reservations, returns to his own country convinced
that the workman who is not wholly responsive to the "financial
incentive" is a troublemaker and a nuisance. And the Chinese
worker lives up to this conviction by breaking plates.[2] Acceptance
of the complaint about the food and collective bargaining of a
logical type conducted at that level would surely have been useless.

[1] Shih Kuo-heng (Cambridge, Mass., Harvard University Press, 1944).
[2] Ibid., Chap. VIII, pp. 111–127; also Chap. X, pp. 151–153.

Yet this is what industry, not only in China, does every day, with the high sanction of State authority and the alleged aid of lawyers and economists. In their behaviour and their statements, economists indicate that they accept the rabble hypothesis and its dismal corollary of financial incentive as the only effective human motive. They substitute a logical hypothesis of small practical value for the actual facts.

The insight gained by the interviewing group, on the other hand, cannot be described as substituting irrational for rational motive, emotion for logic. On the contrary, it implies a need for competent study of complaints and the grievances that provoke them, a need for knowledge of the actual facts rather than acceptance of an outdated theory. It is amusing that certain industrialists, rigidly disciplined in economic theory, attempt to shrug off the Hawthorne studies as "theoretic". Actually the shoe is on the other foot; Hawthorne has re-studied the facts without prejudice, whereas the critics have unquestioningly accepted that theory of man which had its vogue in the nineteenth century and has already outlived its usefulness.

The Hawthorne interview programme has moved far since its beginning in 1929. Originally designed to study the comfort of workers in their work as a mass of individuals, it has come to clear specification of the relation of working groups to management as one of the fundamental problems of large-scale industry. It was indeed this study that first enabled us to assert that the third major preoccupation of management must be that of organizing teamwork, that is to say, of developing and sustaining co-operation.

In summary, certain entirely practical discoveries must be enumerated.

First, the early discovery that the interview aids the individual to get rid of useless emotional complications and to state his problem clearly. He is thus enabled to give himself good advice—a procedure far more effective than advice accepted from another. I have already given instances of this in discussing "emotional release" and the influence on individual attitude of personal history and personal stituation.

Second, the interview has demonstrated its capacity to aid the individual to associate more easily, more satisfactorily, with other persons—fellow workers or supervisors—with whom he is in daily contact.

Third, the interview not only helps the individual to collaborate better with his own group of workers, it also develops his desire and capacity to work better with management. In this it resembles somewhat the action of the Philadelphia colonel.[1] Someone, the interviewer, representing (for the worker) the plant organization outside his own group, has aided him to work better with his own group. This is the beginning of the necessary double loyalty—to his own group and to the larger organization. It remains only for management to make wise use of this beginning.

Fourth, beyond all this, interviewing possesses immense importance for the training of administrators in the difficult future that faces this continent and the world. It has been said that the interviewer has no authority and takes no action. Action can only be taken by the proper authority and through the formally constituted line of authority. The interviewer, however, contributes much to the facilitation of communication both up and down that line. He does this, first, by clearing away emotional distortion and exaggeration; second, his work manifestly aids to exact and objective statement the grievance that lies beyond the various complaints.

Work of this kind is immensely effective in the development of maturity of attitude and judgment in the intelligent and sensitive young men and women who give time to it. The subordination of oneself, of one's opinions and ideas, of the very human desire to give gratuitous advice, the subordination of all these to an intelligent effort to help another express ideas and feelings that he cannot easily express is, in itself, a most desirable education. As a preparation for the exercise of administrative responsibility, it is better than anything offered in a present university curriculum. It is no doubt necessary to train young men and women to present their knowledge and ideas with lucidity. But, if they are to be administrators, it is far more necessary to train them to listen carefully to what others say. Only he who knows how to help other persons to adequate expression can develop the many qualities demanded by a real maturity of judgment.

Finally, there remains the claim made above that the interview has proved to be a source of information of great objective value to management. The three persistent problems of modern large-scale industry have been stated as:

1. The application of science and technical skill to a material product.

---

[1] Chap. III, supra.

2. The systematic ordering of operations.

3. The organization of sustained co-operation.

When a representative of management claims that interview results are merely personal or subjective—and there are many who still echo this claim—he is actually telling us that he has himself been trained to give all his attention to the first and second problems, technical skill and the systematic ordering of operations; he does not realize that he has also been trained to ignore the third problem completely. For such persons, information on a problem, the existence of which they do not realize, is no information. It is no doubt in consequence of this ignorance or induced blindness that strikes or other difficulties so frequently occur in unexpected places. The interview method is the only method extant[1] that can contribute reasonably accurate information, or indeed any information, as to the extent of the actual co-operation between workers—teamwork—that obtains in a given department, and beyond this, the extent to which this co-operation includes management policy or is wary of it. The Hawthorne inquiry at least specified these most important industrial issues and made some tentative steps toward the development of a method of diagnosis and treatment in particular cases.

---

[1] We realize that there are at present in industry many individuals possessed of high skill in the actual handling of human situations. This skill usually derives from their own experience, is intuitive, and is not easily communicable.

CHAPTER V

Absenteeism and Labour Turnover

In the years between 1933 and 1943 many inquiries, greatly varied in character, were undertaken by the Harvard research group. Of these, I shall mention three only—a study of a large department store by F. J. Roethlisberger, John B. Fox, and George F. F. Lombard; a study of unemployment in western Pennsylvania by George C. Homans, John Cooley, and Gordon Bowden; a study of a small, rapidly expanding manufacturing concern by F. J. Roethlisberger, John B. Fox, and Gordon Bowden. I have no doubt that these studies in due course will find their way to publication. The first and second may be said to have given strong support to the belief that the study of working groups is vital to the understanding of any management-worker relationship. The second cannot well be developed until the return of George C. Homans.[1] The third possesses a particular interest, in that it served to demonstrate the urgent need of a systematic ordering of operations as a business grows in size. The group of problems involved in the formal organization of a plant were specified in the preceding chapter (Chapter IV) as second in a list of three of the persistent problems of management and administration. Roethlisberger, Fox, and Lombard have much information on the difficulties created in small manufacturing plants by war-time expansion. Many businesses, especially perhaps in New England, had records of success when their total employment rolls numbered less than 500 persons. The control of such businesses was more or less personal or of a family type; and it worked sufficiently satisfactorily until war-time requirements increased the total personnel to a figure in the neighbourhood of 2,000. Then the lack of systematically ordered procedures showed itself in the sudden emergence of a host of problems that seemed to be personal or psychological until close study revealed the source. A relationship analogous to the family may be effective for a population of 200 persons; but the lack of definition of executive function serves almost to create personal uncertainties and errors when the con-

[1] Lt.-Comdr. George C. Homans, U.S.N.R., on active service. Now (1948) Associate Professor of Social Relations, Harvard University.

cern is overtaken by extremely rapid expansion. The systematic ordering of operations, the second problem of administration named in the last chapter, is important not only for effective work but also as providing a basis upon which co-operation may be established. This fact is generally admitted and questions of organizing method have received much, indeed almost exclusive, attention; for purposes of this book, I return to the topic of human relations in industry, which is generally assumed to be effectively dealt with if operations are properly ordered. Such an attitude in practice—and it is the common practice—means that study of the human situation is usually for the most part neglected.

Early in 1943 great public concern suddenly became manifest with respect to the phenomenon of so-called "absenteeism"; it was believed that war production was seriously diminished by casual and wilful absences of workers from their work. Many alleged "causes" were cited—illness, difficulties of transport, family troubles, shopping problems, and the like. It was also said that larger earnings induced workers to take unjustifiable week-end holidays. When the discussion was at its height—newspapers, Congress, public meetings—we were asked by an official agency to make a study of the situation in three companies in a metal-working industry of great importance to the war. These three companies work almost side by side in a relatively small east coast industrial city—a district traditionally expert in the craft for almost two centuries. The population of the locality is of varied or diverse origin, Lithuanian, Italian, Irish, French-Canadian, and, of course, the Anglo-Saxon Yankee; the war had led to an approximate twelve per cent. increase of the total. But the local tradition apparently held against diversity of origin and the new-comer. Throughout the district there seemed to be a general awareness of what might be expected in this or that department of a metal-working plant. Relative to other parts of the United States, the established order seemed to have been less damaged by modern technical changes.

On arrival in the city we found the general alarm about absences to be as great as elsewhere; we were offered a variety of explanations for the occurrence of absences, based on the personal observations of those living and working in the city. These explanations sometimes came from company officials, sometimes from the workers themselves or their supervisors, sometimes from persons casually encountered. The explanations most frequently offered were that workers were earning a great deal of money; that, by reason of this, they tended to take small excursions in the week-ends; and that there was much conviviality, especially during week-ends. Everyone who gave us such an explanation had one or more stories of actual and verifiable occurrences that illustrated his claim exactly. It was impossible, however, on the basis of these illustrations to decide the comparative incidence or importance of these "causes" of absenteeism.

The office statistics of the three companies did not greatly help us. The customary office statement showed absences in terms of man-hours of work lost. If a worker misses his eight-hour shift, eight man-hours of production have been lost—sometimes this was translated into an agreed equivalent of pounds of metal. This last figure was not wholly reliable; we found instances in which equal losses of man-hours in a casting shop had been followed by a considerable loss of poundage in one case and in another, by no loss at all. In the former event, several furnaces were "down"; in the latter, no furnace scheduled for work had been forced to shut down.

The man-hour figures, to be sure, serve the purpose of giving an executive officer immediate and important information as to the working health of his plant. He receives each week a tabular statement of man-hours lost in each department and the percentage of this loss by comparison with the total man-hours of work planned. So a clerical department may show a 1% or 2% loss, as against a loss of 10% to 14% in sheet mill or casting shop. This shows clearly enough where the problem of casual absences may be reflected in diminished output and indicates a symptom that demands attention. At the foot of such a table, the total man-hours lost in a given week are shown and this loss again is expressed as a percentage of total man-hours planned. In a plant of several thousand workers, this actual total, for example something above 4,000 man-hours in a week, may look formidable—but the percentage expression is misleading. None can pretend that the direct effect upon production of clerical man-hours or casting shop man-hours is equivalent; the two terms cannot even be expressed as numerically related. Yet the inevitable tendency was to assume that the total man-hours lost in a given week were capable of translation into pounds of metal. This tendency was not overt, for its expression would have led to immediate recognition of its absurdity. But that some such idea existed remotely in the thinking of executive officers, the workers themselves, and union organizers was evidenced by the general manifestations of alarm in all these participants about the problem of "absenteeism".

The tables were useful to us, however, in that they supported the statements of responsible executives to the effect that the trouble, whatever it might be, was more acute in the casting shops than elsewhere. We were also informed by the same authorities that the casting shop was the "bottleneck" of the whole industry —every other department was dependent for supply of metal alloy upon the furnaces. Such study as we could make was limited by both time and personnel available; concentration upon the casting shop situation became necessary. Acting upon expert advice, we decided also to study, in part for purposes of comparison, the sheet mills (where slabs of metal are rolled into bars, tubes, and sheets), and, if possible, a department that manufactured the prepared metal.

For a detailed account of our method of procedure, I must refer the reader to *Absenteeism: Management's Problem* by John B. Fox and Jerome F. Scott.[1] The official man-hour tables being useless for purposes of analysis, we decided, with the utmost co-operation of the officers of all three companies, to select, as a preliminary and simple index, that of regular attendance. We hoped to discover something more about the incidence of casual absences amongst the various individuals of a department. And at once we ran into difficulty. Is it possible to distinguish statistically and easily between real sickness and alleged sickness? Inquiry soon showed that records of reasons for absence—where they existed at all—were unreliable. Our concern was with significant approximation rather than with complete accuracy; complete accuracy can be had only in mathematics; in factual determination an approximation is the best that can be achieved. We determined accordingly that, in computing absences, any absence of a number of consecutive days should be scored as one absence. There were a variety of reasons for our adoption of this procedure. For example, published material to date apparently establishes the fact that the greatest single reason for absence in the United States, as in England or Australia, is sickness or injury.[2] Since, in

[1] Harvard Business School, Division of Research, Business Research Studies, No. 29, 1943.
[2] The English *Emergency Report No. 2*, "Hours of Work, Lost Time and Labour Wastage", of the Medical Research Council Industrial Health Research Board (London, H. M. Stationery Office, 1942), supports this statement; so also did figures obtained locally.

the particular study we were making, we were not directly concerned with sickness, it seemed wise to take figures that would, at least to some extent, minimize successive days of absence and maximize frequency of absences, especially absences without permission. By this method considerable confusion was avoided. For example, two male workers were absent for 22 days in 1942. The one was out for 22 successive days with appendicitis and was not otherwise absent during the year; the other was absent 11 times for 2 days, mostly in the week-ends. The first was scored as absent once; the second, as absent 11 times. This simple device not only put order into the study; it also showed group attendance patterns which are usually obscured in any simple statistic by the inclusion of medical cases. And it was the group attendance pattern, irrespective of illness and accident, that we wished to study.

We began by taking out figures for those workers who had been continuously employed throughout 1942: in the casting shops, sheet mills, and one manufacturing department, the majority of these workers—whom we termed "veterans" in the charts—were still in the employment of the same company. The facts thus elicited from company records were surprising not only to us but also to the officers responsible for the records. Chart 1, for instance,

CHART 1. DISTRIBUTION OF 103 VETERANS[1] BY NUMBER OF
ABSENCES[2] IN 1942: COMPANY D[3]—
MANUFACTURING DEPARTMENT

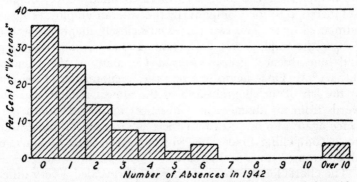

[1] Men hired before January 1, 1942, and on payroll throughout period considered.
[2] Any series of consecutive days absent by one man is counted as one absence.
[3] Subsidiary of Company A.
SOURCE: John B. Fox and Jerome F. Scott, *Absenteeism: Management's Problem* (Harvard Business School, Division of Research, Business Research Studies, No. 29, 1943), Chart 1, p. 4.

shows for a manufacturing subsidiary of Company A (referred to as Company D) the percentage distribution of the so-called veteran group according to frequency of absence. The chart shows that 37 of a total of 103 workers had not been absent at all during the whole year; 26 had been absent once; 15 had been absent twice; 8, 3 times; and so on. The chart gives these absences in the form of percentages of the total group; it shows an almost regular step-down pattern from no absences at all to 5 absences in the 12-month period. Beyond this there are two groups (8 persons in all) whose absences for the year were 6 or more than 10. It is significant that the largest group consists of those persons who were not absent at all; the next largest, those who were absent once; and the next, those who were absent twice. Of the whole group, only 7.8% were absent more than 5 times in the year. We therefore felt entitled to regard these figures as showing that the employees rarely absent prefer to be at work, that their attendance is prevented only by something compelling in external or family circumstance. Further inquiry, of an undirected interview type, confirmed this conclusion during the final stages of the study. Such moralizations as we had heard locally—the stories we had been told—might well apply to the small group, 3.9% of the total, or 4 persons, who were absent over 10 times from work, but could not be reasonably applied in criticism of the whole department.

The next charts (Charts 2 and 3) are similar to the first and give the figures for 1942 in the sheet mills in Companies A and B. In Company A the total veteran (as defined above) employees numbered 166; for Company B, the veteran employees for 1942 numbered 433. The two curves are closely identical; well over 50% of the employees in both companies are in the "no-absence" and "one-absence" groups *combined* (Company A, 56%; Company B, 54.4%). Once again one sees the phenomenon of the cluster at the left of the diagram and of the almost regular step downwards from no absences to 5 absences in the 12-month period. Once again also one sees that there is a special problem, though not of compelling dimensions, with respect to those who have been absent over 10 times in the year.

The charts for the three casting shops revealed a very different situation; it seemed to show that determinants of attendance existed for casters that did not greatly affect the sheet mills and manufacturing. The general opinion held locally was that conditions of work in the casting shops—furnace heat, fumes, and

CHART 2.   DISTRIBUTION OF 166 VETERANS[1] BY NUMBER OF
ABSENCES[2] IN 1942: COMPANY A—SHEET MILL

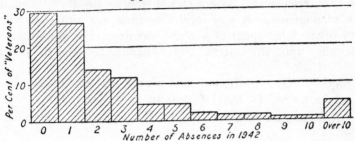

CHART 3.   DISTRIBUTION OF 433 VETERANS[1] BY NUMBER OF
ABSENCES[2] IN 1942: COMPANY B—SHEET MILL

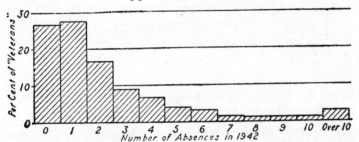

[1] Men hired before January 1, 1942, and on payroll throughout period considered.
[2] Any series of consecutive days absent by one man is counted as one absence.

SOURCE: John B. Fox and Jerome F. Scott, *Absenteeism: Management's Problem,*
Charts 2 and 3, p. 5.

CHART 4.   DISTRIBUTION OF 151 VETERANS[1] BY NUMBER OF
ABSENCES[2] IN 1942: COMPANY A—CASTING SHOP

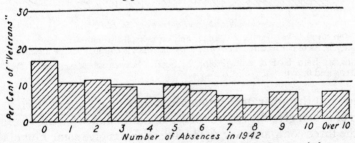

[1] Men hired before January 1, 1942, and on payroll throughout period.
[2] Any series of consecutive days absent by one man is counted as one absence.

SOURCE: John B. Fox and Jerome F. Scott, *Absenteeism: Management's Problem,*
Chart 4, p. 6.

other discomforts—were chiefly responsible for the difference. We
knew also that pressure for production was, if anything, greater
here than elsewhere. This was not due to any direct demand
from management; it was inevitable in a war situation where
every other department of a plant was dependent for supply of
metal alloy upon the casters. The difference between the casting

CHART 5. DISTRIBUTION OF 201 VETERANS[1] BY NUMBER OF
ABSENCES[2] IN 1942: COMPANY B—CASTING SHOP

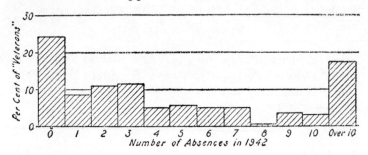

CHART 6. DISTRIBUTION OF 148 VETERANS[1] BY NUMBER OF
ABSENCES[2] IN 1942: COMPANY C—CASTING SHOP

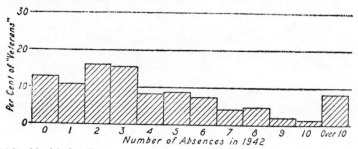

[1] Men hired before January 1, 1942, and on payroll throughout period.
[2] Any series of consecutive days absent by one man is counted as one absence.
SOURCE: John B. Fox and Jerome F. Scott, *Absenteeism: Management's Problem*,
Charts 5 and 6, p. 6.

shops and the other departments is clearly manifest in Charts 4, 5,
and 6, which give the records of regular attendance for the veterans
of the three companies for 1942. These charts give some hint of the
existence of a regular attendance group; the percentage of employees with fewer than 6 absences for the 12 months was 63.5%
for Company A, 65.6% for Company B, and 72.2% for

Company C. But local opinion had led us to expect that the actual physical discomfort of a casting shop would be the chief determining factor. The conditions of work in the Company C shop were much better than those in Companies A and B. Company C had installed a new casting plant and had begun its operation in the closing months of 1941. The furnaces and the moulds could be handled with comparative ease and certainly with less discomfort than in the plants of A and B. Yet the percentage of regular attendance did not show a sufficient difference to be accounted wholly satisfactory.

Simultaneously with this work we had prepared lists of the

CHART 7. ABSENCES[1] OF VETERANS[2] BY QUARTERS, JANUARY, 1942, THROUGH MARCH, 1943: COMPANIES A, B, AND C— CASTING SHOPS

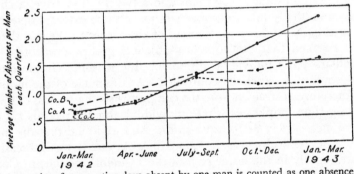

[1] Any series of consecutive days absent by one man is counted as one absence.
[2] Men hired before January 1, 1942, and on payroll throughout period considered.
SOURCE: John B. Fox and Jerome F. Scott, *Absenteeism: Management's Problem*, Chart 12, p. 10.

veteran workers in the three shops which gave the monthly absence record for each of these men. These figures are plotted here by quarters for convenient illustration of the trend. This chart (Chart 7) proved to be of considerable interest. The slight superiority over the other two companies that Company C possessed in 1942 was concentrated in the last few months of the year; furthermore, this superiority took the form of the beginning of a trend of considerable significance. In Company A the increase in absences among the veterans was rapid and persistent. In Company B the increase was steady and considerable. But in Company C, absenteeism rose until the July-September quarter of 1942, and thereafter commenced to fall.   The disparity between the three companies had become notable in the first quarter of 1943, January-March.   Even if we assumed, as we had been urged to do, that the general local situation in this most critical—industrially speaking—year of the war (labour shortage, higher earnings, and the like) was responsible—even if we had assumed this, we were still held by the need to explain why the general labour situation should vigorously affect Companies A and B and yet should seem to be under control in Company C.   The popular explanation was not acceptable, and we turned to closer study of the lists of monthly absences of individual workers.

Guided by our first charts, we had grouped those workers with records of none to 5 absences as regular attendants.   Close inquiry in various instances had given evidence that a man with, for example, 3 absences in a year could account for all 3 by some accident of circumstance—icy roads and a twenty-mile drive, a child or wife suddenly taken ill, or any other of those external determinants usually set down as "causes" of absenteeism.   We had therefore assumed that the none-to-5-absences group constituted the "regulars", the individual difference due to some circumstance that could not be wholly controlled.   At this stage of the inquiry we therefore abstracted from the company lists the records of those casting shop employees whose individual absence records *did not exceed 5 absences in the 15-month period.*   And we found that the incidence of these absences in Companies A and B was increasing more rapidly in the latter part of the 15-month period; in Company C, on the other hand, regular attendants showed improvement after the third quarter of 1942.   In Company A, within the limited group studied were 55 men whose individual absence records did not exceed 5 during 15 months: but, taken quarter by quarter, their absence record rose from 13 in the first quarter of 1942 to 70 in the first quarter of 1943.   In Company B the absence record of 73 men in this classification rose from 27 in the first quarter of 1942 to 68 in the first quarter of 1943.   But in Company C the absence of 70 such men rose from 20 in the first quarter of 1942 to 58 in the third quarter and thereafter fell to 31 in the first quarter of 1943.   These figures again seemed to show that certain elements which were adversely affecting Companies A and B were to some extent under control in Company C.   Chart 8 gives the situation at a glance.

We seemed thus to have learned that the behaviour of the

regular attendants in Companies A and B was affected by the general deterioration; in Company C the improvement in this respect among the regulars seemed to be almost as remarkable. There was need that we should study more closely conditions in Company C in comparison with similar conditions in Companies A and B.

We had not neglected the study of all the workers in the three casting shops. Our special interest in the behaviour of the regular attendants—those who preferred to be at work rather than else-where—was due to our close participation in the Western Electric

CHART 8. ABSENCES[1] OF VETERAN GOOD ATTENDERS[2] BY QUARTERS, JANUARY, 1942, THROUGH MARCH, 1943: COMPANIES A, B, AND C—CASTING SHOPS

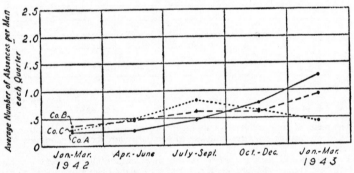

[1] Any series of consecutive days absent by one man is counted as one absence.
[2] Men hired before January 1, 1942, and on payroll throughout period considered who were absent from one to five times in 15 months.

SOURCE: John B. Fox and Jerome F. Scott, *Absenteeism: Management's Problem*, Chart 13, p. 12.

experiments.[1] The final discoveries at Hawthorne of the extent to which the "informal" group influenced individual behaviour[2] had made us alert to the need for knowledge of the attitude and con-duct of the better workers. But we had also prepared for our guidance a chart showing the percentage of absences of all workers (monthly absences expressed as percentage of workers on the pay-roll at that time) from month to month in the casting shops of the three companies. Chart 9 here presented shows these percentages from January, 1942, to June, 1943, inclusive. Here again, taking

[1] Reported, in part, in the last chapter.
[2] F. J. Roethlisberger and William J. Dickson, *Managment and the Worker*, Part IV.

account of all workers, we find an almost startling difference between Company C and the other two.   In the first place, Companies A and B had a higher level of absenteeism at the beginning of 1942.   Second, the general rate of increase was greater.

CHART 9.   ABSENCES[1] OF ALL WORKERS BY MONTHS, JANUARY, 1942, TO JUNE, 1943: COMPANIES A, B[2], AND C— CASTING SHOPS

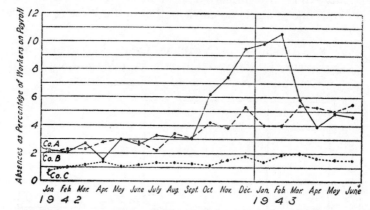

[1] Any series of consecutive days absent by one man is counted as one absence.

[2] Based on available figures adjusted to compare with those of Company A and Company C.

[3] The number of men employed in the three casting shops varied roughly as follows: In Company A there was a rise from 220 at the beginning of 1942 to 250 in June, 1942, at which general level the payroll remained until June, 1943; in Company B there was a rise from 240 in January, 1942, to 270 in March, 1943, and then a drop to 250 in June, 1943; in Company C there was a rise from 200 in January, 1942, to 240 at the end of 1942, and between February and June, 1943, there was a drop to 220.   Allowance is automatically made for these variations on the chart by dividing number of men on payroll into absences.

[4] Estimate based on experience of first two or three weeks in June.

SOURCE: John B. Fox and Jerome F. Scott, *Absenteeism: Management's Problem,* Chart 16, p. 20.

And third, the month-to-month fluctuations were wider.   Business Research Study No. 29, the report on absenteeism, shows that attendance at work in Companies A and B was much more vulnerable to "external causes" than in Company C.[1]   This is especially evident in the charted record of Company A for the four months October, 1942, to the end of January, 1943; in these four months absenteeism quadrupled.

"If we recall that we are looking at the absence record for the

[1] John B. Fox and Jerome F. Scott, *Absenteeism: Management's Problem,* pp. 20–24.

same department in each of these companies; that all are making the same product; that the three are of long standing in the community; that they share the same labour market and environment of housing, transport, and shopping difficulties—if we take account of these factors, then we must attach some significance, for absenteeism, to our findings with regard to differences in administration as between Companies A and C." [1]

Whether we looked at the records of the whole casting shop or of the more regular attendants in it—in either event it was borne in upon us that some difference of method and of internal organization must be, at least in part, responsible for the remarkable difference. Was it possible, simply and directly, to detect this difference?

The answer to this question, which had become clear and specific, was not far to seek. Three findings, which came almost at once, are of special interest:

First: For twenty years foremen had been carefully instructed in Company C that the supervisors' duty had two parts—the one, technical competence; the other, capacity to handle human situations. In other words, the director of training instructed supervisory candidates not only in the technical details of their jobs, but also in the methodical handling of human relationships on the job. Instruction in the latter of these was simple and probably the better for being so. Foremen were taught the very great importance of three elementary rules or methods of approach to human problems. These were:

1. Be patient.
2. Listen.
3. Avoid emotional upsets.

Upon this foundation the communication system of Company C had been built. But, if foremen must be patient and listen, their work must give them time to do so. This led to the second finding.

Second: Management had arranged that foremen should have the aid of certain qualified technical assistants. These assistants took over many of the routine technical responsibilities of the foreman, thus giving him the time he required for the human responsibilities involved in team leadership. This insistence upon adequacy of communication from below upwards to supplement the usual communication from above down had brought certain benefits in its train. Put otherwise, the improvement of com-

[1] Ibid., p. 20.

munication brought to light many problems that had never been specified in the other plants. For instance, each of the four lines of furnaces was manned by a "team" of workers, three shifts. The whole group was paid for its 24-hour achievement—so one shift could make up for difficulties faced and mastered by another. This meant not merely "team-spirit" as an abstraction; it meant in fact that no shift tended to slack off as the end of its period of work approached. A furnace refilled for the men coming on benefited not only the newcomers but also those leaving the job. Officers of the company claimed "teamwork and no buck-passing"

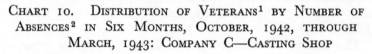

CHART 10. DISTRIBUTION OF VETERANS[1] BY NUMBER OF ABSENCES[2] IN SIX MONTHS, OCTOBER, 1942, THROUGH MARCH, 1943: COMPANY C—CASTING SHOP

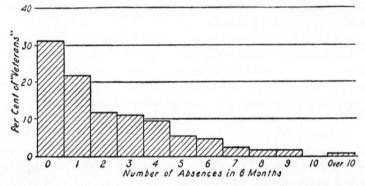

[1] Men hired before January 1, 1942, and on payroll throughout period considered.
[2] Any series of consecutive days absent by one man is counted as one absence.
SOURCE: John B. Fox and Jerome F. Scott, *Absenteeism: Management's Problem,* Chart 19, p. 25.

as the basis of their collaboration, and this was clearly reflected, though no doubt in less explicit fashion, "down the line".

Third: The third part of Company C's method was to have the foreman and the individuals of a shift arrange every week which day "off" (one day in seven) each individual should have. If one worker absented himself unlawfully, the arrangement for the others was upset; the consequence of this system was a pressure exercised by the group on the individual, a pressure that "management would never dare to exercise". The management of Company C thus took definite steps to assure itself that the individual was content with his work and that there should also be mutual responsibility and teamwork.

These three differences of internal organization in Company C led us indirectly to another finding. I have said (page 85) that in the charts of attendance in the three casting shops for 1942 the record of Company C had been something of a disappointment. Local opinion had led us to expect a greater difference because of the better technical facilities and working conditions. We now

CHART 11. DISTRIBUTION OF VETERANS[1] BY NUMBER OF ABSENCES[2] IN SIX MONTHS, OCTOBER, 1942, THROUGH MARCH, 1943: COMPANY B—CASTING SHOP

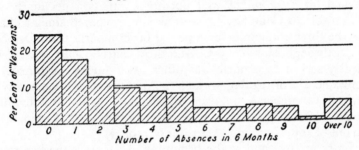

CHART 12. DISTRIBUTION OF VETERANS[1] BY NUMBER OF ABSENCES[2] IN SIX MONTHS, OCTOBER, 1942, THROUGH MARCH, 1943: COMPANY A—CASTING SHOP

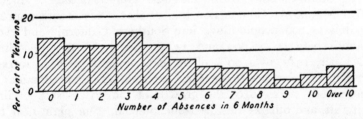

[1] Men hired before January 1, 1942, and on payroll throughout period considered.
[2] Any series of consecutive days absent by one man is counted as one absence.

SOURCE: John B. Fox and Jerome F. Scott, *Absenteeism: Management's Problem*, Charts 20 and 21, p. 25.

realized that, while improved working conditions are perhaps a necessary basis for better teamwork, they do not of themselves lead inevitably to it. The new furnaces in Company C had been put into operation on or about December 1, 1941; and on December 7 had come Pearl Harbour. This country, which had been aiding England in her solitary resistance to Nazi aggression, suddenly found itself at war with both Germany and Japan. And the pressure upon companies such as those described increased enormously. During the first six months of 1942, therefore, Company C was contending with a situation that demanded not only vastly increased production of metal in the casting shop, but also the breaking in of new workers to her adequate but somewhat complex system. For Company C had begun the enrolment of new workers in October, 1941. By the third quarter of 1942, the teams had begun to operate spontaneously; this one may conclude from inspection of Charts 7 and 8. We now realized that the figures quoted for 1942 might well portray a situation peculiarly unfavourable to Company C; we therefore prepared similar charts for the three companies for a period of six months from October, 1942, through March, 1943. And these charts (Charts 10, 11, 12) clearly served to confirm our other observations. Company C shows 89.9% of regular workers (no absences to 5); Company B, 79.3%; Company A, 73.3%. In Company C, only 8 individuals out of 138 had more than 6 absences in 6 months; Company B, 29 out of 169; Company A, 31 out of 150.

Later in 1943 and at the beginning of 1944, we made a somewhat similar study of an important war-time industry in Southern California.[1] Here the situation revealed was very different. To begin with, there is a restless movement of population into the state, out of the state, within the state. Officers of the Los Angeles War Manpower Commission told us that every month approximately 25,000 people move into Southern California and every month between 12,000 and 14,000 people move out. Since October, 1942, over 90% of the newcomers have been workers looking for jobs. Before the war, California was not predominantly industrial; since 1940, the growth of industries—shipbuilding, aircraft, and others—has been phenomenal. One plant near Los Angeles, for instance, increased its total personnel from about 3,000 workers to approximately 50,000 within two years; and this was characteristic of all war industries between December, 1941, and the latter part of 1943. This "explosion", as one executive called it, was concurrent with the loss of many of the best technicians and the best teamworkers to Selective Service; for both these groups are eminently desirable persons from an Army or

[1] Elton Mayo and George F. F. Lombard, *Teamwork and Labor Turnover in the Aircraft Industry of Southern California* (Harvard Business School, Division of Research, Business Research Studies, No. 32, 1944).

Navy point of view. And, it must be remembered, in a young industry the workers, from high executive office to bench, tend to be young; in California, unlike the East, the central "core" of a working team was not made up of older and experienced workmen.

Charts of attendance regularity, taken by departments or shifts, were consequently of small use to us. They certainly showed the probable existence of working teams—the columns at the left of the charts—but, almost always and in every plant studied, they showed an exaggerated group of "irregulars"—the columns at the right. Whereas in the East it was rarely that we found more than 10% of a group irregular (when we did, it marked a situation that called for immediate inquiry), in California a 40% or 50% irregularity was commonly met. And it was this group of irregulars that accounted for the very large labour turnover.

It was consequently necessary that we should ignore the larger groups—departments or shifts—and "go down the line" until we were studying smaller groups of persons actually in daily intimate working association with each other. We were able to get reliable information, and attendance figures, for 71 such groups. And at once we found that such charts no longer showed so large a proportion of "mixed" situations; we had figures for good groups, bad groups, and a few indifferent. I show a specimen of each type of group (Charts 13, 14, and 15).

Our experience of industries in the East and Mid-west justified us in assuming that an attendance rate of less than 5 absences in 12 months implied regularity. On this assumption, we found that of the 71 working groups, 9 scored 100% regularity; and 10 others scored 74%, or better. The bad groups, on the other hand, were very bad—no regularity at all being quite frequently characteristic. Amongst the regular attendance groups, we found three types.

First, the very small group, varying from 2 or 3 to 6 or 7 workers; there were 12 such groups with an almost perfect score. Small size apparently lends itself to the development of intimacy and a group expectation of individual regularity.

Second, a larger group with a central core, as it were, of regulars. The group cited above for good attendance consists of 30 workers; of these, 8 are veterans with an attendance record of 83%, 22 are relative newcomers with a score of 78%.

The *third* type calls for special mention; it comes into being only

NOTE: The horizontal scale on Charts 13, 14, 15, and 16 was designed to represent monthly absence rates by classes A to K as follows:

Classes	Absences per month
A	0–0.09
B	0.1–0.19
C	0.2–0.29
D	0.3–0.39
E	0.4–0.49
F	0.5–0.59
G	0.6–0.69
H	0.7–0.79
I	0.8–0.89
J	0.9–0.99
K	1.0 and over

Thus an employee in Class K would have the equivalent of 12 absences or more per year. An employee of, say, 3 months' service with 2 absences would be in Class G (0.67 absences per month), and so on. As in *Absenteeism: Management's Problem*, we counted absences, not days absent, in order to minimize absences caused by illness and to emphasize the irregular attendant who repeatedly absents himself for brief periods.

CHART 13.   MONTHLY ABSENCE RATES IN DEPARTMENT I,
228 WORKERS,[1] ALL SHIFTS, JANUARY–NOVEMBER, 1943

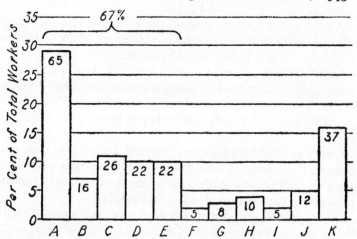

[1] Numbers in columns are number of workers in each class.

SOURCE: Elton Mayo and George F. F. Lombard, *Teamwork and Labor Turnover in the Aircraft Industry of Southern California* (Harvard Business School, Division of Research, Business Research Studies, No. 32, 1944), Chart 5, p. 13.

when someone in authority, or conceived by the workers as representing authority, definitely works to create it.

The chart I show (Chart 16) presents the situation in a small
department in a plant in Southern California. This small group
of persons has a reputation for "working like beavers". Their foreman said that their efficiency (output per man-hour) runs 25%
above that of the average for the plant. A brief glance at the chart
will show that it compares well with anything we can show for
plants in the more established east coast industries. Ninety per

CHART 14. MONTHLY ABSENCE RATES IN DEPARTMENT III,
234 WORKERS,[1] ALL SHIFTS, JANUARY-NOVEMBER, 1943

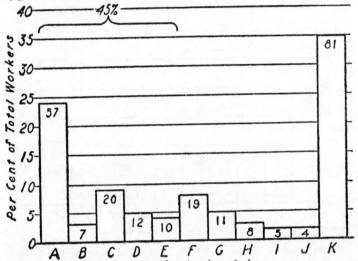

[1] Numbers in columns are number of workers in each class.

SOURCE: Elton Mayo and George F. F. Lombard, *Teamwork and Labor Turnover
in the Aircraft Industry of Southern California* (Harvard Business School, Division of
Research, Business Research Studies, No. 32, 1944), Chart 7, p. 13.

cent. of the workers employed are regular, and by far the greater
number of these have had no absences at all. Indeed, on several
occasions, workers have put in an appearance when suffering from
a high temperature and have had to be sent home by the company
doctor.

This situation has not occurred by chance. The persons
directly responsible are the senior assistant foreman and a "leading
hand". The foreman himself highly approves the work of these
two but is himself much occupied with technical and organiza_

tional details. The assistant foreman and the leading hand both believe, and clearly state, that the achievement of group solidarity is of first importance in a plant, and is actually necessary for sustained production. Their interest, however, is by no means limited to sustained production. On the contrary, both expressed frequently to us pride in the human aspect of their administration. They were alike confident that absenteeism and labour turnover would not become problems in their group.

This fortunate situation has come into being largely as a result of the activities of the leading hand, supported always by the

CHART 15. MONTHLY ABSENCE RATES IN DEPARTMENT II, 374 WORKERS,[1] ALL SHIFTS, JANUARY-NOVEMBER, 1943

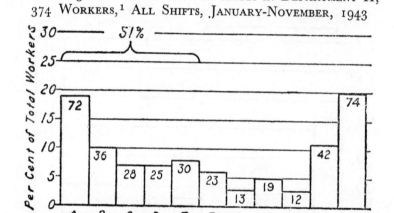

[1] Numbers in columns are number of workers in each class.
SOURCE: Elton Mayo and George F. F. Lombard, *Teamwork and Labor Turnover in the Aircraft Industry of Southern California* (Harvard Business School, Division of Research, Business Research Studies, No. 32, 1944), Chart 6, p. 13.

assistant foreman. The leading hand says that he does "odd jobs", and it is evident that he gives most of his time to facilitating the work of others. His chief activities are, first, helping individual workers; second, the adjustment of technical difficulties; and, third, acting as a medium of relationship for the group with the outside world. For this group the "outside world" means inspectors, time-study men, and even the departmental foreman.

The latter two activities I need not discuss in this place, but the kind of aid the leadman gives the individual worker is of great importance. He begins by listening to a new employee, introduces him to his new companions, and tries to get him congenial work associates. After the newcomer has worked for several days, the leadman gets him a pass and takes him down to the assembly line to see what he has made installed in the complete machine. In addition to this, he listens to any personal problems that may be preoccupying a worker, new or old. He says that line supervision, and probably top management, is not in these days sufficiently

CHART 16. MONTHLY ABSENCE RATES IN DEPARTMENT IV, 55 WORKERS,[1] JANUARY-NOVEMBER, 1943

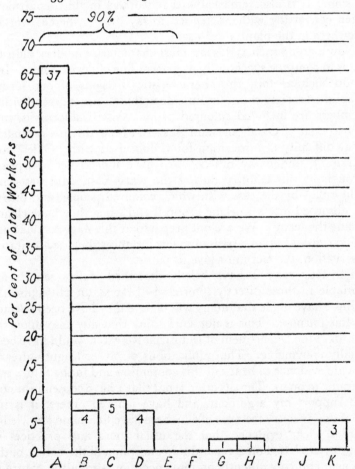

[1] Numbers in columns are number of workers in each class.

SOURCE: Elton Mayo and George F. F. Lombard, *Teamwork and Labor Turnover in the Aircraft Industry of Southern California*, Chart 18, p. 18.

aware of the new demands that changing industrial conditions are making of management in respect of the human problems of administration. In these days, he says, people have "many more things on their minds" than they used to have, and that "strong-arm methods don't work". He gave many examples taken from his own group to illustrate this. And it is remarkable that many members of his group were dissatisfied elsewhere in the plant and would have become "labour turnover" if some company official had not induced them to try working in the department under discussion. It is also remarkable that workers in this department, when conversing with us, tended to say "we", whereas workers elsewhere in the plant always said "I".

Now a group such as this last must characterize modern industry if it is to continue successfully its present line of development. In a group such as this, the characteristic divisions of our former established society count for little or nothing. Amongst individual members are included coloured people, some Californians, men and women of Oklahoma and Arkansas (and there is ordinarily great difficulty of association for Californians with "Okies" and "Arkies"), and many others. We have indeed been surprised throughout this country during the war—East, Mid-west, and California—by the ease with which coloured people, and others, are absorbed into a working group if and when they have clearly "made the team". We are not prepared at this stage to make any generalizations upon a basis of so few instances: but, as a tentative observation, the fact must give us pause.

The four cases I have briefly described—fuller reports are available to those directly interested—bear so directly upon the claims I have made that many will believe they have been selected for this purpose. This is not so; I think that any case upon the records of the Department of Industrial Research would have been equally convincing. The publications of my colleagues already provide evidence to bear out this contention and in the future will continue to do so. The situation is not that I have chosen instances that support my argument, and have ignored others; it is my belief that in every instance of which we have first-hand knowledge there is clear evidence that the usual ideas and practices in industry are based on a general misconception of the nature of the problem and consequently on misconception also of the nature of effective remedy. My selection has been made for two reasons: first, and less important, because in the cases reported I have myself been intimately and continuously concerned; second, because I feel that the instances selected contributed something of significance to our conception of the industrial situation, something that illuminated, or even changed the direction of, our thinking.

What was the nature of this illumination? I think this question can be partially and tentatively answered.

First, in industry and in other human situations the administrator is dealing with well-knit human groups and *not with a horde of individuals*. Wherever it is characteristic, as in the California of 1943, that by reason of external circumstance these groups have little opportunity to form, the immediate symptom is labour turnover, absenteeism, and the like. Man's desire to be continuously associated in work with his fellows is a strong, if not the strongest, human characteristic. Any disregard of it by management or any ill-advised attempt to defeat this human impulse leads instantly to some form of defeat for management itself. In Philadelphia[1] the efficiency experts had assumed the primacy of the financial incentive; in this they were wrong; not until the conditions of working group formation were satisfied did the three financial incentives come into operation at all.

Second, the belief that the behaviour of an individual within the factory can be predicted before employment upon the basis of a laborious and minute examination by tests of his technical and other capacities is mainly, if not wholly, mistaken. Examination of his developed social skills and his general adaptability might give better results. The usual situation is that after employment his relation to "the team" will go far to determine the use he makes of such capacities as he has developed. Operator No. 2 in the Hawthorne test room was the most accomplished worker; No. 4 was remarkable for the number of unnecessary movements she made in the assembly of telephone relays. Yet the latter at many points in the years of experiment almost rivalled the former. She probably accomplished her output at high cost to herself,[2] but the incentive was the experimentally arranged proximity of the best worker, and her desire to stand well with the team.

Third, directly one in an administrative position discards the absurdities of the rabble hypothesis and endeavours to deal directly with the situation that reveals itself on careful study, the results

---

[1] Chap. III, supra.
[2] T. North Whitehead, *The Industrial Worker*, Vol. I.

accomplished are astonishing. In Philadelphia a labour turnover of approximately 250% shrinks to an approximate 5%, production increases, wastage diminishes, absenteeism ceases to be an acute problem. And in California, twenty years later, a leadman can hold his workers and maintain production in the midst of a scene of indescribable human chaos—thousands of workers every week entering and leaving factory employment despite the most stringent Federal regulations.

Finally, these observations do not diminish the gravity of the problems created by the change from an *established* to an *adaptive* society. But the fact that the eager human desire for co-operative society still persists in the ordinary person and can be utilized by intelligent and straightforward management means that these problems can be faced directly and hopefully. Even though progress may be slow, the way is open for us to learn how to handle with success the social problems posed by an *adaptive* industrial civilization.

CHAPTER VI

"Patriotism Is Not Enough; We Must Have No Hatred or Bitterness Towards Anyone"[1]

An eminent physician, writing from Australia, expresses satisfaction that the universities at last show signs of interest in the close study of actual human relationships in the modern world. The letter continues: "Science has developed our knowledge of almost everything except how to live together in peace and amity." The amazing technical development in recent years—air travel, radar, penicillin—puts to shame our utter social incompetence. Men talk to each other by telephone across several thousand miles of sea without wires or any tangible connection. A journey—San Francisco to Sydney in Australia—that twenty years ago took three weeks is now completed in as many days. Certain forms of pneumonia and other diseases have ceased to hold the terrors of a few years back for the patient's immediate relatives. But a world war of some twenty years ago was succeeded by another, still more destructive, more barbaric, more far-flung. And this occurred in spite of the fact that the goodwill and wisdom of the civilized world were supposed to be mobilized at Geneva for the prevention of conflict. The short historic interval between world wars makes one wonder whether the League of Nations did not in some inept fashion actually provoke the conflict despite its admirable intention. Stanley Casson, writing in 1937 and using his historic studies as guide, declared in that year that civilization was "not on the brink of collapse", but had already collapsed.[2] As with Rome, the form persisted for a brief period after the collapse had occurred. Our world as it exists to-day, he says, cannot be called civilized. What we are watching is "a steadily increasing disintegration of all the co-operative efforts of mankind, and an uprush of true barbarism".[3]

Dr. A. V. Hill, the British physiologist, in a speech recently broadcast calls attention to "the terrifying dangers which science, cultivated in secret in the service of political nationalism, is bound

---

[1] Edith Cavell.
[2] *Progress and Catastrophe*, p. 185.
[3] Ibid., p. 205.

to bring. . . . For, if political isolationism and aggressive nationalism are to exploit science and its applications, not for the benefit of mankind but in order to prepare in secret for mutual destruction, they are very likely to succeed; and mankind. . . . may become extinct. . . . The possibilities of injury by physical, chemical and biological methods are frightful beyond any hitherto imagined". Nor can "the decent sense of ordinary men" be trusted to prevent such happenings. For we have seen "an almost complete collapse of previous ethical standards" and "scores of millions of highly educated and intelligent people . . . led into hate and hysteria by the methods of the scientific advertiser and propagandist". The remedy Dr. Hill proposes is "an international brotherhood of scientific men with a common ethical standard".[1]

To those of us who were supposed to have completed our formal education in the closing years of the nineteenth century, this state-ment is reminiscent of what we were then taught. We were told that Europe had become civilized, that the increasing number of highly trained and intelligent persons engaged in scholarly or scientific pursuits which knew no national boundaries entirely pre-cluded the possibility of the recurrence of massive wars. Many of us, relying on the proclaimed intelligence of our academic "leaders of thought", read and believed Sir Norman Angell's *Great Illusion*. And we were utterly surprised by August 4, 1914, and its sequel. Even after 1918, when the first barbaric intrusion upon civilized order had been suppressed, we took comfort in the creation by the League of Nations of an international Committee on Intellectual Co-operation. When a number of persons, each eminent in a highly specialized field, were called to Geneva and, obviously uncomfortable, did not know what to talk about, we merely laughed and still believed that somehow these eminents would find the way. We had not sufficiently realized the truth and relevance of A. N. Whitehead's assertion that there is no substitute for first-hand knowledge.[2] Every specialist knows this in his own field, of course; a mere conference of physicists and chemists does not automatically result in a fully developed physicochemistry, although it is likely to define the points at which laboratory in-vestigation is needed. And when the field is widened to include physiologists, psychologists, classical scholars, and a few statesmen

---

[1] "Scientific Co-operation within the Empire," address delivered at meeting of the Royal Empire Society, *London Calling* (British Broadcasting Corporation), No. 285, March, 1945, p. 16.
[2] Alfred North Whitehead, *Aims of Education & Other Essays*, p. 79.

or political students, the consequence is more likely to be a babel of confusion than the definition of a field for inquiry. Nevertheless the theory that the meeting in conference of a sufficient number of eminent specialists drawn from widely different fields will in some fashion produce the first-hand knowledge required is still widely held, even in universities. Yet such eminent persons, when summoned to Geneva, were merely worried and perplexed by impassioned argument and declamation; they had no notion of any method by which non-logical and noisy troubles could be resolved.

There is no way of dealing effectively with these international or intranational situations other than the way that all the sciences have trod. The first step is the patient, pedestrian development of "first-hand knowledge"[1] or "knowledge of acquaintance".[2] The second step is that of the administrator, the clinician, the artisan —intimate acquaintance with the facts gives rise to skill in handling them. The demonstration of an unquestionably effective skill is immensely important, for it provides the justification, and at first the only justification, for the third step. The third step is the clear statement, for laboratory test and development, of the logical implications of the effective skill. All skill—administrator, clinician, artisan—is based upon the capacity of the operator to select from the mass of facts offered for his inspection two or three that are especially significant for action in the situation. In this manner an effective skill assures the logical relevance and value of the selection or abstraction upon which it is based. The present apparent aimlessness of the social sciences is due to the fact that few of the abstractions they use have been thus developed. No sociologist or psychologist that I know studies an outbreak of "wildcat" strikes in the Detroit area with the intention of looking beyond the symptom to methods of better understanding and control. Yet both management and union leaders are much in need of skilled diagnosis and advice.

The concept of these three steps as chronologically sequent one upon the other is broadly but not wholly true. Something of a conceptual pattern or framework is present in the thinking of the trained observer as he begins his patient, pedestrian toil toward the necessary knowledge-of-acquaintance. This original tentative pattern is always in part mistaken and insufficient; it may be

---

[1] Ibid.
[2] William James, *The Principles of Psychology*, Vol. I, p. 221.

wholly so. The difference between a good observer and one who is not good is that the former is quick to take a hint from the facts, from his early efforts to develop skill in handling them, and quick to acknowledge the need to revise or alter the conceptual framework of his thinking. The other—the poor observer—continues dogmatically onward with his original thesis, lost in a maze of correlations, long after the facts have shrieked in protest against the interpretation put upon them.

The cases I have presented for consideration in connection with the human and social problems of modern industry are, I believe, sufficiently representative of the many other situations we have studied of men and women at work. This claim will be corrected and expanded by my colleagues and successors. We cannot yet be considered to have advanced very far upon the way we have chosen to travel. But sometimes an observation essentially simple carries an importance for practical affairs that extends far beyond anything that can be claimed for it of intellectual illumination. And this, I think, may be said of the finding that modern civilization for approximately two centuries has done nothing to extend and develop human co-operative capacities and, indeed, in the sacred name of the sciences of material development, has unwittingly done much to discourage teamwork and the development of social skill. The almost frenzied cultivation of technical skill at the cost of human discouragement has not been able wholly to defeat the desire of individuals for association in work with others. Such evidence [1] as we have supports the claim of J. N. Figgis that this desire is deep-seated in humanity and sure to find some form of expression. But in developing an adaptive society that shall be able to offer a high standard of material comfort to its least citizen, we have utterly failed to take steps that shall ensure the eager and spontaneous participation of everyone in the effort. Indeed our high technical civilization remains abysmally ignorant of methods by which this necessary co-operative attitude may be provoked. Instead industry has all too frequently converted a readiness to participate into an attitude of wariness, suspicion, hostility, and hatred. So civilization faces the latter part of the twentieth century divided into groups with few bonds of general unity, mutually suspicious, ready at any moment to develop mutual hatreds at the touch of an irresponsible orator or politician.

[1] Elton Mayo and George F. F. Lombard, *Teamwork and Labor Turnover in the Aircraft Industry of Southern California*, p. 28.

It is in this situation that the Hitlers of this world—the destroyers—find their opportunity.

Christopher Dawson, in a passage I have quoted earlier, says that the growing complication of modern mechanized civilization demands a correspondingly higher degree of organization, an organization that cannot be limited to the material elements in the complex. And it must be confessed that, for the most part, this capacity to contrive a higher degree of organization is still to seek. It is far easier for an industrialist to assume the overwhelming importance of material and technical factors and to neglect, or shrug off, the need for active and spontaneous participation in the effort by the workers. Yet it is true that the larger the industrial organization the more dependent is it, not only upon technical advance, but also upon the spontaneous human co-operation of every least member of the group.

F. J. Roethlisberger is of the opinion that our industrial civilization of the present is improvidently living on its capital, upon the store of human goodwill and self-abnegation that many centuries of established routines of living have left us. In a recent paper in the *Harvard Business Review*, he points out that in the industrial situations we have studied we have constantly found, often in the lower levels of administration, "men of extraordinary skill in the direction of securing co-operative effort".[1] The importance of this administrative function "is too little recognized". Indeed "a greater proportion" of such men remain at the lower levels of management because technical competence wins recognition and promotion whereas skill in handling human relations does not. Yet were it not for these men, he claims, "the unleashed forces of modern technology would spin themselves out to doom and destruction". So these men go unnoticed and unrewarded; no provision is made for their replacement when the supply shall fail. And no university calls attention to the fact that material provision is only one of the duties of civilization, the other being the maintenance of co-operative living. Of these two duties it may be said that in any society at a given time the neglected factor becomes the more important. This is our situation now; our theory of civilization acts on the assumption that if technical and material advancement is maintained, human co-operation will *somehow* be inevitable.

[1] F. J. Roethlisberger, "The Foreman: Master and Victim of Double Talk", *Harvard Business Review*, Vol. XXIII, No. 3, Spring, 1945, p. 294.

Morale, the maintenance of co-operative living, is commonly spoken of as an imponderable, an intangible; and these epithets serve to justify the idea that the study of such matters is beneath the notice of the engineer, the economist, the university. Yet the instances I have presented do not seem to support this contemptuous dismissal. Intelligent handling of the situation—not sentimental, but simply intelligent—resulted in major changes of a definitely measurable order in Philadelphia, at Hawthorne in the test room, in Company C, in the leadman's working centre in California. Production increased, wastage diminished, absenteeism and labour turnover diminished—would not such changes in specific instances be taken as triumphs for systematic study in any other area of inquiry? The fact is that those who refer to such matters as imponderable are themselves ignorant of methods by which they can systematically set about the task of improving the co-operative morale in a working department, and are irked by any implication that this is a proper duty of the administrator. Such men therefore rely upon a confident, or even jolly, manner, upon knowing everyone's first name and using it, upon expedients such as saying "Good morning" to everyone they meet. And it is these same persons who express contempt for "sentimental" methods. This, as a substitute for intelligent inquiry and understanding, would be comic in an isolated instance; but, when twentieth-century civilization can, in general, show nothing better, the comic element recedes and tragedy takes its place. There is not much time left us; society, within the nation and without it, is breaking down into groups that show an ever-increasing hostility to each other; irrational hates are taking the place of co-operation. This, historically, has been the precursor of downfall for many valiant civilizations. There is no reason to suppose that our own fate will be otherwise, if we do not at once state explicitly the problem and struggle to develop a better *élite* than we can at present show in public, private, or academic life. Social life resembles biological in at least one aspect; when normal process ceases, pathological growth begins. It is a short step from friendship or tolerance to distrust and hatred when the normal social relationships disintegrate.

At the moment, the outlook for the present and future of civilization is sombre. In saying this, I am not thinking of the war; the democracies have been fortunate in the discovery of military leaders and first-class soldiers to follow their lead who together have taught Germans and Japanese that civilization will not tolerate aggression, tyranny, and soulless brutality. Nor am I thinking of the post-war handling of the problems of Germany and Japan: criminals must be taught that society will not permit crime, nor suffer those beyond the pale of humanity to live in freedom. I am thinking, rather, of the kind of leadership—political, industrial, scientific—we tolerated before the outbreak of the war. France is perhaps an object lesson. A society divided into hostile camps, its leaders venal and contemptuous of humanity, mutual hatred rather than co-operation the mainspring of action, personal reputations dependent on material possession rather than any human quality—what wonder that such a society fell apart instantly at the advent of an aggressor and went down in defeat. Across the English Channel, most fortunately for civilization, the first touch of adversity had the opposite effect. Senseless opposition was abandoned, the exponents of imbecile hatreds were suppressed. An eminent Frenchman, in conversation last year, insisted that "England and civilization were saved by three things". First, by the boys who flew *Spitfires* and the men and women workers that made and repaired them. Second, by two physicists working in a laboratory—radar. Third, by Mr. Winston Churchill and an England that could make an instantaneous and united response to his call for blood, tears, and sweat.

But Dr. A. V. Hill is not the only academic who is apprehensive of our present and future. For the last five or six years a Conference on Science, Philosophy and Religion has been meeting in September in New York. These meetings have been ably organized by the Rev. Dr. Louis Finkelstein with the active assistance of many of the leading academics of the United States. Their discussions have moved with a steady step toward the subject of "Group Tensions"—the increasing hostility, and even hatred, displayed by many and various groups in our society toward each other. For this year, the topic is to be the possibility of developing methods by which this accelerating movement toward disaster may be arrested. Such discussions are admirable and greatly needed: but the difficulty once again is that faced at Geneva. Those scientists and philosophers who are well-equipped to make the third step named above—to make explicit the logic implicit in a developed skill—are without the first-hand knowledge of the facts or the skill that alone can guide them. And those others who, as administrators, may be exercising a rudimentary skill seem at the moment to be handicapped by an inability to express in articulate and logical form the implications of the rudimentary skill they exercise. We have failed to train students in the study of social situations; we have thought that first-class technical training was sufficient in a modern and mechanical age. As a consequence we are technically competent as no other age in history has been; and we combine this with utter social incompetence.

This defect of education and administration has of recent years become a menace to the whole future of civilization. For, just as the will to co-operate is deep-seated in humanity, so also is the readiness to fear and hate an alien or merely another group. I have elsewhere quoted A. R. Radcliffe-Brown's findings in his anthropological studies of the West Australian blackfellow. When he and his blackfellow attendant approached a native camp, the old men of the tribe came out and made meticulous genealogical inquiries into the black attendant's antecedents. If his relationship to the tribe could be proved, he was admitted to the camp. But if such relationship could not be proved, he was not only not admitted but was in danger of his life.[1] And this is characteristic of all primitive peoples. "He who is not for me is against me"; anyone who is not an actual member of the co-operating group is regarded with doubt and suspicion that is easily converted into hostility and hate.

But one does not need exhaustive study of the primitive to confirm this finding; instances exist all about us and form part of our everyday experience. The children's playground, the industrial shop, the churches themselves, will bring an instance to the mind of every reader. In the California study, briefly described in the last chapter, the very strength of the co-operative spirit of the leadman's group seemed to carry with it as corollary or consequence an attitude of doubt or even hostility to other persons in the works. The group was renowned for "keeping to itself". And the relative chaos outside the works served not only to strengthen the group morale but also to accentuate its feeling of difference. War-time California is, no doubt, an extreme instance, but will serve to illustrate a type of human-social problem that will recur and will demand wise administrative handling in the adaptive society of the future. In the established society of our fathers,

[1] Alfred R. Radcliffe-Brown, "Three Tribes of Western Australia", *Journal of the Anthropological Institute*, 1913, p. 152.

easily aroused hostility was characteristic of the relationship between national or local groups but was not too difficult to handle. In the modern technical civilization this same latent hostility has infiltrated the society itself and demands intelligent attention as compared with conventional or routine handling. For the administrator himself in these days is frequently a victim of the emotional doubt or opposition.

Modern civilization is greatly in need of a new type of administrator who can, metaphorically speaking, stand outside the situation he is studying. The administrator of the future must be able to understand the human-social facts for what they actually are, unfettered by his own emotion or prejudice. He cannot achieve this ability except by careful training—a training that must include knowledge of the relevant technical skills, of the systematic ordering of operations, and of the organization of co-operation. Throughout this book I have maintained that the third—co-operation—is the most important now and in the immediate future. This for no other reason than that it is to-day ignored in universities, in industries, and in political statements.

B. M. Selekman, in an essay on "The Strategy of Hate",[1] written in the difficult period that followed the Pearl Harbour attack of December, 1941, points out that the democracies, no less than other groups, have permitted themselves to make use of easily aroused hatred to gain support for a group or measure in politics and industry alike. He says:

> Beyond the family, men also bind themselves variously to neighbourhood, club, school, party, work association, state, church, nation. But just as destructive sentiments can rise even from the cohesive unity of family life to warp and distort individual behaviour, so these other institutions still farther removed from the individual can generate and absorb all kinds of antagonisms and frustrations. We know that industry, *despite the intrinsic co-operation demanded by division of labour*, has also held some of the fiercest conflicts of modern society. [Italics mine, E. M.]

Later he adds:

> . . . if we have learned the perils and boomerang potentialities of Hitler's strategy of hate in international affairs, we have still to carry that lesson over to our own democratic development. Let us only hate one another enough and we shall inflict upon ourselves the mortal injury Hitler himself cannot inflict.[2]

[1] *Harvard Business Review*, Vol. XX, No. 1, Summer, 1942.
[2] Ibid., p. 400.

Thus speaks one with much responsible experience as industrial arbitrator of disputes before he was appointed professor of labour relations. Technical progress and technical organization have enabled the democracies—the "plutodemocracies" of Mussolini and Hitler—to develop, for the most part, beyond an ignorant and peasant type of living, to improve at least to some extent the general material standards of society. But we have failed to develop at an equal step the strategy of co-operation; we have allowed ourselves the easier path, the strategy of hate, that leads inevitably to the City of Destruction. Political leaders, group leaders of all types, have gained followers and momentary support by braying out fear and blame and hate to an extent that remains unrecognized in the popular literature of our time. Indeed many of our so-called "liberal" leaders are almost wholly occupied with devil-hunting, with absurd attempts to fasten the blame for this or that condition upon some persons or groups outside the field of their own immediate acquaintance. Even the universities are not free from this hate-exploitation or from their own private and personal group antagonisms. To blame a person or persons is far easier than to study carefully, and in full detail, a situation. Yet it is only the latter study that can avail to lead us out of the chaos of misery and malice that has overtaken our once proud civilization.

Hitler—a tatterdemalion exponent of hatred—led a nation, perhaps the most technically competent in the world, into a morass of hate and misery. The democracies have attained a high level of technical competence and are justly proud of the achievements of "Science". Yet physics, chemistry, biology, are wholly unaware of the part they have played in the destruction of society. If our social skills had advanced step by step with our technical skills, there would not have been another European war. "Patriotism is not enough; we must have no hatred or bitterness towards anyone".

APPENDIX I
THE POLITICAL PROBLEM
(*May 10th and 11th, 1947*)

I THE MODERNIZATION OF A PRIMITIVE COMMUNITY

ON EVERY hand we are told that the chief political problem of the present is the problem of "Two Worlds". And in almost the same breath the conversation turns to America and Russia as if these were the two worlds in question—and the opposition inevitable. None can deny the obvious difficulty of unity and co-operation between these two giants; but any such hasty foreclosure of the topic makes understanding of the source of difficulty almost impossible, and thus contributes an added item of misunderstanding. There are, of course, two worlds and a conflict of social conceptions and social methods; but the two worlds cannot be geographically identified. In one sense, Western civilization is opposed to Asiatic—with Russia, uneasy and uncertain, straddling the two. In another sense, it is a question of freedom against force —with success and failure to show on either side. But these two worlds interpenetrate each other geographically. China and India can boast scholars as enlightened as any in Europe. Europe can show—especially at this moment—groups numbered by many thousands who are ready to welcome almost any social system that will give certainty of the material necessities of life. Even Russia cannot claim the wholehearted devotion of every Russian to her present political regime. There is evidence everywhere that as general education advances, the desire for personal freedom from dictatorial injunction is increased. As Jean Piaget states in his study of the development of the child's conception of morality, the infant develops from a morality of constraint to a morality of co-operation.[1]

It is almost seventy years since Thomas Hill Green gave his famous lectures on *The Principles of Political Obligation* in Oxford University. In those lectures, as published in 1911, an entire section of forty pages is given to discussion of the thesis that "Will, not force, is the basis of the State".[2] But in the twentieth century we seem to have ignored or forgotten this nineteenth-

[1] *The Moral Judgment of the Child* (London, Kegan Paul, Trench, Trubner & Co., Ltd., 1932), Chap IV.

[2] London, Longmans, Green and Co., Chap. G, p. 121.

century statement. And the neglect cannot be wholly attributed to the fact that an ignoramus like Hitler or Mussolini seized power; the tendency to increase the range of governmental authority had been clearly manifest in the great democracies before the advent of fascism. Mussolini merely accepted a common and superficial conclusion as to the direction of civilized development—and acted on it.

There seems to be little general understanding, that is, articulate understanding, of the two phases—centralized control and normal democratic control—of either administration or government. As a people changes and develops, its government must change and develop also. This change is effected by the advent of a crisis, more or less critical, that demands immediate attention. Such a crisis may be a small affair, affecting only some minor group within the organization; and it may be that routine methods will suffice to its control. But, when the crisis is general and affects a nation, the central democratic authority is expected to assume powers for the time being as arbitrary as those of any tyrant, and must do so. Otherwise the contrivance of an active organization to meet the crisis will be lacking. But when the emergency has passed, the central authority of a democracy, if wise, will relax its grip and will permit a measure of self-determination to return to the peripheral organizations in which development originates. This phasic alternation has been the historic character of the development of the great democracies.

The dynamic character of democracy is very generally misunderstood; it was wholly misunderstood by Mussolini and by Hitler. The years between the two wars were years in which crises, economic and military, were constantly threatening. We seemed to be always preoccupied with the need to stave off some emergency. Mussolini and Hitler misinterpreted these recurrent crises to signify that there are two methods of popular control—the *heroic* and the *civilized*, typically the military and the civilian. And both Mussolini and Hitler, each posturing to himself as hero, chose the former. This easy and superficial decision in favour of military organization has never been valid for any form of government, except in those—usually brief—periods when a momentary heroic control is demanded. At such times heroic control may be briefly needed, but not a hero. Perhaps this is one of the differences between the German and the Russian method.

The victories of peace, unfortunately, are less renowned than

those of war. Moments of dramatic success tend to be associated
in popular thinking with military triumphs and the heroic method.
And the ruler is conceived after the pattern of the Hollywood
actor as one who is wholly occupied in making dramatic decisions.
So a business executive is conceived as one who passes the day
thumping his desk and roaring orders to subordinates. This is not
the administrative process and never has been. But Hitler and
Mussolini were wholly deceived; their proper background was
Hollywood.

The victories of peace rank highest; the terrible and dramatic
moment at Hiroshima would not have been possible had not the
work of many years in quiet laboratories, and in many countries,
been mobilized for purposes of war. In a peaceful world, the
discoveries of nuclear physics had been pointed in quite another
direction. But the atomic bomb, the military utilization of these
discoveries, captured the popular attention. And a large part of
popular theory will, no doubt, continue to misjudge such military
utilization and to regard all forms of successful control as characteristic of the military, the heroic, phase.

But there is no such idea in these pages. As a civilization
develops toward greater complexity, its methods of administration
must develop toward greater complexity also. And the phasic
alternation will characterize not only the whole society but also
all the lesser organizations within it—great and small. Crises may
affect a whole nation or merely a group within it. It is the duty
of a central administration to watch the relations within and
between its constituent groups and to aid, as best it can, the
general co-operative development.

II

A society is a co-operative system; a civilized society is one in
which the co-operation is based on understanding and the will to
work together rather than on force. In any primitive group,
although the will to work together is active and strong, fear and
force nevertheless bulk larger than in a civilization. This fear is
not merely pointed at other groups—even when other groups are
the subject of suspicion or hostility—it is pointed also at the
unknown natural forces that are always capable of defeating
human intentions. Jenks puts this well:

One of the strongest characteristics of primitive man is his fear of the Unknown. He is forever dreading that some act of his may bring down upon him the anger of the gods. He may not fear his fellow man, nor the beasts of the forest; but he lives in perpetual awe of those unseen powers which, from time to time, seem bent on his destruction. He sows his corn at the wrong season; he reaps no harvest, the offended gods have destroyed it all. He ventures up into a mountain, and is caught in a snow-drift. He trusts himself to a raft, and is wrecked by a storm. He endeavours to propitiate these terrible powers with sacrifices and ceremonies; but they will not always be appeased. There are terrors above him and around him.[1]

Jenks continues:

From this state of fear, custom is his first great deliverer. . . .[2]

Writing as a lawyer, he is concerned to demonstrate the origin of law as the articulate expression of accepted customs. Custom, he says, is:

. . . the earliest known stage of Law; it is not enacted, nor even declared: it establishes itself as the result of experience.[3]

His description of the attitude of a primitive society to the world about it and to its own habit of living is sufficiently accurate. "Hence the reverence of primitive societies for custom; hence their terror of the innovator."[4] Man, even at the lowest level of social organization, *finds his personal security in active co-operation* with other members of his group. Hence his suspicion and fear of other groups whose customs differ from his own. In a very primitive group the proximity of disaster is very real—in *Leviathan*, Hobbes says:

. . . worst of all, continual feare, and danger of violent death; And the life of man, solitary, poore, nasty, brutish, and short.[5]

In taking up such a question as the modernization of a primitive society, we have accordingly to be observant of the many different levels of co-operative activity. At the lower levels of culture, fear and force are more nearly descriptive than will. At higher levels, understanding and a will to co-operate are dominant. To some extent Green, in the passage cited above, is defining the direction of civilized development.

---

[1] Edward Jenks, *Law and Politics in the Middle Ages* (2nd ed., London, John Murray, 1919), p. 56.
[2] Ibid.   [3] Ibid., p. 57.   [4] Ibid.
[5] Thomas Hobbes (Everyman's Library ed., London, J. M. Dent & Sons, Ltd.), p. 65.

Rather more than twenty-five years ago—a quarter of a century—Russia threw out the Tsarist regime, and the revolution began. In certain aspects of the development there are echoes of the French Revolution. At first the moderates, the doctrinaires, those who believed in representative government on the English or American pattern, seemed to be in control. As ever, the moderate group proved inadequate to the difficult task; and the controls were taken over by a group of Marxists—the Bolsheviks. Facing civil war and attacks from outside, even these highly disciplined Marxians showed weakness in their ranks, and the first "purgings" took place. The intimate history of this period when it is written will be extraordinarily interesting. At present we have to guess, although the general contour is plain.

The successive purgings, culminating in the flight of Trotsky, who had been largely responsible for victory in the civil war, left in control a group of exceedingly tough-minded rulers. This last group had, in effect, abandoned the doctrinaire Marxist theories. They had learned, and quickly, that the dictatorship of the proletariat did not mean an instantaneous happy Utopia and a classless society. They realized that they were merely at the beginning of an exceedingly difficult undertaking—that of forcing Russia to become a single complex community and not a collection of ill-assorted and widely different social groups. Whereas Tsarism, by police methods, had forced upon Russia the semblance of community, the new rulers determined, by methods not greatly different, to force unity and community to develop from within—to become a reality of co-operation, and the word *Russia* more than a mere name for north-eastern Europe and northern Asia.

The task they faced was colossal. Vera Micheles Dean says that there are nearly two hundred different national and racial groups in Soviet Russia, each having lived formerly in its own traditional fashion.[1] In Tsarist Russia there were at least seventy-six different languages other than Russian,[2] some of which had no written alphabet; and the literacy of the population was very low. It took great courage, and great faith in Russia, to attempt the modernization of a community on so vast a scale. Success or failure, it was indeed a herculean effort.

[1] *Russia: Menace or Promise* (New York, Henry Holt & Co., 1947), p. 5.
[2] Robert Magidoff, "Readers and Writers in Moscow", *The New York Times*, Magazine Section, March 16, 1947.

The revolutionaries were aided in their tutelage of the many different groups by a Marxist training that had led them to discard belief in any existent European pattern of living. That is to say, they realized that industrial and agricultural development could be expedited, first, by a direct relationship to scientific findings and, second, by dissociation from any European system of ownership or any European legal conception of rights and duties. They were thus enabled to present to those whom they tutored a very simple so-called communism that insisted on unity, co-operation, and community. The land must produce for Russia, not merely for a small and local group—and so with industrial manufacture or the conservation of water and natural resources.

Now, a primitive group cannot—in a short period of time—be given understanding of abstract theories or of legal systems. It can however be forced to change its way of living and to adopt another. But it must be a way of living such that every action is related to every other action and to some practical and useful end. That is to say, it must be simple, practicable, communicable in terms of action—and not dependent on logical theory or inference. Northern Russia and Siberia, from Finland to north-eastern Asia, had been peopled by groups practising shamanism. This took form as a primitive code of actions and taboos by which people lived in numberless separate groups. The communism forced upon these groups by the new rulers of Russia was not very different in form from either shamanism or any other primitive way of living. There was no Marxian and abstract theory of the defects of capitalism involved—at least in the primary stages of its communication—it was simply another way of living, similar in kind to that they knew, but possessed of enormous advantages. For example, it enlarged the borders of the social group to include the whole of Russia. No longer was the tribesman's conception of community confined to his native village. Near-by villages were no longer peopled by those who lived by a different code and must therefore be regarded with suspicion or even hostility. Other villages, near-by or remote, lived by the same code and must be regarded as entitled to share the benefits won by all. The task of conversion took years of patient tutelage but, by reason of its essential similarity to the former way of living, was not the herculean effort it might have seemed.

Another advantage accrued from the improved communication with a central authority. Aid sent from the centre slowly improved methods of, for example, agriculture by scientific study and education. The obstinate kulak was removed—and the field was clear for modernization.

Dr. Sun Yat-sen, after some study of Russian achievement, came to the conclusion that methods somewhat similar if applied to China would be marked by three stages. These were:

(1) Military unification.   (3) Constitutional government.[1]
(2) Political tutelage.

Russia, by heroic rather than civilized methods, has made marked progress in the first two stages, military unification and political tutelage. She has provided, and insisted on, education; in twenty-five years she has converted her people from almost total illiteracy into assiduous readers. It is said that over eighty per cent now read eagerly not only the works of Lenin and Stalin —though these of course hold the chief place—but also translations of English, American, French, and other classics. These classics include fiction; apparently books such as *Tom Sawyer* and *Robinson Crusoe* have a Russian appeal.

So much for Russia's immense achievement. One cannot know yet whether Russia's rulers realize the inevitability of Sun Yat-sen's third stage—something of the nature of constitutional government. It would seem that they still think in terms of the heroic method. Every situation is treated as emergency, and may indeed be critical for Russia at this time. The talk is of "victory on the agricultural front", or similar military phrases; rewards are still offered for successful efforts beyond the ordinary in the "battle for wheat". But however justifiable this may be at the moment, there seems to be no evidence that Russia's rulers ever think beyond *emergency—crisis—drive* as a method of leadership. Now, it is relatively easy to persuade a people to co-operate in the face of serious emergency; but the emergency must be an obvious reality, as in England during the war, and not a political contrivance. The latter device may succeed once or twice—but, sooner or later, continued insistence on the heroic method brings in its train weariness, boredom, lack of response. Signs are not lacking that even Russia may at some time have to face just such a reaction.

The problem of government, or administration, does not centre upon organization to meet *emergency;* the real problem is that of

[1] Paul Myron Anthony Linebarger, *The Political Doctrines of Sun Yat-sen* (Baltimore, The Johns Hopkins Press, 1937), p. 211.

the maintenance of *spontaneous co-operation* in times of peace. "Will, not force, is the basis of the State." In these days the main road open to the nations, including Russia, is that of education. Russia has wholeheartedly committed herself to this road; it remains a question, however, whether her leaders know whither it is leading them.

III

And at this point someone may say, "But how can we talk about Russia? We are wholly out of communication with Russians; and such information as we occasionally get from within is inconsistent, contradictory, and unreliable". The reply to which is that of course any information we may get must possess such a character, because what we are watching is a rapid and disorderly growth from a collection of primitive, illiterate, small communities to a geographically large, co-operative, and literate community. For there is no such entity as Russian communism; there is a Russian community; and those of us who are optimistic must hope that we are watching a rapid, somewhat chaotic growth to responsible, self-respecting nationhood.

The event is not new in history. A revolution occurs and there is established a dictatorship of the proletariat. The newcomers celebrate their accession to power by avenging themselves on their enemies, real or imagined. They thus get rid of many of those educated and responsible middle class persons who, in ordinary phrase, "keep things going". And at once the void thus created becomes noticeable, because affairs refuse to manage themselves.

Marx detested "the bourgeoisie": on grounds that will some day probably be shown to have been personal, he regarded the bourgeois as a greedy profit-making exploiter of labour; he considered that the classless society could well do without him. And the revolutionary society speedily discovered that this is doctrinaire nonsense. No society can do without the man who is educated and, moreover, possessed of what is termed nowadays the *know-how*. It is this knowledge that keeps the wheels of industry and agriculture turning. A high official in the English Labour Cabinet, himself a man of education, told his trade-union supporters not many months ago that none of them was eligible for appointment to some reorganization board because none of them had the necessary knowledge of the principles of management. There was at once a howl of indignation, but when he courageously repeated his assertions some months later there is no record of any recrudescence of anger. Perhaps in the meantime the group had canvassed its members to discover which of them was willing to take, and capable of taking, the responsibility.

There is no such entity as Russian communism. The Russian community is developing and, chameleon-like, continually changing its character. The man of education and science, for example, is no longer forced to live, if permitted to live at all, on rations less than those allowed the worker. On the contrary, he is given monetary and other rewards far above the ordinary worker standard—and the value of education itself acknowledged in its extension to every member of the community. Doubtless the scientist is still closely watched by the police—and with reason, from the rulers' point of view; for uneducated persons cannot control the thought and actions of those with superior training.

Indeed it is highly probable that an internal crisis is fast approaching Russia; her next difficulties are more likely to be within Russia than outside. She has enlarged the Russian community; but she has cultivated hostility to all other communities. In other words, she has substituted one variety of primitive control for another; but with the advent of literacy and skill, the primitive type of control is doomed. She has done well to develop wider co-operation and education within her borders, but that very act has made the continuance of primitive methods inconsistent and impossible. There may be progressive development—or there may again be chaos. We must hope for the former alternative.

A great writer of classic times remarked that the primitive, small social organization comes into being for the sake of life itself but continues its development to promote a life directed towards better living.[1] The small and primitive society is always facing the difficulty that other groups, small and large, near or remote, have alien methods of living and must therefore be regarded with doubt, suspicion, hostility. Within the actively co-operating group, the individual experiences an assurance of personal and group security that goes far to maintain a collaborative attitude. But beyond this there is always the threat of danger. Anthropologists have done much in recent years to demonstrate this character of the small community in, for instance, studies of

[1] Aristotle, *Politics*, I, i, 1252^{b}12.

the Australian blackfellow, the Trobriander, the Andaman Islander, and many others. These different organizations are described as "cultures"—social cultures—and, historically speaking, *there have been many cultures but only one civilization.* This claim demands brief explanation. The more we study the history of ancient peoples in Mediterranean Europe, Asia, Africa, the more astounded are we by the high development of technical skill of many and various kinds in these ancient peoples. Yet all these cultural developments disappeared, humanly speaking; they are represented now merely by relics that are excavated and studied by the scholar.

Even the American continent can show its Mayan and other cultures. These cultures seem always to have collapsed, at least finally, as a result of invasion from without—a fact of observation that has led to many curious theories of an aging of the social organism. Yet it is obvious that the development of what is termed high morale and skill within a given group demands a balanced relation with other and outside groups for its perpetuation. This fact can be observed—in microcosm—even within an industrial organization. In a chaotic industrial situation, if one group possesses a high morale, if its members are actively co-operating among themselves, the effect is to make them doubtful or suspicious of other departments and the people in them. I suppose that everyone responsible for a large-scale business organization has had some personal experience of this kind. One's feeling of personal security seems to vary directly, and almost mathematically, with the area of active co-operation within which one lives and works. This has been studied in school and playground by the child study group in the University of Toronto.[1] It is also a fact of ordinary observation in Toronto and elsewhere that those who have been intelligent and active members of many groups possess, not only superior independence of judgment, but also a greater capacity for ease of co-operation with other persons and groups.

It seems to be characteristic of primitive groups, and to have been characteristic of highly developed ancient cultures, that the area of active collaboration should be definitely limited geographically. And this apparently is one of many factors that have

[1] University of Toronto Studies, Child Development Series, No. 18, *An Evaluation of Adjustment Based upon the Concept of Security,* by Mary D. Salter (Toronto, University of Toronto Press, 1940).

contributed to downfall. Russia seems to have overcome this limitation within her borders; but unless she can devise means of actively relating her own development to developments elsewhere in the world, one must suppose that her destiny, near or remote, is that of Crete or Ur. In the modern world of improved means of communication, this need becomes even more imperative than in ancient times.

Note: Those who find this general topic important will be interested in a recent paper by Sidney B. Fay, "The Idea of Progress", *The American Historical Review*, Vol. LII, No. 2, January, 1947.

II. Change and Its Social Consequences

There have been many cultures, but only one civilization. European culture in the fifth and, again, in the tenth century faced crises at least as serious as those which afflict us now. The one threat of chaos followed the fall of Rome; the other followed the collapse of the Carolingian Empire. And the world was smaller then than now. There was no United States to maintain and develop existing social standards; no Canada, South Africa, Australia to support such standards. Relative to the world as it then was, the crises of the fifth and tenth centuries were more wholesale than that we face at present. And it was then that the Christian Church arose to maintain and develop civilization.

Christopher Dawson says, "At the very moment of the fall of the Empire in the West, St. Augustine, in his great book, *Of the City of God*, had set forth the programme which was to inspire the ideals of the new age. He viewed all history as the evolution of two opposite principles embodied in two hostile societies, the heavenly and the earthly cities, Sion and Babylon, the Church and the World".[1] "The State is not condemned as such," but its highest achievement is earthly prosperity and human wisdom. Yet in so far as the State is Christian it subserves the ends of the heavenly city: in other words, it is "a subordinate society", the spiritual society is supreme.

A professor of religious history tells me that Augustine's doctrine was Iranian in origin and apocalyptic. That is to say, he expected a Last Day when the Kingdom of God should be established on earth and the Babylons swept away; and those who had served the cause of Sion should be rewarded. I have no doubt that a very simple form of this doctrine was accepted by the Europe of that time; but the simplicity is unimportant as compared with the practical effect of his teaching.

Max Radin, writing in the first number of *The Pacific Spectator*, describes the part played by Christianity in what he terms the *High Middle Age*. He says, "But over and above being a guildsman or a knight or a peasant, every man had another aspect. He was

[1] *The Making of Europe* (London, Sheed & Ward, 1945), p. 192.

not, properly speaking, a citizen, but he was a member of a society that theoretically included the whole world and actually did include most of western and central Europe. He was a Christian".[1]

However simple and apocalyptic the doctrine in origin and acceptance, it had the effect on Western civilization that Radin describes. It transformed what had been merely another culture into a civilization. Every man felt himself to be participant in the work of the Church and felt therefore that his chief duty was that of co-operation with every other person of any diverse race or kingdom in the service of Sion. And in small agrarian centres rose those great grey abbeys and churches, many of which still stand as witness that the builders were, even in the most humble daily round, consecrated to the service of a far-reaching conception of human destiny. For many centuries, and in spite of wars and disturbances, the doctrine of human co-operation remained the guiding spirit of the developing civilization.

The findings of the older psychology, for example that of James Ward, William James, J. F. Herbart, are more in accord with the medieval ideal than the odd excursions of some modern psychologists into the psychotechnical area. In his article on psychology in the ninth edition of the *Encyclopedia Britannica*, Ward points to the human need for what he, following Herbart, calls *complication*. The human individual, to retain interest in living, must continuously throughout his existence complicate, or make more complex, his relationship to the world of men and things about him. He is of course forced by his limitations to some degree of specialization; he cannot simultaneously develop knowledge and skill in all directions. Furthermore, the growth in capacity must include social as well as technical skills—human relationships as well as abstract sciences or philosophy. This last, human relationships, is perhaps the great contribution of Janet, Freud, and the psychiatrists generally. The medieval ideal of civilization safeguarded this human need by setting no bounds to human participation in the civilized activities of others. No four or five year plan was allowed to interfere with the almost infinite possibilities of human social development.

Western civilization, then, may be regarded as the one outstanding experiment in the development of the almost endless

[1] "Education for Conversation", *The Pacific Spectator* (Stanford University, California), Vol. I, No. 1, Winter, 1947, p. 6.

possibilities of human social capacity. From the Augustinian point of view, no easy realization of an ideal of merely material comfort can be sufficient; any present accomplishment must fall short of what is possible and be open to improvement. Scholars and the church began the arduous task by instruction in the *Trivium*—grammar, logic, rhetoric. This instruction was one of the most important contributions to general education ever made; it is still the important element in all education. The *Trivium* taught intelligent students to express their thoughts in articulate fashion and, having expressed them, to subject their thinking to rigorous logical criticism. This led to discussion, learned disputation, and the improved communication of ideas. And this again, in due time, led beyond the learned disputation of mere assertions to investigation of the facts about which assertions were made. Finally the scientists and the adventure of systematic discovery appeared upon the scene; and, with the scientist's advent, the modern period of rational scepticism may be considered to have begun. It is of some interest to note, however, that the scientist has wholly accepted one aspect of the teachings of the church: he does not make final assertions; he does not regard knowledge as ever complete; he is clearly aware that any discovery he may make is not only open to revision and restatement but that it inevitably opens up new areas for investigation. Discovery is an endless adventure.

As this work proceeded, the early and simple apocalyptic doctrine of man's duty became untenable. Max Radin, in the article I have already quoted, points out that when many persons began to doubt the reality of the other world, when also they ceased to believe in the authority of the clergy, the unfortunate effect was that the faith in universal human co-operation was disastrously weakened. The effect has been, according to another scholar, Sidney B. Fay, that "our tremendous material progress has not been accompanied by any corresponding advance in other fields. . . . In moral and spiritual matters millions of men, having lost the strength and guidance which they used to draw from the teachings of the institutional church, are morally adrift or spiritually indifferent. They have not yet discovered a better way of life than that indicated by the essential principles of Christianity, but they find these principles intertwined with unacceptable dogmas. They have not learned how to reinterpret and adapt Christian values to the social and economic environment of the present, which is entirely different from the small communities in which Christian experience was first formulated". [1]

Put in other words this means that from the sixteenth century onwards we began a rapid descent from a real civilization towards the mere cultures—the types of social organization that change and pass, leaving only historic traces. The tendency to exaggerate the importance of technical and material discovery and to ignore study of the social and collaborative aspect was strengthened by the development, from 1752 onwards, of a gross misinterpretation of Quesnay's teachings and the doctrines of the French physiocrats. Quesnay's *Tableau Economique* and his *Maximes* were misinterpreted to mean that the only effective human motive was self-interest, that study of social organization was, strictly speaking, unnecessary.

This was not Quesnay's doctrine: he was a clinician, physician at the Court of Louis XV of France, and a careful, professional observer of human beings. He claimed that there is a natural and essential order of society such that, if a number of individuals work together to achieve a common purpose, a harmony of interest will develop amongst them to which individual self-interest will be subordinated. This is a very different doctrine from the claim that individual self-interest is the solitary human motive. Moreover, in our industrial studies we, like many others, have found it to be as true to-day as in Quesnay's time that individual self-interest is eagerly subordinated to the group. Whether as anthropologists we study a primitive race or as industrialists we study some part of the modern complex and chaotic scheme, we find, either in the natural wilds or in the modern city, groups of individuals who find their happiness and such sense of personal security as may be in the subordination of an individual to a common interest. The solitary who works alone is always a very unhappy person.

The importance assigned to humanly inadequate economic theories during the eighteenth and nineteenth centuries was one of the major disasters the cause of civilization has suffered. It is always the larger that controls the lesser purpose, and with the disappearance of the larger purpose of a Christian civilization in which all nations or races should find a place and function—with the disappearance of this ideal, the ancient rivalry between

[1] "The Idea of Progress", *The American Historical Review*, Vol. LII, No. 2, January, 1947, p. 244.

different groups and cultures revived in full force. A common purpose that shall unite the different nations in a single quest, a common ideal that shall reconcile the various groups within a particular geography—these have disappeared, leaving in their place only the ancient military type of unity that presents a hostile front to all who differ. And as the will to co-operate diminished, the sense of personal security diminished also.

In the modern world the sense of security must depend on intelligent organization that takes careful account of all the group interests involved. As investigators, we have often noticed that where co-operation is maintained between the individual and his group, the group and the union, the union and management, the personal sense of security and absence of discontent in the individual run high. The International Ladies Garment Workers Union is an instance. No money wages can purchase the content and quiet thus gained. But where this character is absent, the contrary is true. Management no doubt has in the past often failed to understand the importance of gaining the trust and confidence—the co-operation—of its workers by straight dealing and a real interest in their many and various problems. But management is not the only offender. The unions themselves know far better how to organize for warfare against management than for peaceful co-operation with management. Yet, if any group essential to achievement of the purpose of an organization is thus excluded, the inevitable consequence is a feeling of personal insecurity in the union members themselves. Indeed, on looking over the whole field, one can assert that unions in the present are for the most part repeating the mistakes that management has made. The military, the heroic, method of organizing for emergency is the easiest way to secure immediate co-operation. But the exclusion of a group—the management group—that is needed for complete organization of joint work implies hostility and leads in the individual worker either to a feeling of incomplete security or of active insecurity. By this road arrive those "wildcat" strikes that are the present plague of union organizers. The medieval ideal of the co-operation of all is the only satisfactory source of civilized procedure. Militant tactics are invariably the sign of imperfect organization, of imperfect understanding of the principles of organization. This criticism applies both to the international situation and to those situations where strikes or similar troubles afflict the even tenor of our way.

Fay says that the churches have failed to study the changing character of our civilization. It is not for me but rather for the theologians and pastors to study the extent to which they have permitted themselves to expect the early apocalyptic beliefs of Augustine's time to maintain a sway over the minds of men. Perhaps we in the universities have failed to supply the requisite material for the consideration of the churches; perhaps foolish rationalistic oversimplifications of the nature of man have offended the religious sense of human dignity. But, since we need the churches' help badly in the chaotic modern world, perhaps we can begin to supply them with observations worthy of their attention.

Either from the point of view of the churches, then, or from the point of view of responsible management, the outstanding need of the modern world is the need for investigation and study of organization and the principles of intelligent administration. If we are to lay aside the strong and simple religious feeling of medieval times as the chief organizing principle of civilization, we can only substitute intelligent understanding of all the necessary elements involved in human organization on the modern scale. The understanding required involves two main groups of problems and one contributory:

1. The scientific and technical problems of supplying the community's economic and material needs.
2. The scientific and technical problems of effective communication and co-operation.

Finally there is a contributory group of problems, namely:

3. The problems involved in the systematic ordering of operations.

Only by developing knowledge and practice in these three areas shall we be able to contrive an issue from our present discontents.

The immense changes of the last two centuries have disturbed all the traditional social balances. Material and technical achievements have outpaced free communication between groups and the capacity for spontaneous co-operation. Study of the social facts is only now beginning—at a critical moment when the general ignorance of the facts of social organization has become alarming. Owing to this general ignorance, the political leaders in many countries have introduced another unfortunate complication by relapsing on the ancient idea of compulsion by central authority. This has affected even those countries that nominally retain the forms of democratic government.

Now compulsion has never succeeded in rousing eager and spontaneous co-operation. In Byzantium it may have seemed to succeed for several centuries, owing in part to obvious external need, and in part to an apparently efficient civil service. But even in Byzantium the popular will to collaborate ultimately withered and died under the conditions of external and internal compulsion: and another culture disappeared. The will to survive and co-operate must come from within; will, not force, is the basis of the State. At the moment the churches, like the rest of us, are in need of new knowledge; and the urgent problem, social and political, of the present is where we can look for the new knowledge that shall aid the churches and all of us in understanding.

And, at this point, I am happy to be able to turn away from my topic and to look at the work of the Graduate School of Business Administration, of which I have been a member for twenty-one years. I shall not speak of my personal debt to the School, to my colleagues of the Faculty, to Harvard University, and to this country for the opportunity of work offered—although I am grateful beyond adequate expression to all. I shall confine my attention to some observations I have made during almost a quarter of a century.

This School has for many years been occupied with studies that unquestionably contribute a beginning of the understanding we so badly need. The movement began simply enough in 1919 when Dean Wallace Donham and one after another of his Faculty decided that the material used for instruction in business administration must consist of actual cases gathered from business itself. This innovation was a move away from academic generalizations, insufficiently supported by adequate evidence; a move in the direction of actuality. A few highly intelligent young men were sent out to collect cases, the project in charge of Dr. M. T. Copeland. It is of interest that one of the first of these young men was named Donald K. David, now Dean of the School. Inevitably the cases collected led the Faculty members themselves to visit the situations described in order to verify various aspects of the reports. By this road came gradually the knowledge that human situations are infinitely more complicated than textbook descriptions. I shall not attempt to describe the growth of understanding that followed. Indeed, since I only joined the Faculty in 1926, when the movement was well under way, I cannot claim to have played any part in it. I did not even know that I was similarly occupied until much later—although I believe that my younger colleagues have contributed something of value to the latest developments. The final step—the effective implementation of the real purpose of the School, namely, the study of human organizations and administrative principles in all their aspects—was probably hastened by the war. During the war many members of the Staff discovered, perhaps to their surprise, that they were more than fitted to apply their knowledge to the service of the cause. Perhaps some other person better equipped for the task than I am will some day give adequate attention to the work this School has done. Harvard University has already recognized it. But I should like, in saying farewell to my colleagues, to acknowledge the debt that I, and my associates, owe them. I have every confidence that they will continue work so well begun and that their initiative will provoke and stimulate similar studies elsewhere.

APPENDIX II

STUDIES OF THE DEPARTMENT OF INDUSTRIAL RESEARCH GRADUATE SCHOOL OF BUSINESS ADMINISTRATION HARVARD UNIVERSITY

by Professor GEORGE F. F. LOMBARD

1926–1945

A BRIEF description of the major studies of the Department of Industrial Research may be of interest to other research students at this time. These studies have not been fully reported for a variety of reasons. Important among the latter is the fact that studies of what is important to a particular person or group of persons are difficult to report without revealing the names of those who have willingly contributed to the researches under the promise that their anonymity will be preserved. The passage of time and the collection of a wider range of data make problems such as these easier to overcome. Some of the studies here listed are being prepared for publication; it may be possible to issue others later.

The Department of Industrial Research was formed in 1926, when a special research committee (later called the Committee on Industrial Physiology) was appointed at Harvard University with the financial help of the Laura Spelman Rockefeller Memorial (later The Rockefeller Foundation) to organize and direct research into effort and fatigue in industry and into the industrial efficiency of individuals. From the beginning it was clear that there were two distinct, although closely related, fields of inquiry. One type of inquiry about human beings at work could be conducted under laboratory conditions, inquiries into, e.g., biochemical changes occurring in the blood stream under different conditions of work, temperature, humidity, etc. Another type of inquiry concerned with workers and their work in an industrial plant itself could not be conducted under strict laboratory conditions. Here the "total situation" of an individual worker had to be studied in his concrete environment, both physical and social. For this type of inquiry the approach had to be more clinical than "experimental" in the strict laboratory sense. The Fatigue Laboratory was organized to carry out the former studies; the Department of Industrial Research, the latter.

Elton Mayo has characterized explanations of human behaviour in industry at the time when this work began as follows:

. . . The industrial arena was haunted by individuals each of whom seemed assured that the abstractions he expressed—economics, politics, psychology of efficiency—were adequate to the special problem he studied. All these logics had to be tentatively set aside on the ground that they might be derivations rather than the achievement of logico-experimental investigation. In every instance *the particular situation* had to be studied, and without preconceived determination. In every instance care had to be exercised to account for *the simple and the obvious*, for the simple and obvious facts are so firmly established in the awareness of industry that they are apt to be disregarded.[1]

The work, then, had to start, not with known facts whose uses were to be discovered, but with inquiries to discover what the simple obvious facts of human situations were that were important when an aspect of the problem was to secure action. These simple and obvious facts were of three kinds: physiological, personal, and social. The Fatigue Laboratory worked with facts of the first category. Problems of the personal and social became the concern of the Department of Industrial Research.

Activities of the Department may be divided into three periods. The first, extending approximately from 1926 to 1932, was a period of intensive, exploratory research. In the second period, from about 1932 to 1936, the chief activities of members of the Department were assessing the results of the exploratory period, testing newly formulated hypotheses through more research, and stating the implications of the researches for business administration. In the third period, beginning about 1936, members of the Department began to emphasize more than in earlier years the development of ways of communicating to students of administration the methods and points of view which the studies had developed. The activities of these three periods were by no means mutually exclusive. Research workers were trained in the first period, and research studies were made in the last. Nevertheless, there was some difference in emphasis in the activities of members of the Department during these three periods. This difference reflected stages in the growth of the Department's understanding of the problems of securing action through human beings in industrial situations.

[1] "Industrial Research", *Harvard Business School Alumni Bulletin*, Vol. XVI, No. 2, 1940, p. 87.

Early Exploratory Research: 1926 to 1932

The earliest studies (numbered 1 and 2 below) were chiefly useful in delimiting the need for the longer and more intensive studies
that followed. At the same time they marked out three of the
major lines of study which members of the Department were to
follow in later years.

1. *Exploratory studies of physiological, personal, and social factors in a
work situation.* Some aspects of this study, the relations between
the expenditure of energy and output as affected by emotion and
attentive effort, have been published in "The Quantitative
Measurement of Human Efficiency under Factory Conditions",
by Osgood S. Lovekin, in *The Journal of Industrial Hygiene.* [1]

2. *Another early study explored the relation to a work situation of the
broad aspects of community life.* In a small town, the home of a large
industry, members of several racial and class groups which were
geographically and socially separate in distinct residential areas
were brought together in the factory in a way that limited the
effects of administrative action which ignored these factors, often
seemingly irrelevant to issues arising in the business. In a similar
way action which started in the factory often affected the wider
community. This study is partially reported in *The Wertheim
Lectures on Industrial Relations, 1928.* [2]

Perhaps it is not using too much hindsight to say that these
first studies began to clarify that the determinants of action in an
organization pertain to (1) the individuals and (2) the groups
which co-operate or fail to co-operate and (3) the methods the
administrator uses to get action. These aspects of the problem
were much more fully explored in the longer studies of the period.

3. *Studies in the personal adjustment of students at the Graduate School
of Business Administration.* These studies carried on throughout the
three periods of the Department's history. Altogether, nearly four
hundred students were interviewed. In early years, members of
the Department active in this work spent a great deal of time reading and discussing the literature of psychopathology and anthropology. Author after author was studied and his conclusions
tested against the experience of the researchers in handling cur-

[1] Vol. XII, No. 4, April, 1930.
[2] "Maladjustment of the Industrial Worker", by Elton Mayo, one of a series of
lectures on various phases of industrial relations published in a volume by the Jacob
Wertheim Research Fellowship for the Betterment of Industrial Relations (Cambridge,
Mass., Harvard University Press, 1929), pp. 165–196.

rent situations. Differences in the reported results of other investigators and hypotheses of the research group were noted and thoroughly discussed.

The results of this study gave additional support to the conclusions of the Western Electric studies which were reported in the chapter on the interviewing method in *Management and the Worker*.[1] Indeed, this chapter may be looked on as a report on the methodology developed during both studies. These studies of students explored the structure of an individual's thinking and its relation to his capacity to take co-operative action with others for a common purpose. These studies concentrated in particular on the problems of those who have difficulty in so contributing their efforts. This negative side of the ingredients of co-operation, in conjunction with the other studies, helped throw light on the nature of an individual's adjustment to group life.

4. *Studies carried out in connection with the Western Electric Company*. These studies, among the most important on which members of the Department collaborated, many aspects of which have been adequately reported, will not be discussed here, except to point out that in the beginning the experimenters were concerned with determining how factors in the physical environment, such as lighting and rest periods, affected the way in which workers co-operated in the job at hand (the early test-room studies). These experiments pointed to a different variable, the attitudes of workers to their jobs, as being controlling, and led to the interviewing programme. The latter in connection with the next study to be mentioned showed a need to explore the determinants of co-operation in a social group: the factors that make for social integration and unity of purpose, on the one hand, or disruption and discord, on the other. This aspect of the study at the Western Electric Company became known as the Bank Wiring Test Room.

5. *The studies of what became known as "Yankee City"*. These researches are reported in six volumes in the "Yankee City Series" published by the Yale University Press.[2] These studies were

---

[1] F. J. Roethlisberger and William J. Dickson (Cambridge, Mass., Harvard University Press, 1939), Chap. XIII.

[2] W. Lloyd Warner and Paul S. Lunt, *The Social Life of a Modern Community* (Yankee City Series, Vol. I, 1941); W. Lloyd Warner and Paul S. Lunt, *The Status System of a Modern Community* (Yankee City Series, Vol. II, 1942); W. Lloyd Warner and Leo Srole, *The Social Systems of American Ethnic Groups* (Yankee City Series, Vol. III, 1945); W. Lloyd Warner and J. O. Low, *The Social System of the Modern Factory* (Yankee City Series, Vol. IV) in preparation; W. Lloyd Warner, *American Symbol Systems* (Yankee City Series, Vol. V) in preparation; W. Lloyd Warner, *Data Book for the Yankee City Series* (Yankee City Series, Vol. VI) in preparation.

focused on the determinants of co-operation in a modern community in its widest sense. The point of view of the studies, stated
in a few sentences and without qualification, was that "society is a
group of mutually interacting individuals. Hence, if any relationship of a given social configuration is stimulated, it will influence
all other parts and in turn will be influenced by them".[1] Furthermore, "most, if not all, societies have a fundamental structure or
structures which integrate and give characteristic form to the rest
of the society"[2] and "determine the basic outlook of an individual",[3] that is, his adjustment or maladjustment to society.

Formulating and Testing New Hypotheses: 1932 to 1936

By this time the major lines of growth in the Department's programme, as suggested by early studies, were beginning to emerge.
It was becoming clear, for example, that a major part of an
administrator's task was to provide satisfactions for those contributing their services to the organization as well as to promote the
purposes of the enterprise itself. It seemed that an administrator's
function was not to consider these as equally desirable alternatives
but to integrate both in the action he determined was necessary.
The satisfactions which an individual demands of his work are
related to his ways of thinking as developed by his own personal
experiences and to the social codes of his group. The ways in
which such personal and social facts as these were related to a
point of action and their implications for the techniques of
administration had to be articulated in detail. Since many of
these concepts of co-operative phenomena had to do with the
relations of individuals and groups to action in any society, not
just an industrial one, these hypotheses had to be tested in a
variety of situations, both business and non-business, and refined
in the light of new data; for in research, studies in contrast often
light up the simple and obvious but as yet unobserved.

6. *A community situation in the South.* These studies, published as
Deep South, by Allison Davis, Burleigh B. Gardner, and Mary R.
Gardner,[4] describe the caste-class system in the deep South and
in the terms of this analysis re-examine the South's economic and
political systems.

7. *Studies of the human and social problems of a community primarily*

---

[1] W. Lloyd Warner and Paul S. Lunt, *The Social Life of a Modern Community*, p. 13.
[2] Ibid., p. 36.   [3] Ibid., p. 35.
[4] Chicago, The University of Chicago Press, 1941.

not industrial. These studies, reports of which have been published in *The Irish Countryman*, by Conrad M. Arensberg,[1] and in *Family and Community of Ireland*, by Arensberg and Solon T. Kimball,[2] analyzed several aspects of community life in Ireland, including the economic, in terms of the family relationships which ordered that society.

8. *Studies at the Norfolk Prison Colony.* These studies developed, in collaboration with others, a classification for the treatment of prisoners based not on the crime they had committed but on the underlying factors in their situation which resulted in crime. This classification is described on pages 136 and 137 of *The Development of Penological Treatment at Norfolk Prison Colony in Massachusetts*, by Walter H. Commons, Thomas Yahkub, and Edwin Powers.[3]

9 *An extension of the study of an individual's social adjustment.* In this period, to give the researchers a wider background of familiarity with personal situations other than those found in a graduate school of a large university, investigations were begun in conjunction with the out-patient department of a large metropolitan hospital. These studies, carried on for a number of years, enabled members of the Department to check the results of their studies of individuals against the situations of a broad cross section of the population. A general restatement of the results of this investigation can be found in Elton Mayo's paper, "Frightened People".[4]

10. *Studies of unemployment.* Other studies of the period included clinical case studies of unemployment, which resulted in teaching material and articles by Professor Benjamin M. Selekman. These studies further explored the relationships existing between an individual, the organization employing him, and the wider community.

Communicating a Point of View: 1936–1945

In 1935 and later years, members of the Department participated in Professor Philip Cabot's Week-End Discussion Groups for Business Executives, a series of meetings designed to present problems of human and labour relations from several points of view. In 1936 the Department offered its first course, Human Problems of Administration, for students in the Harvard Business School. These activities initiated the Department's experiments

---

[1] New York, The Macmillan Company, 1937.
[2] Cambridge, Mass., Harvard University Press, 1940.
[3] New York, Bureau of Social Hygiene, Inc., 1940.
[4] *Harvard Medical Alumni Bulletin*, Vol. XIII, No. 2, 1939.

in training graduate students and men of experience, other than research workers, in the point of view which the research programme had developed. These experiments in instruction later continued at the post-graduate level at Radcliffe College, at the undergraduate level at Harvard College, in several of the war-time training schools established at the Harvard Business School, and at other schools. These courses, several of which at first emphasized the handling of special human problems by "staff" experts, moved rapidly in the direction of making a contribution to the techniques used by a "line" administrator in taking action.

Because experience showed the effectiveness of the case discussion method as a teaching medium, members of the Department gave more and more attention to developing such material. One result of these efforts was the book entitled *Social Problems in Labor Relations*, by Paul Pigors, L. C. McKenney, and T. O. Armstrong. [1] The Department has also developed a considerable volume of mimeographed case material, particularly in recent years. A number of the research studies mentioned below were undertaken with the development of such material as a primary objective.

Among the research studies of this period, the following may be mentioned. The studies were all directly focused on the techniques of administration in a wide variety of situations in business.

11. *Studies of the relationships of head-office organizations in large corporations to manufacturing or other field organizations.* These studies placed particular attention on the personnel function and came to emphasize the importance of foreman-worker relations in personnel matters.

12 *Studies of community resettlement in a depressed coal region.* These studies have been reported in an article entitled "Community Resettlement in a Depressed Coal Region", by F. L. W. Richardson, Jr.[2] They explored practical aspects of community planning in a concrete situation.

13. *Studies of executive compensation.* In these studies the situations of over one hundred executives in different organizations as explored in a non-directed interviewing programme were related to their views on compensation. The study developed the relationship between the social organization of the companies studied and

---

[1] New York, McGraw-Hill Book Co., Inc., 1939.
[2] *Applied Anthropology*, Part I, Vol. I, No. 1, October, 1941; Part II, Vol. I, No. 3, April-June, 1942.

the compensation systems which they used. The investigation showed that the way a compensation system was administered was as important in determining its results as an incentive as was the system itself.

14. *Studies of management, salesgirl, and customer relationships in a department store.* These studies came to centre on the relations between salesgirl and customers. This relationship, foreign to a factory situation, was found to be significant in determining the volume and the type of service a salesgirl gave as well as in determining the form of the executive organization.

15. *Studies of an industrial community seriously affected by unemployment resulting from technological change.* Extensive field work in such a community was carried on, but the work was interrupted by the war.

16. *Clinical studies of management-union-community relations as revealed in arbitration proceedings.* The purpose of these studies was to explore the totality of factors in all their interrelations that enter into that area of human relations that is known as labour relations. A full report of these studies by Professor Benjamin M. Selekman is in preparation.

17. *Studies of management-worker relations under the conditions of rapid expansion in industry that existed during the early war period.* These studies were made in two parts:

(a) A comparative study of twelve to fifteen rapidly expanding plants. The results of this study were incorporated in the Job Relations Training Programme of the Training Within Industry Division of the then Office of Production Management.

(b) An intensive study of one rapidly expanding organization. This study explored in detail the ways in which an expansion programme affected the techniques of administration and form of organization that had been found successful in a "family-organized" company of three hundred to four hundred persons.

Certain aspects of these studies contributed to Professor Roethlisberger's article, "The Foreman: Master and Victim of Double Talk".[1]

18. *Studies of absenteeism in war industries.* These studies have been published in *Absenteeism: Management's Problem*, by John B. Fox and Jerome F. Scott.[2] These studies explored the extent to which

---

[1] *Harvard Business Review*, Vol. XXIII, No. 3, Spring, 1945.
[2] Harvard Business School, Division of Research, Business Research Studies, No. 29, 1943.

management can control the absences of workers in spite of factors external to the work situation which tend to increase them. The report showed that favourable results will occur when the workers, if given a chance by management, develop this responsibility for disciplining themselves.

19. *Studies of labour turnover.* These studies have been reported in *Teamwork and Labour Turnover in the Aircraft Industry of Southern California,* by Elton Mayo and George F. F. Lombard.[1] This study characterized the objective of an administrator's job in the area of human relations as building the persons under him into an effectively working team and developed a tentative classification of teams based on how they are formed.

These varied studies contributed many new insights to the Department's understanding of the problems of organizing, conducting, and communicating the results of research studies in certain aspects of administration and of developing related training programmes.

[1] Harvard Business School, Division of Research, Business Research Studies, No. 32, 1944.

INDEX

Routledge Social Science Series

Routledge & Kegan Paul   London and Boston

68–74 Carter Lane London EC4V 5EL
9 Park Street Boston Mass 02108

Contents

*Authors wishing to submit manuscripts for any series in
this catalogue should send them to the Social Science Editor,
Routledge & Kegan Paul Ltd, 68–74 Carter Lane,
London EC4V 5EL*

●*Books so marked are available in paperback*
All books are in Metric Demy 8vo format (216 × 138mm approx.)

International Library of Sociology

General Editor John Rex

GENERAL SOCIOLOGY

Barnsley, J. H. The Social Reality of Ethics. *464 pp.*
Belshaw, Cyril. The Conditions of Social Performance. *An Exploratory Theory. 144 pp.*
Brown, Robert. Explanation in Social Science. *208 pp.*
● Rules and Laws in Sociology. *192 pp.*
Bruford, W. H. Chekhov and His Russia. *A Sociological Study. 244 pp.*
Cain, Maureen E. Society and the Policeman's Role. *326 pp.*
Gibson, Quentin. The Logic of Social Enquiry. *240 pp.*
Glucksmann, M. Structuralist Analysis in Contemporary Social Thought. *212 pp.*
Gurvitch, Georges. Sociology of Law. *Preface by Roscoe Pound. 264 pp.*
Hodge, H. A. Wilhelm Dilthey. *An Introduction. 184 pp.*
Homans, George C. Sentiments and Activities. *336 pp.*
Johnson, Harry M. Sociology: *a Systematic Introduction. Foreword by Robert K. Merton. 710 pp.*
Mannheim, Karl. Essays on Sociology and Social Psychology. *Edited by Paul Kecskemeti. With Editorial Note by Adolph Lowe. 344 pp.*
 Systematic Sociology: *An Introduction to the Study of Society. Edited by J. S. Erös and Professor W. A. C. Stewart. 220 pp.*
Martindale, Don. The Nature and Types of Sociological Theory. *292 pp.*
●**Maus, Heinz.** A Short History of Sociology. *234 pp.*
Mey, Harald. Field-Theory. *A Study of its Application in the Social Sciences. 352 pp.*
Myrdal, Gunnar. Value in Social Theory: *A Collection of Essays on Methodology. Edited by Paul Streeten. 332 pp.*
Ogburn, William F., and **Nimkoff, Meyer F.** A Handbook of Sociology. *Preface by Karl Mannheim. 656 pp. 46 figures. 35 tables.*
Parsons, Talcott, and **Smelser, Neil J.** Economy and Society: *A Study in the Integration of Economic and Social Theory. 362 pp.*
●**Rex, John.** Key Problems of Sociological Theory. *220 pp.*
 Discovering Sociology. *278 pp.*
 Sociology and the Demystification of the Modern World. *282 pp.*
●**Rex, John** (Ed.) Approaches to Sociology. *Contributions by Peter Abell, Frank Bechhofer, Basil Bernstein, Ronald Fletcher, David Frisby, Miriam Glucksmann, Peter Lassman, Herminio Martins, John Rex, Roland Robertson, John Westergaard and Jock Young. 302 pp.*
Rigby, A. Alternative Realities. *352 pp.*
Roche, M. Phenomenology, Language and the Social Sciences. *374 pp.*
Sahay, A. Sociological Analysis. *220 pp.*
Urry, John. Reference Groups and the Theory of Revolution. *244 pp.*
Weinberg, E. Development of Sociology in the Soviet Union. *173 pp.*

FOREIGN CLASSICS OF SOCIOLOGY

●**Durkheim, Emile.** Suicide. *A Study in Sociology. Edited and with an Introduction by George Simpson. 404 pp.*
Professional Ethics and Civic Morals. *Translated by Cornelia Brookfield. 288 pp.*
●**Gerth, H. H.,** and **Mills, C. Wright.** From Max Weber: *Essays in Sociology. 502 pp.*
●**Tönnies, Ferdinand.** Community and Association. (*Gemeinschaft und Gesellschaft.) Translated and Supplemented by Charles P. Loomis. Foreword by Pitirim A. Sorokin. 334 pp.*

SOCIAL STRUCTURE

Andreski, Stanislav. Military Organization and Society. *Foreword by Professor A. R. Radcliffe-Brown. 226 pp. 1 folder.*
Coontz, Sydney H. Population Theories and the Economic Interpretation. *202 pp.*
Coser, Lewis. The Functions of Social Conflict. *204 pp.*
Dickie-Clark, H. F. Marginal Situation: *A Sociological Study of a Coloured Group. 240 pp. 11 tables.*
Glaser, Barney, and **Strauss, Anselm L.** Status Passage. *A Formal Theory. 208 pp.*
Glass, D. V. (Ed.) Social Mobility in Britain. *Contributions by J. Berent, T. Bottomore, R. C. Chambers, J. Floud, D. V. Glass, J. R. Hall, H. T. Himmelweit, R. K. Kelsall, F. M. Martin, C. A. Moser, R. Mukherjee, and W. Ziegel. 420 pp.*
Jones, Garth N. Planned Organizational Change: *An Exploratory Study Using an Empirical Approach. 268 pp.*
Kelsall, R. K. Higher Civil Servants in Britain: *From 1870 to the Present Day. 268 pp. 31 tables.*
König, René. The Community. *232 pp. Illustrated.*
●**Lawton, Denis.** Social Class, Language and Education. *192 pp.*
McLeish, John. The Theory of Social Change: *Four Views Considered. 128 pp.*
Marsh, David C. The Changing Social Structure of England and Wales, 1871-1961. *288 pp.*
Mouzelis, Nicos. Organization and Bureaucracy. *An Analysis of Modern Theories. 240 pp.*
Mulkay, M. J. Functionalism, Exchange and Theoretical Strategy. *272 pp.*
Ossowski, Stanislaw. Class Structure in the Social Consciousness. *210 pp.*
Podgórecki, Adam. Law and Society. *About 300 pp.*

SOCIOLOGY AND POLITICS

Acton, T. A. Gypsy Politics and Social Change. *316 pp.*
Hechter, Michael. Internal Colonialism. *The Celtic Fringe in British National Development, 1536–1966. About 350 pp.*
Hertz, Frederick. Nationality in History and Politics: *A Psychology and Sociology of National Sentiment and Nationalism. 432 pp.*

Kornhauser, William. The Politics of Mass Society. *272 pp. 20 tables.*

Laidler, Harry W. History of Socialism. *Social-Economic Movements: An Historical and Comparative Survey of Socialism, Communism, Co-operation, Utopianism; and other Systems of Reform and Reconstruction. 992 pp.*

Lasswell, H. D. Analysis of Political Behaviour. *324 pp.*

Mannheim, Karl. Freedom, Power and Democratic Planning. *Edited by Hans Gerth and Ernest K. Bramstedt. 424 pp.*

Mansur, Fatma. Process of Independence. *Foreword by A. H. Hanson. 208 pp.*

Martin, David A. Pacifism: *an Historical and Sociological Study. 262 pp.*

Myrdal, Gunnar. The Political Element in the Development of Economic Theory. *Translated from the German by Paul Streeten. 282 pp.*

Wootton, Graham. Workers, Unions and the State. *188 pp.*

FOREIGN AFFAIRS: THEIR SOCIAL, POLITICAL AND ECONOMIC FOUNDATIONS

Mayer, J. P. Political Thought in France from the Revolution to the Fifth Republic. *164 pp.*

CRIMINOLOGY

Ancel, Marc. Social Defence: *A Modern Approach to Criminal Problems. Foreword by Leon Radzinowicz. 240 pp.*

Cain, Maureen E. Society and the Policeman's Role. *326 pp.*

Cloward, Richard A., and **Ohlin, Lloyd E.** Delinquency and Opportunity: *A Theory of Delinquent Gangs. 248 pp.*

Downes, David M. The Delinquent Solution. *A Study in Subcultural Theory. 296 pp.*

Dunlop, A. B., and **McCabe, S.** Young Men in Detention Centres. *192 pp.*

Friedlander, Kate. The Psycho-Analytical Approach to Juvenile Delinquency: *Theory, Case Studies, Treatment. 320 pp.*

Glueck, Sheldon, and **Eleanor.** Family Environment and Delinquency. *With the statistical assistance of Rose W. Kneznek. 340 pp.*

Lopez-Rey, Manuel. Crime. *An Analytical Appraisal. 288 pp.*

Mannheim, Hermann. Comparative Criminology: *a Text Book. Two volumes. 442 pp. and 380 pp.*

Morris, Terence. The Criminal Area: *A Study in Social Ecology. Foreword by Hermann Mannheim. 232 pp. 25 tables. 4 maps.*

Rock, Paul. Making People Pay. *338 pp.*

● **Taylor, Ian, Walton, Paul,** and **Young, Jock.** The New Criminology. *For a Social Theory of Deviance. 325 pp.*

SOCIAL PSYCHOLOGY

Bagley, Christopher. The Social Psychology of the Epileptic Child. *320 pp.*

Barbu, Zevedei. Problems of Historical Psychology. *248 pp.*

Blackburn, Julian. Psychology and the Social Pattern. *184 pp.*

●**Brittan, Arthur.** Meanings and Situations. *224 pp.*

Carroll, J. Break-Out from the Crystal Palace. *200 pp.*

●**Fleming, C. M.** Adolescence: Its Social Psychology. *With an Introduction to recent findings from the fields of Anthropology, Physiology, Medicine, Psychometrics and Sociometry. 288 pp.*

● The Social Psychology of Education: *An Introduction and Guide to Its Study. 136 pp.*

Homans, George C. The Human Group. *Foreword by Bernard DeVoto. Introduction by Robert K. Merton. 526 pp.*

◉ Social Behaviour: *its Elementary Forms. 416 pp.*

●**Klein, Josephine.** The Study of Groups. *226 pp. 31 figures. 5 tables.*

Linton, Ralph. The Cultural Background of Personality. *132 pp.*

●**Mayo, Elton.** The Social Problems of an Industrial Civilization. *With an appendix on the Political Problem. 180 pp.*

Ottaway, A. K. C. Learning Through Group Experience. *176 pp.*

Ridder, J. C. de. The Personality of the Urban African in South Africa. *A Thermatic Apperception Test Study. 196 pp. 12 plates.*

●**Rose, Arnold M.** (Ed.) Human Behaviour and Social Processes: *an Interactionist Approach. Contributions by Arnold M. Rose, Ralph H. Turner, Anselm Strauss, Everett C. Hughes, E. Franklin Frazier, Howard S. Becker, et al. 696 pp.*

Smelser, Neil J. Theory of Collective Behaviour. *448 pp.*

Stephenson, Geoffrey M. The Development of Conscience. *128 pp.*

Young, Kimball. Handbook of Social Psychology. *658 pp. 16 figures. 10 tables.*

SOCIOLOGY OF THE FAMILY

Banks, J. A. Prosperity and Parenthood: *A Study of Family Planning among The Victorian Middle Classes. 262 pp.*

Bell, Colin R. Middle Class Families: *Social and Geographical Mobility. 224 pp.*

Burton, Lindy. Vulnerable Children. *272 pp.*

Gavron, Hannah. The Captive Wife: *Conflicts of Household Mothers. 190 pp.*

George, Victor, and **Wilding, Paul.** Motherless Families. *220 pp.*

Klein, Josephine. Samples from English Cultures.

1. Three Preliminary Studies and Aspects of Adult Life in England. *447 pp.*

2. Child-Rearing Practices and Index. *247 pp.*

Klein, Viola. Britain's Married Women Workers. *180 pp.*

The Feminine Character. *History of an Ideology. 244 pp.*

McWhinnie, Alexina M. Adopted Children. *How They Grow Up. 304 pp.*

● **Myrdal, Alva,** and **Klein, Viola.** Women's Two Roles: *Home and Work. 238 pp. 27 tables.*

Parsons, Talcott, and **Bales, Robert F.** Family: Socialization and Inter-action Process. *In collaboration with James Olds, Morris Zelditch and Philip E. Slater. 456 pp. 50 figures and tables.*

SOCIAL SERVICES

Bastide, Roger. The Sociology of Mental Disorder. *Translated from the French by Jean McNeil. 260 pp.*

Carlebach, Julius. Caring For Children in Trouble. *266 pp.*

Forder, R. A. (Ed.) Penelope Hall's Social Services of England and Wales. *352 pp.*

George, Victor. Foster Care. *Theory and Practice. 234 pp.*
Social Security: *Beveridge and After. 258 pp.*

George, V., and **Wilding, P.** Motherless Families. *248 pp.*

● **Goetschius, George W.** Working with Community Groups. *256 pp.*

Goetschius, George W., and **Tash, Joan.** Working with Unattached Youth. *416 pp.*

Hall, M. P., and **Howes, I. V.** The Church in Social Work. *A Study of Moral Welfare Work undertaken by the Church of England. 320 pp.*

Heywood, Jean S. Children in Care: *the Development of the Service for the Deprived Child. 264 pp.*

Hoenig, J., and **Hamilton, Marian W.** The De-Segregation of the Mentally Ill. *284 pp.*

Jones, Kathleen. Mental Health and Social Policy, 1845-1959. *264 pp.*

King, Roy D., Raynes, Norma V., and **Tizard, Jack.** Patterns of Residential Care. *356 pp.*

Leigh, John. Young People and Leisure. *256 pp.*

Morris, Mary. Voluntary Work and the Welfare State. *300 pp.*

Morris, Pauline. Put Away: *A Sociological Study of Institutions for the Mentally Retarded. 364 pp.*

Nokes, P. L. The Professional Task in Welfare Practice. *152 pp.*

Timms, Noel. Psychiatric Social Work in Great Britain (1939-1962). *280 pp.*

● Social Casework: *Principles and Practice. 256 pp.*

Young, A. F. Social Services in British Industry. *272 pp.*

Young, A. F., and **Ashton, E. T.** British Social Work in the Nineteenth Century. *288 pp.*

SOCIOLOGY OF EDUCATION

Banks, Olive. Parity and Prestige in English Secondary Education: a Study in Educational Sociology. *272 pp.*

Bentwich, Joseph. Education in Israel. *224 pp. 8 pp. plates.*

● **Blyth, W. A. L.** English Primary Education. *A Sociological Description.*
1. Schools. *232 pp.*
2. Background. *168 pp.*

Collier, K. G. The Social Purposes of Education: *Personal and Social Values in Education. 268 pp.*

Dale, R. R., and **Griffith, S.** Down Stream: *Failure in the Grammar School.* *108 pp.*

Dore, R. P. Education in Tokugawa Japan. *356 pp. 9 pp. plates.*

Evans, K. M. Sociometry and Education. *158 pp.*

●**Ford, Julienne.** Social Class and the Comprehensive School. *192 pp.*

Foster, P. J. Education and Social Change in Ghana. *336 pp. 3 maps.*

Fraser, W. R. Education and Society in Modern France. *150 pp.*

Grace, Gerald R. Role Conflict and the Teacher. *About 200 pp.*

Hans, Nicholas. New Trends in Education in the Eighteenth Century. *278 pp. 19 tables.*

● Comparative Education: *A Study of Educational Factors and Traditions.* *360 pp.*

Hargreaves, David. Interpersonal Relations and Education. *432 pp.*

● Social Relations in a Secondary School. *240 pp.*

Holmes, Brian. Problems in Education. *A Comparative Approach. 336 pp.*

King, Ronald. Values and Involvement in a Grammar School. *164 pp.*

School Organization and Pupil Involvement. *A Study of Secondary Schools.*

●**Mannheim, Karl,** and **Stewart, W. A. C.** An Introduction to the Sociology of Education. *206 pp.*

Morris, Raymond N. The Sixth Form and College Entrance. *231 pp.*

●**Musgrove, F.** Youth and the Social Order. *176 pp.*

●**Ottaway, A. K. C.** Education and Society: An Introduction to the Sociology of Education. *With an Introduction by W. O. Lester Smith. 212 pp.*

Peers, Robert. Adult Education: *A Comparative Study. 398 pp.*

Pritchard, D. G. Education and the Handicapped: *1760 to 1960. 258 pp.*

Richardson, Helen. Adolescent Girls in Approved Schools. *308 pp.*

Stratta, Erica. The Education of Borstal Boys. *A Study of their Educational Experiences prior to, and during, Borstal Training. 256 pp.*

Taylor, P. H., Reid, W. A., and **Holley, B. J.** The English Sixth Form. *A Case Study in Curriculum Research. 200 pp.*

SOCIOLOGY OF CULTURE

Eppel, E. M., and **M.** Adolescents and Morality: *A Study of some Moral Values and Dilemmas of Working Adolescents in the Context of a changing Climate of Opinion. Foreword by W. J. H. Sprott. 268 pp. 39 tables.*

●**Fromm, Erich.** The Fear of Freedom. *286 pp.*

● The Sane Society. *400 pp.*

Mannheim, Karl. Essays on the Sociology of Culture. *Edited by Ernst Mannheim in co-operation with Paul Kecskemeti. Editorial Note by Adolph Lowe. 280 pp.*

Weber, Alfred. Farewell to European History: *or The Conquest of Nihilism. Translated from the German by R. F. C. Hull. 224 pp.*

SOCIOLOGY OF RELIGION

Argyle, Michael and **Beit-Hallahmi, Benjamin.** The Social Psychology of Religion. *About 256 pp.*

Nelson, G. K. Spiritualism and Society. *313 pp.*

Stark, Werner. The Sociology of Religion. *A Study of Christendom.*
Volume I. *Established Religion. 248 pp.*
Volume II. *Sectarian Religion. 368 pp.*
Volume III. *The Universal Church. 464 pp.*
Volume IV. *Types of Religious Man. 352 pp.*
Volume V. *Types of Religious Culture. 464 pp.*

Turner, B. S. Weber and Islam. *216 pp.*

Watt, W. Montgomery. Islam and the Integration of Society. *320 pp.*

SOCIOLOGY OF ART AND LITERATURE

Jarvie, Ian C. Towards a Sociology of the Cinema. *A Comparative Essay on the Structure and Functioning of a Major Entertainment Industry. 405 pp.*

Rust, Frances S. Dance in Society. *An Analysis of the Relationships between the Social Dance and Society in England from the Middle Ages to the Present Day. 256 pp. 8 pp. of plates.*

Schücking, L. L. The Sociology of Literary Taste. *112 pp.*

Wolff, Janet. Hermeneutic Philosophy and the Sociology of Art. *About 200 pp.*

SOCIOLOGY OF KNOWLEDGE

Diesing, P. Patterns of Discovery in the Social Sciences. *262 pp.*

●**Douglas, J. D.** (Ed.) Understanding Everyday Life. *370 pp.*

●**Hamilton, P.** Knowledge and Social Structure. *174 pp.*

Jarvie, I. C. Concepts and Society. *232 pp.*

Mannheim, Karl. Essays on the Sociology of Knowledge. *Edited by Paul Kecskemeti. Editorial Note by Adolph Lowe. 353 pp.*

Remmling, Gunter W. (Ed.) Towards the Sociology of Knowledge. *Origin and Development of a Sociological Thought Style. 463 pp.*

Stark, Werner. The Sociology of Knowledge: *An Essay in Aid of a Deeper Understanding of the History of Ideas. 384 pp.*

URBAN SOCIOLOGY

Ashworth, William. The Genesis of Modern British Town Planning: *A Study in Economic and Social History of the Nineteenth and Twentieth Centuries. 288 pp.*

Cullingworth, J. B. Housing Needs and Planning Policy: *A Restatement of the Problems of Housing Need and 'Overspill' in England and Wales. 232 pp. 44 tables. 8 maps.*

Dickinson, Robert E. City and Region: *A Geographical Interpretation* *608 pp. 125 figures.*

The West European City: *A Geographical Interpretation. 600 pp. 129 maps. 29 plates.*

● The City Region in Western Europe. *320 pp. Maps.*

Humphreys, Alexander J. New Dubliners: *Urbanization and the Irish Family. Foreword by George C. Homans. 304 pp.*

Jackson, Brian. Working Class Community: *Some General Notions raised by a Series of Studies in Northern England. 192 pp.*

Jennings, Hilda. Societies in the Making: *a Study of Development and Re-development within a County Borough. Foreword by D. A. Clark. 286 pp.*

●**Mann, P. H.** An Approach to Urban Sociology. *240 pp.*

Morris, R. N., and **Mogey, J.** The Sociology of Housing. *Studies at Berinsfield. 232 pp. 4 pp. plates.*

Rosser, C., and **Harris, C.** The Family and Social Change. *A Study of Family and Kinship in a South Wales Town. 352 pp. 8 maps.*

RURAL SOCIOLOGY

Chambers, R. J. H. Settlement Schemes in Tropical Africa: *A Selective Study. 268 pp.*

Haswell, M. R. The Economics of Development in Village India. *120 pp.*

Littlejohn, James. Westrigg: *the Sociology of a Cheviot Parish. 172 pp. 5 figures.*

Mayer, Adrian C. Peasants in the Pacific. *A Study of Fiji Indian Rural Society. 248 pp. 20 plates.*

Williams, W. M. The Sociology of an English Village: *Gosforth. 272 pp. 12 figures. 13 tables.*

SOCIOLOGY OF INDUSTRY AND DISTRIBUTION

Anderson, Nels. Work and Leisure. *280 pp.*

●**Blau, Peter M.,** and **Scott, W. Richard.** Formal Organizations: *a Comparative approach. Introduction and Additional Bibliography by J. H. Smith. 326 pp.*

Eldridge, J. E. T. Industrial Disputes. *Essays in the Sociology of Industrial Relations. 288 pp.*

Hetzler, Stanley. Applied Measures for Promoting Technological Growth. *352 pp.*

Technological Growth and Social Change. *Achieving Modernization. 269 pp.*

Hollowell, Peter G. The Lorry Driver. *272 pp.*

Jefferys, Margot, *with the assistance of Winifred Moss.* Mobility in the Labour Market: *Employment Changes in Battersea and Dagenham. Preface by Barbara Wootton. 186 pp. 51 tables.*

Millerson, Geoffrey. The Qualifying Associations: *a Study in Professionalization. 320 pp.*

Smelser, Neil J. Social Change in the Industrial Revolution: *An Application of Theory to the Lancashire Cotton Industry, 1770-1840. 468 pp. 12 figures. 14 tables.*

Williams, Gertrude. Recruitment to Skilled Trades. *240 pp.*

Young, A. F. Industrial Injuries Insurance: *an Examination of British Policy. 192 pp.*

DOCUMENTARY

Schlesinger, Rudolf (Ed.) Changing Attitudes in Soviet Russia.
   2. The Nationalities Problem and Soviet Administration. *Selected Readings on the Development of Soviet Nationalities Policies. Introduced by the editor. Translated by W. W. Gottlieb. 324 pp.*

ANTHROPOLOGY

Ammar, Hamed. Growing up in an Egyptian Village: *Silwa, Province of Aswan. 336 pp.*

Brandel-Syrier, Mia. Reeftown Elite. *A Study of Social Mobility in a Modern African Community on the Reef. 376 pp.*

Crook, David, and **Isabel.** Revolution in a Chinese Village: *Ten Mile Inn. 230 pp. 8 plates. 1 map.*

Dickie-Clark, H. F. The Marginal Situation. *A Sociological Study of a Coloured Group. 236 pp.*

Dube, S. C. Indian Village. *Foreword by Morris Edward Opler. 276 pp. 4 plates.*
   India's Changing Villages: *Human Factors in Community Development. 260 pp. 8 plates. 1 map.*

Firth, Raymond. Malay Fishermen. *Their Peasant Economy. 420 pp. 17 pp. plates.*

Firth, R., Hubert, J., and **Forge, A.** Families and their Relatives. *Kinship in a Middle-Class Sector of London: An Anthropological Study. 456 pp.*

Gulliver, P. H. Social Control in an African Society: a Study of the Arusha, Agricultural Masai of Northern Tanganyika. *320 pp. 8 plates. 10 figures.*
   Family Herds. *288 pp.*

Ishwaran, K. Shivapur. *A South Indian Village. 216 pp.*
   Tradition and Economy in Village India: *An Interactionist Approach. Foreword by Conrad Arensburg. 176 pp.*

Jarvie, Ian C. The Revolution in Anthropology. *268 pp.*

Jarvie, Ian C., and **Agassi, Joseph.** Hong Kong. *A Society in Transition. 396 pp. Illustrated with plates and maps.*

Little, Kenneth L. Mende of Sierra Leone. *308 pp. and folder.*
   Negroes in Britain. *With a New Introduction and Contemporary Study by Leonard Bloom. 320 pp.*

11

Lowie, Robert H. Social Organization. *494 pp.*

Mayer, Adrian, C. Caste and Kinship in Central India: *A Village and its Region. 328 pp. 16 plates. 15 figures. 16 tables.*

Peasants in the Pacific. *A Study of Fiji Indian Rural Society. 248 pp.*

Smith, Raymond T. The Negro Family in British Guiana: *Family Structure and Social Status in the Villages. With a Foreword by Meyer Fortes. 314 pp. 8 plates. 1 figure. 4 maps.*

SOCIOLOGY AND PHILOSOPHY

Barnsley, John H. The Social Reality of Ethics. *A Comparative Analysis of Moral Codes. 448 pp.*

Diesing, Paul. Patterns of Discovery in the Social Sciences. *362 pp.*

●**Douglas, Jack D.** (Ed.) Understanding Everyday Life. *Toward the Reconstruction of Sociological Knowledge. Contributions by Alan F. Blum. Aaron W. Cicourel, Norman K. Denzin, Jack D. Douglas, John Heeren, Peter McHugh, Peter K. Manning, Melvin Power, Matthew Speier, Roy Turner, D. Lawrence Wieder, Thomas P. Wilson and Don H. Zimmerman. 370 pp.*

Jarvie, Ian C. Concepts and Society. *216 pp.*

Pelz, Werner. The Scope of Understanding in Sociology. *Towards a more radical reorientation in the social humanistic sciences. 283 pp.*

Roche, Maurice. Phenomenology, Language and the Social Sciences. *371 pp.*

Sahay, Arun. Sociological Analysis. *212 pp.*

Sklair, Leslie. The Sociology of Progress. *320 pp.*

International Library of Anthropology

General Editor Adam Kuper

Brown, Paula. The Chimbu. *A Study of Change in the New Guinea Highlands. 151 pp.*

Lloyd, P. C. Power and Independence. *Urban Africans' Perception of Social Inequality. 264 pp.*

Pettigrew, Joyce. Robber Noblemen. *A Study of the Political System of the Sikh Jats. 284 pp.*

Van Den Berghe, Pierre L. Power and Privilege at an African University. *278 pp.*

International Library of Social Policy

General Editor Kathleen Jones

Bayley, M. Mental Handicap and Community Care. *426 pp.*

Butler, J. R. Family Doctors and Public Policy. *208 pp.*

Holman, Robert. Trading in Children. *A Study of Private Fostering. 355 pp.*

Jones, Kathleen. History of the Mental Health Service. *428 pp.*

Thomas, J. E. The English Prison Officer since 1850: *A Study in Conflict. 258 pp.*

Woodward, J. To Do the Sick No Harm. *A Study of the British Voluntary Hospital System to 1875. About 220 pp.*

International Library of Welfare and Philosophy

General Editors Noel Timms and David Watson

● **Plant, Raymond.** Community and Ideology. *104 pp.*

Primary Socialization, Language and Education

General Editor Basil Bernstein

Bernstein, Basil. Class, Codes and Control. *2 volumes.*
1. *Theoretical Studies Towards a Sociology of Language. 254 pp.*
2. *Applied Studies Towards a Sociology of Language. About 400 pp.*

Brandis, W., and **Bernstein, B.** Selection and Control. *176 pp.*

Brandis, Walter, and **Henderson, Dorothy.** Social Class, Language and Communication. *288 pp.*

Cook-Gumperz, Jenny. Social Control and Socialization. *A Study of Class Differences in the Language of Maternal Control. 290 pp.*

● **Gahagan, D. M.,** and **G. A.** Talk Reform. *Exploration in Language for Infant School Children. 160 pp.*

Robinson, W. P., and **Rackstraw, Susan D. A.** A Question of Answers. *2 volumes. 192 pp. and 180 pp.*

Turner, Geoffrey J., and **Mohan, Bernard A.** A Linguistic Description and Computer Programme for Children's Speech. *208 pp.*

Reports of the Institute of Community Studies

Cartwright, Ann. Human Relations and Hospital Care. *272 pp.*
● Parents and Family Planning Services. *306 pp.*
Patients and their Doctors. *A Study of General Practice. 304 pp.*
● **Jackson, Brian.** Streaming: *an Education System in Miniature. 168 pp.*
Jackson, Brian, and **Marsden, Dennis.** Education and the Working Class: *Some General Themes raised by a Study of 88 Working-class Children in a Northern Industrial City. 268 pp. 2 folders.*
Marris, Peter. The Experience of Higher Education. *232 pp. 27 tables.*
Loss and Change. *192 pp.*

Marris, Peter, and **Rein, Martin.** Dilemmas of Social Reform. *Poverty and Community Action in the United States. 256 pp.*

Marris, Peter, and **Somerset, Anthony.** African Businessmen. *A Study of Entrepreneurship and Development in Kenya. 256 pp.*

Mills, Richard. Young Outsiders: *a Study in Alternative Communities. 216 pp.*

Runciman, W. G. Relative Deprivation and Social Justice. *A Study of Attitudes to Social Inequality in Twentieth-Century England. 352 pp.*

Willmott, Peter. Adolescent Boys in East London. *230 pp.*

Willmott, Peter, and **Young, Michael.** Family and Class in a London Suburb. *202 pp. 47 tables.*

Young, Michael. Innovation and Research in Education. *192 pp.*

●**Young, Michael,** and **McGeeney, Patrick.** Learning Begins at Home. *A Study of a Junior School and its Parents. 128 pp.*

Young, Michael, and **Willmott, Peter.** Family and Kinship in East London. *Foreword by Richard M. Titmuss. 252 pp. 39 tables.*
The Symmetrical Family. *410 pp.*

Reports of the Institute for Social Studies in Medical Care

Cartwright, Ann, Hockey, Lisbeth, and **Anderson, John L.** Life Before Death. *310 pp.*

Dunnell, Karen, and **Cartwright, Ann.** Medicine Takers, Prescribers and Hoarders. *190 pp.*

Medicine, Illness and Society

General Editor W. M. Williams

Robinson, David. The Process of Becoming Ill. *142 pp.*

Stacey, Margaret, *et al.* Hospitals, Children and Their Families. *The Report of a Pilot Study. 202 pp.*

Monographs in Social Theory

General Editor Arthur Brittan

●**Barnes, B.** Scientific Knowledge and Sociological Theory. *About 200 pp.*

Bauman, Zygmunt. Culture as Praxis. *204 pp.*

● **Dixon, Keith.** Sociological Theory. *Pretence and Possibility. 142 pp.*

●**Smith, Anthony D.** The Concept of Social Change. *A Critique of the Functionalist Theory of Social Change. 208 pp.*

Routledge Social Science Journals

The British Journal of Sociology. *Edited by Terence P. Morris. Vol. 1, No. 1, March 1950 and Quarterly. Roy. 8vo. Back numbers available. An international journal with articles on all aspects of sociology.*
Economy and Society. *Vol. 1, No. 1. February 1972 and Quarterly. Metric Roy. 8vo. A journal for all social scientists covering sociology, philosophy, anthropology, economics and history. Back numbers available.*
Year Book of Social Policy in Britain, The. *Edited by Kathleen Jones. 1971. Published annually.*

Printed in Great Britain by Unwin Brothers Limited
The Gresham Press Old Woking Surrey
A member of the Staples Printing Group